MATHS CONNECT G

Sue Bright

Alexandra Hewitt

Dave Kirkby

Mavis Rayment

Catherine Roe

Bev Stanbridge

Heinemann Educational Publishers
Halley Court, Jordan Hill, Oxford OX2 8EJ
Part of Harcourt Education

Heinemann is a registered trademark of
Harcourt Education Limited

First published 2005

08 07 06 05
10 9 8 7 6 5 4 3 2 1

British Library Cataloguing in Publication Data is available
from the British Library on request.

ISBN 0 435 53496 3

Designed by Bridge Creative
Typeset by Tech-Set Ltd, Gateshead, Tyne and Wear
Original illustrations © Harcourt Education Limited, 2004
Illustrated by Tech-Set Ltd and Bigtop Design
Cover design by mccdesign ltd
Printed in Italy by Printer Trento srl

Acknowledgements
Every effort has been made to contact copyright holders of material reproduced in this book. Any omissions
will be rectified in subsequent printings if notice is given to the publishers.

Consultant
Jackie Fairchild

The authors and publishers would like to thank the following for permission to use photographs:
p63 Harcourt Education Ltd/Martin Sookias, p93 Alamy Images, p103 Action Plus, p124 Getty Images,
p161 Getty Images

Cover photo: Getty images ©

Publishing team

Editorial		Design	Production
Amanda Halden	Neelaksh Sadhoo	Phil Leafe	Siobhan Snowden
Naomi Anderson	Joanna Shock		
Lindsey Besley	Ian Crane	**Picture Research**	
Saskia Besier	Carol Harris	Jane Hance	
Maggie Rumble	Katherine Pate	Chrissie Martin	
Eleanor Hodge	Laurice Suess		

Tel: 01865 888058 email: info.he@heinemann.co.uk

MATHS CONNECT 3 G

Contents   v

How to use this book   viii

Unit 1	A1/2	Sequences, functions and graphs	2
Unit 2	N1	Fractions, decimals and ratio	14
Unit 3	A3	Equations and formulae	32
Unit 4	SSM1	Geometrical reasoning and constructions	44
Unit 5	HD1	Handling data	62
Unit R1		Revision exercises 1	74
Unit 6	SSM2	Measures, areas and volumes	78
Unit 7	N2	Place value and calculations	90
Unit 8	A4	Powers, roots and graphs	106
Unit 9	HD2	Probability	124
Unit 10	SSM3	Transformations	132
Unit R2		Revision exercises 2	144
Unit 11	A5	Formulae and graphs	148
Unit 12	N3	Problem solving	160
Unit 13	HD3	Collecting, displaying and analysing data	170
Unit 14	SSM4	3-D objects and nets	182
Unit 15	HD4	More probability	194
Unit R3		Revision exercises 3	206

Index   212

Contents

A1/2 Sequences, functions and graphs

1.1	Sequences	2
1.2	The general term	4
1.3	Finding the general term	6
1.4	Mappings	8
1.5	Finding the function	10
1.6	Graphs of functions	12

N1 Fractions, decimals and ratio

2.1	Multiplying and dividing integers	14
2.2	Ordering fractions	16
2.3	Adding and subtracting fractions	18
2.4	Multiplying and dividing by fractions	20
2.5	Ordering decimals	22
2.6	Ratio	24
2.7	Ratio and direct proportion	26
2.8	Percentages	28
2.9	Percentage increase and decrease	30

A3 Equations and formulae

3.1	Solving equations 1	32
3.2	Forming equations 1	34
3.3	Solving equations 2	36
3.4	Forming equations 2	38
3.5	Substitution into expressions	40
3.6	Direct proportion	42

SSM1 Geometrical reasoning and constructions

4.1	Angles	44
4.2	Calculating angles	46
4.3	Quadrilaterals	48
4.4	Angle problems	50
4.5	Construction	52
4.6	Perpendiculars	54
4.7	Drawing triangles	56
4.8	Exploring constructions	58
4.9	Loci	60

HD1 Handling data

5.1	Planning an investigation 1	62
5.2	Processing data 1	64
5.3	Working with data	66
5.4	Pie charts	68

5.5	Drawing diagrams	70
5.6	Interpreting information	72

R1 Revision exercises 1   74

SSM2 Measures, areas and volumes

6.1	Mid-points	78
6.2	Metric equivalents	80
6.3	Areas	82
6.4	More areas	84
6.5	Volume 1	86
6.6	Volume 2	88

N2 Place value and calculations

7.1	Mental calculations 1	90
7.2	Mental calculations 2	92
7.3	Multiplying and dividing by 0.1 and 0.01	94
7.4	Rounding	96
7.5	Adding and subtracting decimals	98
7.6	Multiplying decimals	100
7.7	Dividing decimals	102
7.8	Square roots	104

A4 Powers, roots and graphs

8.1	Cubes and cube roots	106
8.2	Powers of 10	108
8.3	Prime factors	110
8.4	Index notation	112
8.5	Substitution and powers	114
8.6	Drawing graphs	116
8.7	The gradient	118
8.8	Plotting real-life graphs	120
8.9	Interpreting real-life graphs	122

HD2 Probability

9.1	Probability	124
9.2	Possible outcomes 1	126
9.3	Estimating probabilities	128
9.4	Comparing probabilities	130

SSM3 Transformations

10.1	Combining transformations	132
10.2	Symmetries	134
10.3	Congruence	136
10.4	Enlargement	138
10.5	Scale factors and ratio	140
10.6	Scale drawings	142

R2 Revision exercises 2   144

A5 Formulae and graphs

11.1	Simplifying expressions	148
11.2	More simplifying	150
11.3	Substitution into formulae	152
11.4	Constructing formulae	154
11.5	Drawing distance–time graphs	156
11.6	Interpreting distance–time graphs	158

N3 Problem solving

12.1	Solving ratio, proportion and percentage problems	160
12.2	Solving geometrical problems	162
12.3	Mixed problems	164
12.4	Multistep problems	166
12.5	Extended problems	168

HD3 Collecting, displaying and analysing data

13.1	Planning an investigation 2	170
13.2	Processing data 2	172
13.3	Representing data 1	174
13.4	Interpreting data 1	176
13.5	Writing your report	178
13.6	Evaluating your investigation	180

SSM4 3-D objects and nets

14.1	Cuboids	182
14.2	2-D representations of 3-D objects	184
14.3	3-D reflection symmetry	186
14.4	Nets	188
14.5	More nets	190
14.6	Surface area	192

HD4 More probability

15.1	Planning a probability investigation	194
15.2	Experimental probabilities	196
15.3	Possible outcomes 2	198
15.4	Representing data 2	200
15.5	Interpreting data 2	202
15.6	Writing a report	204

R3 Revision exercises 3

206

Index

212

Matching charts linking the content of the lessons in each Unit to the *Sample medium-term plans for mathematics* and the Year 9 teaching programme from the *Framework for teaching mathematics* are available on the web at **www.heinemann.co.uk**

How to use this book

This book is divided up into 15 colour-coded Units. **Algebra** Units are green, **Number** Units are orange, **Space, Shape and Measure** Units are blue and **Handling Data** Units are red. There are also three sections of Revision Exercises, colour-coded light blue. These are placed after each group of five units, and they test the knowledge and skills you have covered in those units. Each lesson is on its own double page spread.

1.1 Sequences

⊕ Find terms of a sequence and say whether it is ascending or descending, finite or infinite

⊕ Find the next term in a sequence of numbers or shapes

Key words
sequence
term
consecutive
infinite
finite

Lesson targets tell you what you will learn in the lesson.
To help you to remember the important vocabulary, there is also a **key words box** here.

A number **sequence** is a set of numbers in a given order, e.g. 1, 2, 3, 4, 5, …

Each number in a sequence is called a **term** .

Terms next to each other are called **consecutive terms** .

Sequences may be **ascending** (e.g. 2, 4, 6, 8, …) or **descending** (e.g. 18, 15, 12, 9, …).

The sequence 1, 2, 3, 4, 5 … is **infinite** . We could go on counting forever.

The sequence 10, 12, 14 … 98 is **finite** . The dots mean that there are missing terms and that the sequence continues in the same way until the final value, 98, is reached.

In the **explanation box**, you can see a summary of the key ideas that are covered in the lesson. The key words are highlighted in yellow.

Example 1 Here is a sequence of diagrams.
Spot the pattern and draw the next two terms in the sequence.

Each time two more dots are added:

This is the 5th term.

This is the 6th term.

The **worked examples** show you methods of answering the exercise questions. On the blue paper, you can see the kind of working you should be writing in your exercise book. The **hint boxes** help to explain how you can calculate the answers.

The **exercise** for each lesson is made up of three types of question:

- **practice** questions, which allow you to practise the basic skills
- **problem** questions, which encourage you to apply the skills you have learned
- **investigation** questions, which give you practice at solving open-ended problems.

The following features are found in the exercise:

Consecutive terms are terms that are next to each other.

Hint boxes give tips and reminders to help you with the questions

Questions you should try without the help of a calculator are marked with this symbol

Questions that require you to use a calculator are marked with this symbol.

If there is no symbol, you can choose whether or not to use a calculator.

1.1 Sequences

⊕ Find the next few terms in sequences for which the difference between consecutive terms is not always the same

Remember:
We can generate a **sequence** given the first term and the **term-to-term** rule.

For example: First term = 5   Term to term rule = −2
The sequence is:

First term	Second term	Third term	Fourth term	Fifth term	Sixth term	Seventh term	Eighth term
5	5 − 2 = **3**	3 − 2 = **1**	1 − 2 = **⁻1**	⁻1 − 2 = **⁻3**	⁻3 − 2 = **⁻5**	⁻5 − 2 = **⁻7**	⁻7 − 2 = **⁻9**

Example 1

Generate the first eight terms of the sequence with first term 1 and term-to-term rule 'add 5'.

The sequence is:

First term	Second term	Third term	Fourth term	Fifth term	Sixth term	Seventh term	Eighth term
1	1 + 5 = **6**	6 + 5 = **11**	11 + 5 = **16**	16 + 5 = **21**	21 + 5 = **26**	26 + 5 = **31**	31 + 5 = **36**

Example 2

Write down the first three terms of the sequence with first term 25 and term-to-term rule '×2'.

First term = 25 — We are told the first term is 25.

Second term = 25 × 2 = 50 — To find the second term we multiply the **first** term by 2.

Third term = 50 × 2 = 100 — To find the third term we multiply the **second** term by 2.

Example 3

By looking at the pattern of differences, write down the next term in the sequence:
3, 4, 6, 9, 13, 18, …

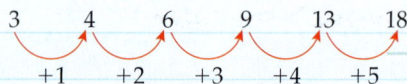

3   4   6   9   13   18
 +1 +2 +3 +4 +5

First write out the sequence and work out the differences between **consecutive** terms.

'Consecutive' means 'next to each other'.

From the pattern of differences, we can see that we are adding the consecutive numbers 1, 2, 3, 4, 5, …

18 + 6 = 24 — To find the next term we need to add 6 to 18.

Exercise 1.1

1 Write down the first five terms of each of the following sequences:
   a) First term = 10   Term-to-term rule = +3
   b) First term = 100   Term-to-term rule = −20
   c) First term = 60   Term-to-term rule = +0.5
   d) First term = 1   Term-to-term rule = +0.2
   e) First term = 5   Term-to-term rule = −2
   f) First term = ⁻8   Term-to-term rule = +3

2 By looking at the pattern of differences between terms, write down the next three terms for each of the sequences below:
   a) 50, 56, 62, 68, 74, …   **b)** 10, 8, 6, 4, …   **c)** 80, 92, 104, 116, …
   d) 32, 22, 12, 2, …   **e)** ⁻100, ⁻80, ⁻60, ⁻40, …   **f)** ⁻3, ⁻6, ⁻9, ⁻12, …

3 Copy and complete the table to generate the first 5 terms of the sequence with first term 2 and term-to-term rule '×3':

First term	Second term	Third term	Fourth term	Fifth term
2	$2 \times 3 = 6$	$6 \times 3 = \ldots$	………	………

4 Write down the first five terms of each of the following sequences:
   a) First term = 2   Term-to-term rule = ×2
   b) First term = 1   Term-to-term rule = ×10
   c) First term = 1   Term-to-term rule = ×5
   d) First term = 64   Term-to-term rule = ÷2
   e) First term = 3   Term-to-term rule 'add consecutive odd numbers'
   f) First term = 50   Term-to-term rule 'subtract consecutive integers'

> Consecutive odd numbers are 1, 3, 5, 7, …

> Integers are whole numbers, 1, 2, 3, …

5 a) Copy and complete the diagram to show the pattern of differences for this sequence:

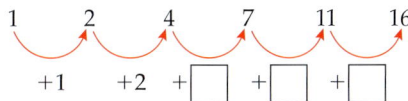

   b) Follow the pattern to write down the next three terms in the sequence.

6 Use the method in **Q5** to find the next three terms for each of the sequences below:
   a) 3, 5, 8, 12, 17, …   **b)** 0, 2, 6, 12, 20, …
   c) 1000, 990, 970, 940, 900, …   **d)** 50, 40, 20, ⁻10, …

> The differences will all be subtractions.

7 Jandeep and Alice both receive 50p pocket money in 2005.
   Alice's parents increase the amount of her pocket money by 50p each year.
   a) How much pocket money will Alice receive in
      i) 2006   **ii)** 2007   **iii)** 2008?

   Jandeep's parents double his pocket money each year.
   b) How much pocket money will Jandeep receive in
      i) 2006   **ii)** 2007   **iii)** 2008?

   c) In what year will Alice receive £16?

> Write out the sequence.

   d) In what year will Jandeep receive £16?

⊕ Generate a sequence given the general term

You can generate a sequence by giving the first **term** and a term-to-term rule. For example, if the first term is 1000 and the term-to-term rule $\div 10$, the sequence is: 1000, 100, 10, 1, 0.1, …

You can also generate a sequence from the **general term**, written as $T(n)$. It is a formula for calculating any term in the sequence.

For example, the general term of a sequence is $T(n) = 2n - 4$.

To find terms of the sequence we replace the n with the term number:

$T(1) = 2 \times 1 - 4 = -2$ For the first term, the term number is 1, so replace the n with 1.

$T(2) = 2 \times 2 - 4 = 0$ $T(2)$ is the second term.

$T(3) = 2 \times 3 - 4 = 2$

You can use the general term to find any term in the sequence.

To find the 100th term replace the n with 100:

$T(100) = 2 \times 100 - 4 = 196$

Example 1   The general term of a sequence is $T(n) = 4n - 2$. Find:

   a) $T(1)$ **b)** $T(2)$ **c)** $T(25)$

a) $T(1) = 4 \times 1 - 2 = 2$

b) $T(2) = 4 \times 2 - 2 = 6$

c) $T(25) = 4 \times 25 - 2 = 98$

We substitute the value of n into the general term.

Example 2   The general term of a sequence is:

   $T(n) = 6 - 3n$

   a) Find the first five terms of the sequence.

   b) Write down the first term and the term-to-term rule for this sequence.

a) $T(1) = 6 - 3 \times 1 = 3$

$T(2) = 6 - 3 \times 2 = 0$

$T(3) = 6 - 3 \times 3 = {}^-3$

$T(4) = 6 - 3 \times 4 = {}^-6$

$T(5) = 6 - 3 \times 5 = {}^-9$

b) The first term of the sequence is 3.

The pattern of differences is:

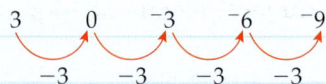

3   0 $^-3$ $^-6$ $^-9$

   -3 -3 -3 -3

The term-to-term rule is -3.

To get from one term to the next you subtract 3.

Exercise 1.2

1 Find the first five terms of each of the following sequences.

   i) $T(n) = n + 4$ **ii)** $T(n) = n$ **iii)** $T(n) = 3n - 2$

   iv) $T(n) = 4n + 12$ **v)** $T(n) = 2n$ **vi)** $T(n) = 1 - n$

> The first five terms are $T(1)$, $T(2)$, ..., $T(5)$.

2 Find $T(1)$, $T(10)$ and $T(20)$ of each of the following sequences:

   a) $T(n) = n + 3$ **b)** $T(n) = n - 5$ **c)** $T(n) = 2n + 3$

   d) $T(n) = 3n - 7$ **e)** $T(n) = 4n$ **f)** $T(n) = 9 - 2n$

3 **a)** Describe each of the sequences in **Q1** by giving the first term, $T(1)$, and the term-to-term rule.

   b) How does the general term help you to find the term-to-term rule?

> Compare the general term with the term-to-term rule for each sequence.

4 Describe the following sequences by giving the first term and the term-to-term rule:

> You do not need to write out the sequence.

   a) $T(n) = 4n + 5$ **b)** $T(n) = 100n$

   c) $T(n) = 25n - 25$ **d)** $T(n) = 3 - 2n$

5 Lord Number uses the general term $T(n) = 100n - 4$ to calculate a new combination for his safe each day.

   On 1 January the combination is: $T(1) = 100 \times 1 - 4 = 96$

   On 2 January the combination is: $T(2) = 100 \times 2 - 4 = 196$

   a) What is the combination on 3 January?

   b) What is the combination on 31 January?

   c) What is the combination on 15 February?

   d) What is the highest number that the code will take this year?

> 1 February is the 32nd day of the year.
>
> How many days are there in this year?

6 James uses the following spreadsheet to generate the sequence:

   $T(n) = 10 - 2n$

   a) Write down the values which should occur in cells B3, B4 and B5.

   b) James generates the sequence by writing a formula in column B which refers to column A. What formula should he enter in cell B1?

	A	B	C	D
1	1	8		
2	2	6		
3	3	...		
4	4	...		
5	5	...		

Investigation

7 Look at the sequences in **Q1**.

   a) Which sequences are ascending (going up)?

   b) Which sequences are descending (going down)?

   c) How can you tell (without generating terms of the sequence) whether a sequence will be ascending or descending?

Finding the general term

⊕ Find the general term of a sequence

The **general term** (or ***n*th term**) of a **sequence** is given in the form:

$T(n) = 3n + 5$

We find the terms of the sequence by substituting the values $n = 1, 2, 3, \ldots$ into the general term.

The terms in this sequence are: 8, 11, 14, 17, 20, …

The difference between **consecutive terms** in this sequence is 3. This is the same as the value in front of the *n* in the general term.

To find the general term of a sequence we look at the difference between consecutive terms.

Example 1 Find the general term of this sequence.
Use this to calculate the number of dots in the 10th term.

Term Number	1	2	3	4	5
Sequence	•	• • •	• • • • • • • •	• • • • • • • • • •	• • • • • • • • • • •

n	1	2	3	4	5
$T(n)$	1	4	7	10	13
Multiples of 3	3	6	9	12	15

From the diagrams, we can see that 3 dots are added each time. The difference between consecutive terms is 3.

The general term: $T(n) = 3n - 2$

The 10th term: $T(10) = 3 \times 10 - 2$

$= 30 - 2$

$= 28$ dots

We compare the sequence to the multiples of 3.

Each term of the sequence is two less than the multiples of 3.
E.g. $T(1) = 3 \times 1 - 2 = 1$

Example 2 Find the general term of the following sequence: 9, 13, 17, 21, 25, …

n	1	2	3	4	5
$T(n)$	9	13	17	21	25
Multiples of 4	4	8	12	16	20

The difference between consecutive terms is 4.

Each term in the sequence is 5 more than the multiple of 4.

The general term: $T(n) = 4n + 5$

Compare the sequence to the multiples of 4.

Exercise 1.3

1 A sequence of numbers starts: 7, 9, 11, 13, 15, …

    a) Copy the table below and complete the second row.

n	1	2	3	4	5
T(n)	7	…	…	…	…
Multiples of …					

    b) What is the difference between consecutive terms?

    c) Complete the third row of the table.

    d) How much must you add to the sequence of multiples to find your original sequence?

    e) Copy and complete the general term of the sequence T(n) = …n………

> Which multiples will you compare the sequence to?

2 A sequence of numbers starts: 2, 7, 12, 17, 22, …

    a) Copy the table below and complete the second row.

n	1	2	3	4	5
T(n)	2	…	…	…	…
Multiples of …					

    b) What is the difference between consecutive terms?

    c) Complete the third row of the table.

    d) How much must you subtract from the sequence of multiples to find your original sequence?

    e) Copy and complete the general term of the sequence T(n) = …n………

3 **a)** Draw the next two patterns in the sequence.

    b) Write down a general term for the number of circles in each pattern, explaining why it works.

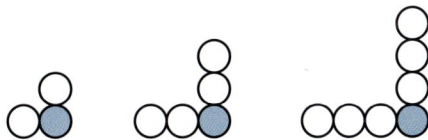

4 Look at this pattern.

    a) How many circles are there in the next pattern?

    b) How many circles are there in the 10th pattern?

    c) How many circles are there in the 100th pattern? Explain how you know.

    d) Find a general term for the number of circles in the nth pattern, explaining why it works.

5 Find the general term of each of the following sequences.

    a) 5, 10, 15, 20, 25, …

    b) 11, 21, 31, 41, 51, …

    c) 1, 3, 5, 7, 9, 11, …

    d) 7, 17, 27, 37, 47, …

    e) 20, 17, 14, 11, …

    f) 12, 9, 6, 3, 0, …

> You could use the method in **Q1**.

6 Find the 10th term of each of the sequences in **Q5**.

Mappings

- ⊕ Write functions using symbols
- ⊕ Draw mapping diagrams for functions

A **function** shows the relationship between two sets of values.

For example, the function: $y = x - 5$

shows that the value of y is always 5 less than the value of x.

You can write this function as a **mapping** $x \rightarrow x - 5$ and draw a mapping diagram.

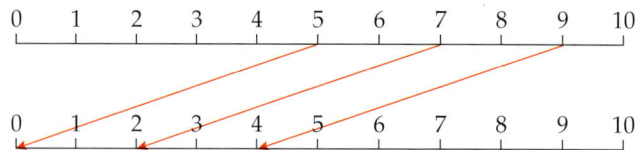

Example 1   Draw a mapping diagram for the mapping $x \rightarrow 2x - 1$.

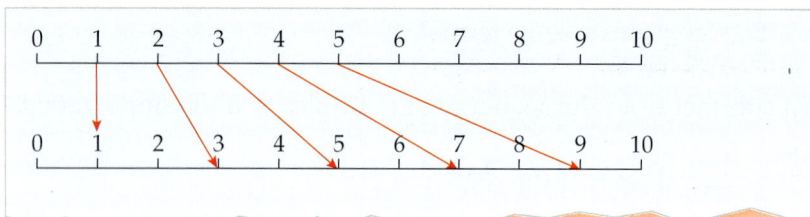

1 maps to
$2 \times 1 - 1 = 1$.
2 maps to
$2 \times 2 - 1 = 3$.

Example 2   Susie calculates her monthly phone bill (in pounds) by multiplying the number of minutes she has spent on the phone by 0.15 and adding £10.

    a) How much will her bill be if she has spent:
        i) 10 minutes
        ii) 15 minutes on the phone in a month?

    b) Represent the information as a mapping and draw a mapping diagram.

a) **i)** $10 \times 0.15 + £10 = £11.50$

      ii) $15 \times 0.15 + £10 = £12.25$

To calculate a bill, multiply by 0.15 and add 10.

b) $x \rightarrow 0.15x + 10$

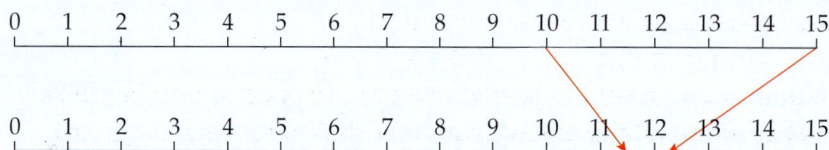

Exercise 1.4

1 Copy and complete separate mapping diagrams to show each of the following:

    a) $x \to 2x$ **b)** $x \to 3x - 2$ **c)** $x \to 2x - \frac{1}{2}$ **d)** $x \to x - 2$

2 A helicopter pilot uses the following table to work out how far he can fly on a given weight of fuel.

    a) What is the mapping that connects the amount of fuel to the distance flown?

        A mapping begins with $x \to$.

    b) How far can a helicopter fly with 5 kg of fuel?

    c) How far can a helicopter fly with 30 kg of fuel?

kg		Distance in km
1	→	0.5
10	→	5
15	→	7.5
20	→	10
50	→	25

3 To calculate his monthly pocket money, Zac uses the function:

$$p = a + 0.5$$

where p = amount of pocket money in pounds and a = his age in years.

    a) Work out how much pocket money he will receive when he is:

        i) 7 years old   **ii)** 10 years old   **iii)** 18 years old

    b) Write the function as a mapping.

    c) Copy and complete the mapping diagram below:

```
0   1   2   3   4   5   6   7   8   9   10


0   1   2   3   4   5   6   7   8   9   10
```

4 To convert from centimetres to metres we use the function $m = \dfrac{c}{100}$ where m = distance in metres and c = distance in cm.

    a) Use the function to convert the following distances from cm to metres.

        i) 200 cm   **ii)** 5600 cm   **iii)** 320 cm   **iv)** 425 cm

    b) Write the function as a mapping.

Investigations

5 **a)** Write each of the following functions as mappings:

        i) $y = 2x$ **ii)** $y = 3x$ **iii)** $y = 4x$ **iv)** $y = 5x$

    b) Draw a pair of number lines from 0 to 20.

    c) Draw the mappings you found in part **a)** on this pair of number lines.

    d) Which arrow have you drawn four times?

    e) Why is this?

6 **a)** Write each of the following functions as mappings:

        i) $y = x + 1$ **ii)** $y = x + 2$ **iii)** $y = x + 3$

    b) Display the mappings you found in part **a)** on separate pairs of number lines.

    c) What do you notice about all the arrows you have drawn for each diagram?

    d) Why does this happen?

Finding the function

◈ Given inputs and outputs, find the function

A **function** machine shows the relationship between two sets of numbers.

For example: **Input** ⟶ ×4 ⟶ −3 ⟶ **Output**

If we input the number 5 into this function machine the output is $5 \times 4 - 3 = 17$.

When you know some inputs and outputs of a function machine you can find the function. You look at the sequence of the outputs and find the general term of this sequence.

Example Find the missing functions in this function machine:

1, 2, 3, 4 ⟶ ? ⟶ ? ⟶ 1, 4, 7, 10

First draw up a table of inputs and outputs:

Input (n)	1	2	3	4
Output (sequence)	1	4	7	10
Multiples of 3	3	6	9	12

We can draw the function machine, filling in the missing functions:

1, 2, 3, 4 ⟶ ×3 ⟶ −2 ⟶ 1, 4, 7, 10,

The difference between terms in the sequence (the outputs) is 3 so we compare the sequence to the multiples of 3.

The multiples of 3 are always two more than the term in the sequence. So the general term of the sequence is: $T(n) = 3n - 2$.

Exercise 1.5

1 a) Copy the table of inputs and outputs for this function machine:

1, 2, 3, 4 ⟶ ? ⟶ ? ⟶ 3, 5, 7, 9

Input (n)	1	2		
Output (sequence)	3			
Multiples of ...				

b) Complete the first two rows.   Fill in the inputs and outputs.

c) What is the difference between consecutive terms in the output sequence?

d) Use your answer to part **c)** to fill in the bottom row of the table.   The difference between consecutive terms tells you which multiples to compare the sequence to.

e) Compare the values in the bottom two rows of the table to find the general term of the sequence of outputs.

f) Draw the function machine and write in the missing functions.

2 Find the missing functions in the following function machines.

Use the method in **Q1**.

a) $1, 2, 3, 4 \longrightarrow \boxed{?} \longrightarrow \boxed{?} \longrightarrow 5, 7, 9, 11$

b) $1, 2, 3, 4 \longrightarrow \boxed{?} \longrightarrow \boxed{?} \longrightarrow 8, 11, 14, 17$

c) $1, 2, 3, 4 \longrightarrow \boxed{?} \longrightarrow \boxed{?} \longrightarrow 6, 11, 16, 21$

3 $2, 1, 4, 3 \longrightarrow \boxed{?} \longrightarrow \boxed{?} \longrightarrow 15, 5, 35, 25$

a) Copy the table of inputs and outputs for this function machine:

Input (n)	1	2	3	4
Output (sequence)	5			
Multiples of ...				

Although the inputs are not in ascending order, we know that $2 \to 15$, $1 \to 5$, etc. Write the inputs in ascending order in your table of values, with their corresponding outputs.

b) Complete the first two rows.

c) What is the difference between consecutive terms in the output sequence?

d) Use your answer to part **c)** to fill in the bottom row of the table.

e) Compare the values in the bottom two rows of the table to find the general term of the sequence of outputs.

f) Draw the function machine and write in the missing functions.

4 Sometimes two operations in a function machine can be combined into one.
Choose different inputs and find the outputs for each function machine.
Look at your inputs and outputs. Which single operation could replace the two operations?

a) $\text{Input} \longrightarrow \boxed{\times 4} \longrightarrow \boxed{\times 2} \longrightarrow \text{Output}$

b) $\text{Input} \longrightarrow \boxed{-3} \longrightarrow \boxed{-7} \longrightarrow \text{Output}$

c) $\text{Input} \longrightarrow \boxed{\div 2} \longrightarrow \boxed{\div 5} \longrightarrow \text{Output}$

5 By choosing inputs and outputs for the following function machines decide whether it is possible to simplify the machines:

a) $\text{Input} \longrightarrow \boxed{\times 10} \longrightarrow \boxed{\div 5} \longrightarrow \text{Output}$

b) $\text{Input} \longrightarrow \boxed{\div 2} \longrightarrow \boxed{+3} \longrightarrow \text{Output}$

c) $\text{Input} \longrightarrow \boxed{+7} \longrightarrow \boxed{-3} \longrightarrow \text{Output}$

d) Experiment with other combinations of operations.
Find a rule for which pairs of operations can be combined to one operation.

Graphs of functions

◈ Plot graphs of linear functions

A **function** is a way of expressing a relationship between two sets of values.

We can represent a function by drawing a **graph**.

Example　A chocolate factory makes 200 bars of chocolate per hour.

　　a)　Write down in words the function for calculating the number of chocolate bars made in a certain number of hours.

　　b)　Draw a graph to show how many chocolate bars are made during an eight-hour shift.

a)　Number of chocolate bars = 200 × time in hours

b)

x (time in hours)	y (number of chocolate bars)
0	200 × 0 = 0
4	200 × 4 = 800
8	200 × 8 = 1600

For example, to calculate the number of chocolate bars made in 4 hours we calculate 200 × 4.

In general, to calculate the number of chocolate bars made we multiply the time in hours by 200.

The x-axis will go from 0 to 8. First calculate some points on the graph.

By choosing the largest and smallest x-values we can see that the y-axis must go from 0 to 1600.

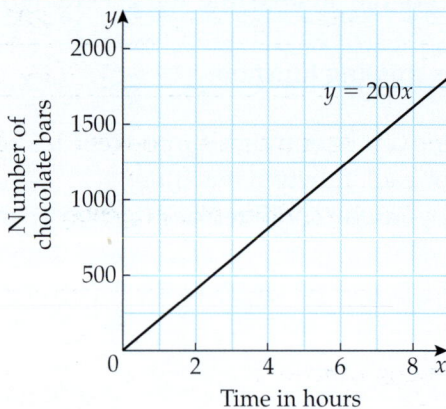

Exercise 1.6

You will need graph paper for this exercise.

1　a)　Jeremy earns 10p per newspaper delivered on his paper round.
　　　Copy and complete the following function for calculating how much Jeremy is paid (in pounds):

　　　　Earnings = …. × number of newspapers delivered.

How do you write 10p in pounds?

　　b)　Jeremy can deliver up to 300 papers in one morning.
　　　Copy the table below. Choose appropriate x-values and calculate the y-values.

x (number of papers delivered)			
y (Earnings in £s)			

Choose three x-values spread out over the range of possible values of x.

　　c)　Draw a pair of axes with a suitable scale to plot the points from your table.

　　d)　Plot the points to draw a graph showing how much Jeremy earns for different numbers of papers.

2 Use the graph you drew for **Q1** to answer the following questions:
   a) How much will Jeremy earn if he delivers:
      i) 20   **ii)** 150   **iii)** 225 newspapers?
   b) How many newspapers did Jeremy deliver when he earned:
      i) £10   **ii)** £25   **iii)** £15.50?

3 The graph below shows the cost of taxi journeys of different distances.
   a) What is the cost for a journey of:
      i) 10 miles   **ii)** 30 miles   **iii)** 35 miles?
   b) Describe in words how to calculate
      the cost of a journey when you know
      the distance.
   c) What distance can you travel for:
      i) £10   **ii)** £7   **iii)** £20?
   d) Copy and complete the following function:

   Journey distance = …….. × cost

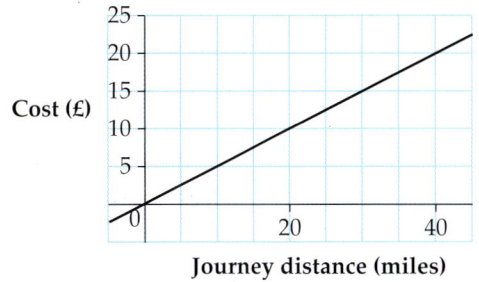
Cost (£)

Journey distance (miles)

4 To calculate the cost of a bag of Pick 'n' Mix, a cashier uses the following function.

   Cost (in pence) = weight in grams × 1.5

   a) Copy and complete the following table for the cost of different bags:

Weight (in grams)	50	250	20	100	200
Cost (in pence)	50 × 1.5 = …	………….	………….	………….	………….

   b) Draw a graph to show the cost of a bag of Pick 'n' Mix weighing between 0 and 200 g.
   c) How heavy is a bag that costs:
      i) £1   **ii)** £2   **iii)** £1.70?   Convert each cost into pence.

Investigation

5 To convert between km and m we use the following function:
   Distance in m = 1000 × distance in km
   a) Write down the function for converting from m to km.
      This is called the **inverse function**.
   b) How does this function relate to the function for converting from km to m?
   c) Look at the functions for **Q1**, **Q3** and **Q4**.
      For each question, write down both the function
      and the inverse function.

Multiplying and dividing integers

⊕ Multiply positive and negative numbers

⊕ Divide positive and negative numbers

Multiplication	Division
$^+ve \times {}^+ve = {}^+ve$	$^+ve \div {}^+ve = {}^+ve$
$^-ve \times {}^-ve = {}^+ve$	$^-ve \div {}^-ve = {}^+ve$
$^+ve \times {}^-ve = {}^-ve$	$^+ve \div {}^-ve = {}^-ve$
$^-ve \times {}^+ve = {}^-ve$	$^-ve \div {}^+ve = {}^-ve$

To multiply or divide two **integers** , first multiply or divide the number parts, and then decide on the correct sign.

Rules of signs for multiplication and division:

If both signs are the same, then the **product** is **positive** .

If both signs are different, then the product is **negative** .

Product is another word for the answer to a multiplication.

For example: $^-4 \times {}^-3 = {}^+12$
$(4 \times 3 = 12$, and the signs are the same, so the product is positive)
$$^-20 \div {}^+5 = {}^-4$$
$(20 \div 5 = 4$, and the signs are different, so the answer is negative)

Example 1 $^-8 \times {}^+2 = {}^-16$

    a) Write down two division facts from this multiplication fact.

    b) Check your answers with the rules of dividing integers.

  a) $^-16 \div {}^-8 = {}^+2$

       $^-16 \div {}^+2 = {}^-8$

  b) $^-16 \div {}^-8 \ (16 \div 8 = 2,\ \text{sign } {}^+ve) = {}^+2$

       $^-16 \div {}^+2 \ (16 \div 2 = 8,\ \text{sign } {}^-ve) = {}^-8$

Same signs make ^+ve
Different signs make ^-ve

Example 2   Work out **a)** $^-3 \times {}^-4$ **b)** $^+7 \times {}^-3$
                   c) $(^-4)^2$ **d)** $^-5 \times {}^+4 \times {}^-2$

  a) $^-3 \times {}^-4 \ (3 \times 4 = 12,\ \text{sign } {}^+ve) = {}^+12$

  b) $^+7 \times {}^-3 \ (7 \times 3 = 21,\ \text{sign } {}^-ve) = {}^-21$

  c) $^-4 \times {}^-4 \ (4 \times 4 = 16,\ \text{sign } {}^+ve) = {}^+16$

  d) $^-5 \times {}^+4 \times {}^-2 \ (5 \times 4 = 20,\ \text{sign } {}^-ve) = {}^-20 \times {}^-2$

       $^-20 \times {}^-2 \ (20 \times 2 = 40,\ \text{sign } {}^+ve) = {}^+40$

$(^-4)^2$ means $^-4 \times {}^-4$

Exercise 2.1

1 Copy and complete these multiplications.

a) $^-3 \times {}^+2 =$

b) $^+4 \times {}^+6 =$

c) $^+5 \times {}^-9 =$

d) $^+8 \times {}^-10 =$

e) $^-6 \times {}^-3 =$

f) $^-10 \times {}^-10 =$

2 $^+6 \times {}^-4 = {}^-24$

a) Write down two division facts from this multiplication fact.

b) Check your answers with the rules of dividing integers.

3 a) Copy and complete this multiplication table

$\times$	$^-4$	$^-3$	$^-2$	$^-1$	0	$^+1$	$^+2$	$^+3$	$^+4$
$^-4$	$^+16$								
$^-3$								$^-9$	
$^-2$			$^+4$						
$^-1$									
0					0				
$^+1$									
$^+2$									$^+8$
$^+3$	$^-12$								
$^+4$				$^-4$					

b) Write down any patterns you notice in   i) the numbers   ii) the signs.

4 Work out

a) $^-3 \times {}^-5$

b) $^+16 \div {}^-2$

c) $^-2 \times {}^+3 \times {}^+4$

d) $\dfrac{^-8}{^-4}$

e) $^+3 \times {}^-8 \times {}^-2$

f) $\dfrac{^+20}{^-5}$

5 Find the value of   a) $(^+2)^2$ b) $(^-5)^2$ c) $(^-9)^2$

6 Copy and complete these multiplication pyramids. Each number is found by multiplying the two numbers below it.

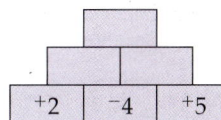

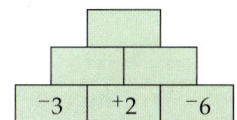

| $^+2$ | $^-4$ | $^+5$ |

| $^-3$ | $^+2$ | $^-6$ |

7 Copy and complete these sentences

a) When multiplying integers, if the signs are the same the answer is ....

b) When dividing integers, if the signs are .... the answer is positive.

c) When multiplying integers, if the signs are different the answer is ....

d) When dividing integers, if the signs are .... the answer is negative.

8 Using the sign change key on a calculator, work out

$\times$	$^-62$	$^+39$	$^-124$
$^+82$			
$^-247$			
$^+76$			

$\div$	$^-144$	$^+216$	$^-444$
$^-6$			
$^+12$			
$^-4$			

9 a) Write down as many multiplications as you can that have an answer of $^-10$.

b) Write down two divisions that give the answer $^-10$.

c) Now do the same for an answer of $^-12$.

Ordering fractions

- Order fractions by converting them to decimals
- Order fractions by converting them to equivalent fractions with a common denominator
- Order fractions by positioning them on a number line

Key words
fraction
numerator
denominator
equivalent
  fraction
common
  denominator

There are several methods for ordering this set of **fractions** : $\frac{3}{5}, \frac{7}{10}, \frac{3}{4}, \frac{5}{8}$
Here are two:

Method 1: Convert the fractions to decimals by dividing the **numerator** by the **denominator**

i.e. $\frac{3}{5} = 0.6$ $\frac{7}{10} = 0.7$ $\frac{3}{4} = 0.75$ $\frac{5}{8} = 0.625$

Show them on a number line

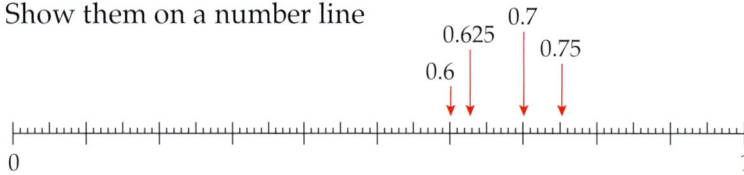

Method 2: Convert them to **equivalent fractions** with a **common denominator**.

The denominators of the four fractions are: 5, 10, 4, 8
The lowest common multiple of these is 40.

$\frac{3}{5} = \frac{24}{40}$ Multiply numerator and denominator by 8.

$\frac{7}{10} = \frac{28}{40}$ Multiply numerator and denominator by 4.

$\frac{3}{4} = \frac{30}{40}$ Multiply numerator and denominator by 10.

$\frac{5}{8} = \frac{25}{40}$ Multiply numerator and denominator by 5.

Writing them in order: $\frac{24}{40}, \frac{25}{40}, \frac{28}{40}, \frac{30}{40}$ or $\frac{3}{5}, \frac{5}{8}, \frac{7}{10}, \frac{3}{4}$.

Example $\frac{4}{20}$ $\frac{4}{5}$ $\frac{3}{10}$

a) Change these fractions into
    i) decimals   ii) equivalent fractions with a common denominator.
b) Show them on separate number lines.
c) Write the fractions in order from smallest to largest.

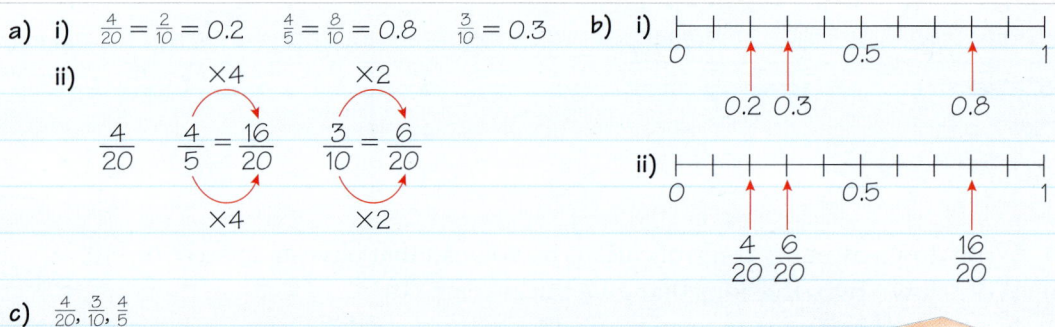

a) i) $\frac{4}{20} = \frac{2}{10} = 0.2$ $\frac{4}{5} = \frac{8}{10} = 0.8$ $\frac{3}{10} = 0.3$

    ii)
    $$\frac{4}{20} \qquad \overset{\times 4}{\frac{4}{5} = \frac{16}{20}} \qquad \overset{\times 2}{\frac{3}{10} = \frac{6}{20}}$$

b) i)

    ii)

c) $\frac{4}{20}, \frac{3}{10}, \frac{4}{5}$

Exercise 2.2

1 $\frac{1}{2}$ $\frac{3}{4}$ $\frac{3}{20}$

   a) Change these fractions into decimals.

   b) Show them on a number line.

   c) Write the fractions in order from smallest to largest.

2 Find these equivalent fractions.

   a) $\frac{3}{8} = \frac{}{24}$ **b)** $\frac{4}{7} = \frac{}{21}$ **c)** $\frac{4}{5} = \frac{}{40}$ **d)** $\frac{1}{6} = \frac{}{30}$

3 0 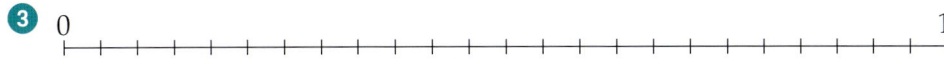 1

   a) Make a copy of this number line and place the following fractions on it.

      $\frac{7}{24}$ $\frac{1}{2}$ $\frac{2}{3}$ $\frac{3}{4}$ $\frac{3}{8}$ $\frac{1}{6}$ $\frac{5}{12}$

   b) Now put them in order from the smallest to the largest.

> Change them into equivalent fractions with a common denominator.

4 What would be the lowest common denominator for these pairs of fractions?

   a) $\frac{1}{3}$ and $\frac{2}{5}$ **b)** $\frac{2}{3}$ and $\frac{3}{4}$ **c)** $\frac{3}{7}$ and $\frac{2}{5}$ **d)** $\frac{3}{4}$ and $\frac{4}{5}$

5 By changing into equivalent fractions with a common denominator, find the largest fraction in each pair in **Q4**.

6 $\frac{2}{3}$ $\frac{5}{6}$ $\frac{3}{4}$

   a) Change these fractions into equivalent fractions with a common denominator.

   b) Show them on a number line.

   c) Write them in order from smallest to largest.

7 Which of these fractions is closest to 1?

      $\frac{7}{8}$ $\frac{23}{25}$ $1\frac{1}{10}$ $1\frac{3}{20}$

8 Use the signs $<$, $>$ or $=$ to complete the following:

   a) $\frac{1}{3}$ [ ] $\frac{2}{9}$ **b)** $\frac{5}{8}$ [ ] $\frac{4}{5}$ **c)** $\frac{1}{4}$ [ ] 0.23   **d)** 1.3 [ ] $1\frac{3}{10}$

9 John eats $\frac{2}{5}$ of a bar of chocolate and Sami eats $\frac{5}{12}$ of a bar. Who eats the most chocolate?

10 **a)** Find a fraction that is halfway between $\frac{3}{5}$ and $\frac{13}{15}$.

      It might help to place them on a number line.

   b) Find a fraction that is halfway between 0.25 and $\frac{5}{12}$.

> What fraction is the same as 0.25?

Adding and subtracting fractions

- ⊕ Add fractions by converting them to equivalent fractions with a common denominator
- ⊕ Subtract fractions by converting them to equivalent fractions with a common denominator

We can easily add and subtract **fractions** when they have the same **denominator**.

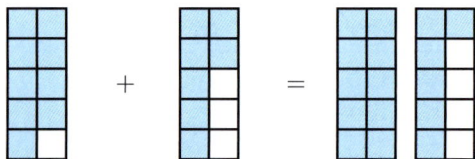

$$\frac{9}{10} + \frac{7}{10} = \frac{16}{10} = 1\frac{6}{10}$$
$$= 1\frac{3}{5}$$

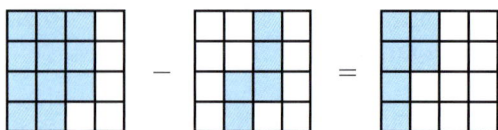

$$\frac{11}{16} - \frac{5}{16} = \frac{6}{16} = \frac{3}{8}$$

If the fractions have different denominators, then convert them to **equivalent fractions** which all have the same **(common) denominator**.

When choosing a common denominator, it is easier to choose the smallest possible common denominator. This is the **lowest** (smallest) **common multiple** of the denominators.

Suppose you need to add the fractions $\frac{2}{3}$, $\frac{7}{12}$ and $\frac{5}{8}$.

Their denominators are 3, 12 and 8.
The lowest common multiple of 3, 12 and 8 is 24.

So, find equivalent fractions with denominators of 24:
$$\frac{2}{3} = \frac{16}{24}, \frac{7}{12} = \frac{14}{24}, \frac{5}{8} = \frac{15}{24}$$

Add these together: $\frac{16}{24} + \frac{14}{24} + \frac{15}{24} = \frac{45}{24} = 1\frac{21}{24}$ or $1\frac{7}{8}$.

Example 1 Work out **a)** $\frac{3}{8} + \frac{7}{8}$ **b)** $\frac{2}{3} - \frac{1}{4}$ **c)** $2\frac{1}{2} - 1\frac{2}{3}$

a) $\frac{3}{8} + \frac{7}{8} = \frac{10}{8} = 1\frac{2}{8}$ or $1\frac{1}{4}$

Same denominator so just add the numerators.

b) $\frac{2}{3} - \frac{1}{4}$

$\overset{\times 4}{\frac{2}{3} = \frac{8}{12}}$ $\overset{\times 3}{\frac{1}{4} = \frac{3}{12}}$
$\underset{\times 4}{}$ $\underset{\times 3}{}$

$\frac{2}{3} - \frac{1}{4} = \frac{8}{12} - \frac{3}{12} = \frac{5}{12}$

The lowest common multiple of 3 and 4 is 12.

c) $2\frac{1}{2} - 1\frac{2}{3} = \frac{5}{2} - \frac{5}{3}$

$\frac{5}{2} - \frac{5}{3} = \frac{15}{6} - \frac{10}{6}$
$= \frac{5}{6}$

Change to improper fractions.

$\overset{\times 3}{\frac{5}{2} = \frac{15}{6}}$ $\overset{\times 2}{\frac{5}{3} = \frac{10}{6}}$
$\underset{\times 3}{}$ $\underset{\times 2}{}$

Exercise 2.3

1 Work out

a) $\frac{4}{5} + \frac{3}{5}$

b) $\frac{5}{7} - \frac{2}{7}$

c) $\frac{3}{10} + \frac{4}{10} + \frac{7}{10}$

d) $\frac{1}{3} + \frac{5}{6}$

e) $\frac{3}{4} - \frac{1}{8}$

f) $\frac{3}{5} - \frac{7}{20}$

2 Find the value of

a) $\frac{2}{3} + \frac{1}{4}$

b) $\frac{1}{2} + \frac{2}{5}$

c) $\frac{2}{3} + \frac{1}{5}$

d) $\frac{3}{4} - \frac{1}{6}$

e) $\frac{4}{7} - \frac{1}{3}$

f) $\frac{5}{6} - \frac{4}{5}$

3 Write as improper fractions

a) $3\frac{1}{2}$

b) $2\frac{1}{4}$

c) $1\frac{5}{6}$

d) $2\frac{3}{5}$

4 Work out

a) $1\frac{1}{2} + 2\frac{1}{4}$

b) $2\frac{1}{3} + 1\frac{2}{5}$

c) $2\frac{3}{4} - 1\frac{3}{8}$

d) $2\frac{1}{6} - 1\frac{1}{4}$

5 In Megan's garden $\frac{1}{2}$ was a grass lawn and $\frac{1}{3}$ was a flower bed.

a) How much garden was lawn and flower bed altogether?

b) How much garden is left?

6 Ali ate $\frac{5}{12}$ of a pizza and Susie ate $\frac{1}{4}$.

a) How much did they eat altogether?

b) How much pizza was left?

7 Three friends were putting their favourite music onto a tape. Pat filled $\frac{3}{8}$ of the tape and Sean $\frac{5}{12}$. What fraction of the tape is left for Raffi?

8 What is the perimeter of this rectangle?

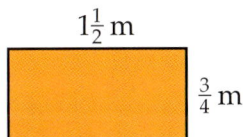

$1\frac{1}{2}$ m

$\frac{3}{4}$ m

Perimeter is all the way round.

9 Mr. Green has $3\frac{1}{2}$ m of wood.
He uses $1\frac{3}{4}$ m.
How much wood has he left?

Investigation

10 a) Find the differences between the fractions in this sequence.

$$\frac{1}{2} \qquad \frac{2}{3} \qquad \frac{3}{4} \qquad \frac{4}{5} \qquad \frac{5}{6}$$

b) Can you guess what the next difference will be?

c) Continue the sequence and check to see if you were right.

Take the largest from the smallest in each pair.

Look for a pattern.

Multiplying and dividing by fractions

- ⊕ Multiply an integer by a fraction
- ⊕ Divide an integer by a fraction
- ⊕ Know how to calculate fractions of quantities

To find $\frac{3}{4}$ of £32, first find $\frac{1}{4}$ of £32, then multiply this by 3.

So, $\frac{1}{4}$ of £32 = £8 and $\frac{3}{4}$ of £32 = £8 × 3 = £24

Multiplying by a fraction :

$\frac{3}{4}$ of £32 is the same as $\frac{3}{4}$ × £32

To find $\frac{3}{4}$ × £32, write it as $\frac{3}{4}$ × $\frac{32}{1}$, and **cancel** if possible.

$$\frac{3}{\underset{1}{4}} \times £\frac{\overset{8}{32}}{1} = £\frac{24}{1} = £24$$

> Cancel by dividing by 4. When no further cancelling is possible, multiply the **numerators** together, and the **denominators** together.

Dividing by a fraction:

$3 \div \frac{1}{4} = ?$

This is the same as asking 'How many quarters are there in 3?'.

There are 4 quarters in 1, so there are 3 × 4, or 12 quarters in 3.

$3 \div \frac{1}{4} = 12$	$3 \times \frac{4}{1} = 12$
$5 \div \frac{1}{3} = 15$	$5 \times \frac{3}{1} = 15$
$10 \div \frac{1}{5} = 50$	$10 \times \frac{5}{1} = 50$

From this list we can see that dividing by a fraction is equivalent to multiplying by the same fraction with the numerator and denominator switched:

So, for example, $32 \div \frac{1}{4} = \frac{32}{1} \times \frac{4}{1} = \frac{128}{1} = 128$ and $60 \div \frac{3}{5} = \frac{60}{1} \times \frac{5}{3} = \frac{100}{1} = 100$

Example   Work out   **a)** $\frac{3}{5}$ of £40   **b)** $7 \div \frac{1}{5}$

a) $\frac{3}{5}$ of £40 = $\frac{3}{5}$ × £40

There are two ways of calculating this:

Method 1	Method 2
$\frac{1}{5}$ of 40 = $\frac{40}{5}$ = £8	$\frac{3}{5} \times \frac{40}{1}$
$\frac{3}{5}$ of 40 = 3 × £8	$\frac{3}{\underset{1}{5}} \times \frac{\overset{8}{40}}{1} = \frac{24}{1}$
= £24	= £24

> £40 is written as $\frac{40}{1}$ as a fraction.

> Cancel any numerator with any denominator.

b) $7 \div \frac{1}{5} = 7 \times \frac{5}{1}$

> Dividing by $\frac{1}{5}$ is the same as multiplying by $\frac{5}{1}$.

Method 1	Method 2
5 fifths in 1	$\frac{7}{1} \times \frac{5}{1} = \frac{35}{1}$
5 × 7 = 35	= 35
35 fifths in 7	

Exercise 2.4

1. Simplify these fractions by cancelling down to their lowest form.
   a) $\frac{15}{20}$
   b) $\frac{8}{10}$
   c) $\frac{14}{21}$
   d) $\frac{16}{20}$
   e) $\frac{9}{24}$

2. Work out
   a) $\frac{2}{3}$ of £27
   b) $\frac{4}{5}$ of 55 g
   c) $\frac{3}{8}$ of 32 m
   d) $\frac{4}{9}$ of 72 ℓ

3. Calculate
   a) $28 \times \frac{1}{4}$
   b) $18 \times \frac{4}{9}$
   c) $\frac{5}{6} \times 36$
   d) $80 \times \frac{3}{8}$

4. Find the value of
   a) $4 \div \frac{1}{3}$
   b) $11 \div \frac{1}{5}$
   c) $9 \div \frac{1}{6}$
   d) $15 \div \frac{1}{4}$

5. Copy and complete these sentences
   a) $\frac{3}{7}$ of £30 is the same as $\frac{3}{7} \times$ ......
   b) $24 \times \frac{5}{9}$ is the same as ...... $\times$ 24
   c) $6 \div \frac{1}{8}$ is the same as 6 ...... $\frac{8}{1}$
   d) Dividing by $\frac{1}{20}$ is the same as multiplying by ......

6. Zoë collects £93 for April Cosmetics. She receives $\frac{1}{3}$ of this amount in pay. How much does she get paid?

7. At his party Ray expects everyone to eat $\frac{1}{5}$ of a pizza. He has 6 pizzas. How many people could he invite?

8. Fazir spends $\frac{3}{8}$ of his pocket money on magazines. If he gets £4 pocket money, how much does he spend on magazines?

9. a) What is the area of this bookmark?
   b) What would be the area of 12 bookmarks?

   12 inches

   $\frac{7}{8}$ inch

10. Benji spends $\frac{2}{3}$ of his pocket money and saves the rest. This week he spent £5. How much did he save?

   What fraction does he save?

11.

   $\frac{1}{2}$ of 8

   Answer 4

   $2 \div \frac{1}{2}$

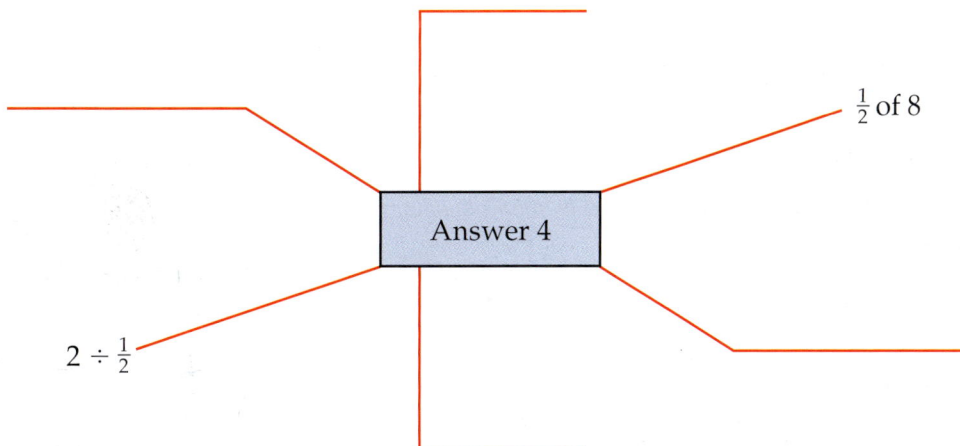

   Find four more fraction facts to complete the diagram.

Ordering decimals

- Put decimal numbers in order by comparing their digits
- Position decimal numbers on a number line
- Use accurately the symbols $<, >, \leqslant, \geqslant$
- Find a number halfway between two others

Compare the size of these decimal numbers:

A: 2.48
B: 2.47
C: 2.476

Compare their digits , starting from the left to the right.

| Compare whole numbers (the same) | Compare tenths digits (the same) | Compare hundredths digits (A is the largest, B, C the same) | Compare thousandths digits (C is larger than B) |

So the order is B, C, A, i.e. 2.47, 2.476, 2.48

We can write $2.47 < 2.476 < 2.48$ ———— smallest to largest
Or $2.48 > 2.476 > 2.47$ ———— largest to smallest

And position them on a number line:

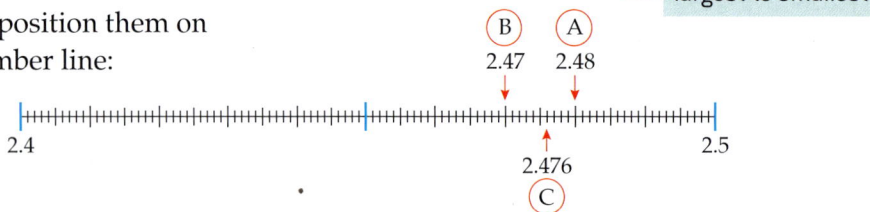

B   A
2.47 2.48

```
|++++|++++|++++|++++|++++|++++|++++|++++|++++|++++|
2.4                                              2.5
```
2.476
C

To find a number exactly halfway between two numbers use the number line:
For example,   halfway between A and C is 2.478
              halfway between B and C is 2.473

$x \geqslant 2.48$ means x is a number greater than or equal to 2.48.
$x \leqslant 2.47$ means x is a number less than or equal to 2.47.

Example 1   Place these decimals in order from smallest to largest: 5.323, 5.32, 5.319, 5.4

A 5.323
B 5.32 ⟵———— B is the next smallest
C 5.319
D 5.4

B has nothing in the thousandths column and A has a 3.

Units are the same
C is the smallest
D is the largest

In order C B A D = 5.319, 5.32, 5.323, 5.4

Example 2   List all the possible values for x using one or two decimal places: $3.2 \leqslant x < 3.24$

3.2, 3.21, 3.22, 3.23 ————

$3.2 \leqslant x$ means the number can also equal 3.2.

Exercise 2.5

1 Put the correct sign $<$ or $>$ between these numbers
   a) 6.37   6.371
   b) 0.328   0.238
   c) 4.239   4.193
   d) 3.664   3.6641
   e) $^-$1.35 $^-$1.349
   f) 0.6042   0.60402

2 Write these numbers from smallest to largest
   a) 0.263   0.259   0.26   0.3
   b) 7.43   7.426   7.438   7.443
   c) 2.847   2.839   2.845   2.84   2.83

3 Copy each number line and place the numbers on it.

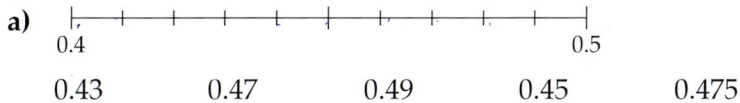

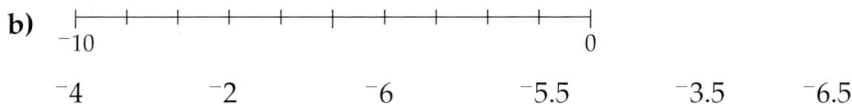

   a)
   0.4   0.5

      0.43   0.47   0.49   0.45   0.475

   b)
   $^-$10   0

      $^-$4 $^-$2 $^-$6 $^-$5.5 $^-$3.5 $^-$6.5

   c)
   $^-$2 $^-$1

      $^-$1.3 $^-$1.55 $^-$1.05 $^-$1.68 $^-$1.72 $^-$1.13

4 $9.133 < x \leqslant 9.42$
   Are these numbers possible values for x?
   a) 9.132   b) 9.42   c) 9.267   d) 9.133   e) 9.4199

5 Place these numbers in this number sentence to make it true: ____ $<$ ____ $<$ ____
   a) 4.25   4.205   4.2   b) 3.129   3.124   3.13   c) $^-$6.27 $^-$6.32 $^-$6.23

6 List the possible values for x.
   a) $^-5 < x < ^-1$ (using whole numbers)
   b) $1.3 < x \leqslant 1.8$ (using numbers with one decimal place)
   c) $5.27 \leqslant x < 5.33$ (using numbers with two decimal places)
   d) $^-3.47 \leqslant x \leqslant ^-3.468$ (using numbers with three decimal places)

> Numbers with one decimal place have one number after the decimal point.

7 These are the results of an experiment to find at which temperature (°C) different liquids freeze.
   $^-$0.1 $^-$0.02 $^-$0.34 $^-$0.024 $^-$0.002 $^-$0.06
   Place them in descending order.

> Put the coldest last.

8 Which number is halfway between these numbers? You can use a number line to help.
   a) 0.7 and 0.8   b) 0.32 and 0.33   c) 6.324 and 6.328
   d) $^-$4.32 and $^-$4.38   e) 5.26 and 5.264   f) 1.31 and 1.37

- Simplify a ratio to an equivalent ratio by cancelling
- Divide a quantity into two or more parts in a given ratio

The **proportion** of red pegs is $\frac{4}{12}$ or $\frac{1}{3}$.
The proportion of blue pegs is $\frac{8}{12}$ or $\frac{2}{3}$.

A proportion compares one part (e.g. blue pegs) with the whole (all pegs).

The **ratio** of red pegs to blue pegs is 4 : 8 or 1 : 2
The ratio of blue pegs to red pegs is 8 : 4 or 2 : 1

A ratio compares one part (blue pegs) with another part (red pegs).

Ratios can be simplified by **cancelling**.
Ratios can have more than two parts.

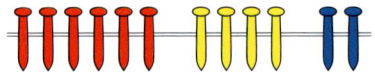

The ratio of red to yellow to blue pegs is: 6 : 4 : 2 or, by cancelling, 3 : 2 : 1.

Example 1 Write in their simplest form

a) 30 : 6   b) 120 : 100 : 40   c) 75p : £2

a) 30 : 6
        5 : 1
Cancel by dividing by 6.

b) 120 : 100 : 40
    12 : 10 : 4
     6 :   5 : 2
Cancel by dividing by 10.
Cancel by dividing by 2.

c) 75p : £2
    75 : 200
     3 : 8
Change them both into pence then cancel by dividing by 25.

Example 2 Jamina has a big bag of coloured pens. She wants to use 30 of them to make a pattern of red and blue pens in the ratio 3 : 2. How many of each colour will she need?

Red : Blue   Total
  3 : 2   5 pens
×2   ×2 (to make 10)
  6 : 4   10 pens
×3   ×3 (to make 30)
 18 : 12   30 pens

She will need 18 red pens and 12 blue pens.

You could multiply by 6 to do this in one step:
$5 \times 6 = 30$

Exercise 2.6

1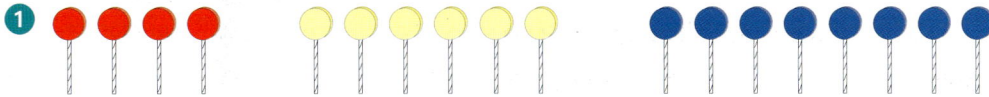

    a) How many lollypops are there altogether?

    b) What proportion are red?

    c) What is the ratio of red to blue lollypops?

    d) What is the ratio of yellow to blue lollypops?

    e) What is the ratio of blue to red to yellow lollypops?

> Make sure your answers are in their simplest terms.

2 Simplify these ratio by cancelling.

    a) $35:15$ **b)** $8:32$ **c)** $7:14:21$ **d)** $48:36$ **e)** $9:15:21$ **f)** £2:40p

3 Ali has a big bag of sweets. He wants to make a pattern of red and yellow sweets in the ratio $5:3$. If he uses 40 sweets, how many of each colour will he use?

4 In Jed's street there are 27 dogs and 36 cats. Write the ratio of cats to dogs in its simplest form.

5 A survey of Year 9 pupils' favourite types of food gave the following results.

Food	Pizza	Burgers	Fried Chicken
Number	80	60	160

    a) What is the ratio of Pizza to Fried Chicken?

    b) What is the ratio of Pizza to Burgers?

    c) What is the ratio of Burgers to Pizza to Fried Chicken?

> Remember to cancel down.

6 A school trip needs 2 teachers for every 32 pupils.

    a) Write this as a ratio in its simplest form.

    b) The Headteacher has said that 6 teachers can go on the trip. How many pupils can go?

7 Simon, 8 years old, Rachel, 12 years old, and Scott, 16 years old, are given pocket money by their Grandfather in the ratio of their ages.

    a) Write the ratio in its simplest form.

    b) If Simon gets £2, how much does their Grandfather give them altogether each week?

    c) How much does he give in 4 weeks?

    d) How many weeks will it be before he has given £81 between them?

8 Simplify these ratios by cancelling down. Remember to change your units first.

    a) $3\,m:50\,cm$ **b)** $10\,min:1\,hour$ **c)** $250\,g:2\,kg$ **d)** $2\,\ell:75\,ml$

9 I have £55 to share out between Yasmin and Ben in the ratio $6:5$.
How much will each get?

> Look back at Example 2 to help you.

Investigation

10 **a)** Find the ratio of right to left handed people in your class.

    b) Do a survey similar to **Q5** to find some favourites in your class. Show your results as ratios in their lowest terms.

Ratio and direct proportion

⊕ Understand the relationship between ratio and proportion

⊕ Solve problems using direct proportion

Unit means 'one'.

In the **unitary method** we solve problems by first considering one item.

For example, if 6 tickets cost £54, then we can find the cost of 5 tickets, 20 tickets, 11 tickets, or any number of tickets, by first finding the cost of 1 ticket.

If 6 tickets cost £54, then 1 ticket costs £54 ÷ 6 = £9

So   5 tickets cost £45   (5 × 9)
        20 tickets cost £180   (20 × 9)
        11 tickets cost £99   (11 × 9)

The cost of the tickets is in **direct proportion** to the number of tickets.

The **ratio** of tickets to cost is 1 : £9.

For every ticket we buy, the cost goes up by £9.

Example 1 To make 25 gingerbread men you need 400 g of flour, 225 g of sugar and 50 g of ginger. I want to make 35 gingerbread men for my party. How much of each ingredient will I need?

Flour	25 men need 400 g
	1 man needs 400 ÷ 25 = 16 g
	35 men need 35 × 16 = 560 g
Sugar	25 men need 225 g
	1 man needs 225 ÷ 25 = 9 g
	35 men need 35 × 9 = 315 g
Ginger	25 men need 50 g
	1 man needs 50 ÷ 25 = 2 g
	35 men need 35 × 2 = 70 g
I need 560 g flour, 315 g sugar and 70 g ginger.	

Take each ingredient separately.

Example 2 The cost of 7 pens is £2.10. What is the cost of 5 pens?

7 pens cost   210p

1 pen costs $\dfrac{210}{7}$

5 pens cost $\dfrac{210}{7} \times \dfrac{5}{1} = \dfrac{\overset{30}{\cancel{210}}}{\underset{1}{\cancel{7}}} \times \dfrac{5}{1} = \dfrac{150}{1}$

= £1.50

Change into pence.

Exercise 2.7

1 Find the following:
   a) If 6 pizzas cost £14.70, how much will 10 cost?
   b) If 9 drinks cost £3.42, how much will 5 cost?
   c) If 14 cinema tickets cost £32.90, how much will 8 cost?
   d) If 8 bus tickets cost £6.08, what will 3 cost?
   e) If 53 m of ribbon cost £11.66, what will 24 m cost?
   f) If 12 litres of paint cost £10.44, what will 7 litres cost?

2 Paul works 18 hours a week and earns £80.10.
   a) How much does he earn per hour?
   b) How much would he be paid for a 38 hour week?

3 To mix 1 cocktail drink you need 100 ml of lemonade, 75 ml of orange juice and 25 ml of cranberry juice.
   a) Write the ratio of lemonade to orange juice to cranberry juice without simplifying.
   b) If I want to make 12 cocktail drinks, how much of each ingredient will I need?

4 To cook a 5 pound pumpkin takes 2 hours.
   How long would it take to cook a 2 pound pumpkin?

   Change your hours into minutes.

5 To make green paint you mix 8 ℓ of yellow paint with 3 ℓ of blue. How much yellow paint would I need for these amounts of blue paint.
   a) 6 ℓ   **b)** 1 ℓ   **c)** 5 ℓ   **d)** 7 ℓ

6 On a visit to America I got $1.71 for £1.
   a) How many dollars would I get for £35?
   b) How many pounds would I get for $30? Give your answer to the nearest penny.

7 To make 20 cheese scones I use 480 g of flour, 240 g of butter and 110 g of cheese.
   How much of each ingredient will I need to make 12 scones?

8 The large cog in a clock turns 4 times when the small cog turns 9 times.
   a) How many times will the small cog turn if the large one turns 16 times?
   b) If the small cog turns 54 times, how many times will the big cog turn?

9 A 500 g packet of cornflakes costs £1.75. A 300 g packet costs £1.25. Which is the better value?

   Which packet costs less for 1 g or 100 g?

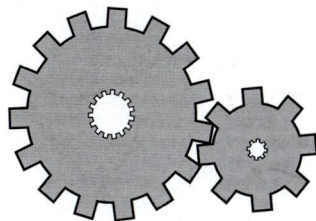

Investigation

10 Compare the prices for different items in your local supermarket. Is it always best to buy the biggest packet?

Percentages

- Understand that percentage can mean 'so many hundredths'
- Calculate percentages of numbers, quantities and measurements using written methods and using a calculator
- Express one number as a percentage of another

Key words
percentage
fraction
decimal
cancelling
unitary method

% is shorthand for 'per cent'. It means 'out of one hundred' or 'so many hundredths'.

35% means '35 out of every 100'

A **percentage** (35%) can be written as a **fraction** ($\frac{35}{100}$), and as a **decimal** (0.35).

Here are three methods for finding a percentage of a quantity, for example, 35% of £80.

Method 1   Write the percentage as a fraction and multiply using **cancelling** :

$$35\% \text{ of } £80 = \frac{35}{100} \times \frac{80}{1} = £28 \qquad \frac{\overset{7}{\cancel{35}}}{\underset{\underset{1}{20}}{\cancel{100}}} \times \frac{\overset{\overset{4}{\cancel{8}}}{\cancel{80}}}{1} = \frac{28}{1} = £28$$

Method 2   Write the percentage as a decimal and multiply, using a calculator:

$$35\% \text{ of } £80 = 0.35 \times 80 = £28 \qquad \boxed{0}\ \boxed{.}\ \boxed{3}\ \boxed{5}\ \boxed{\times}\ \boxed{8}\ \boxed{0}\ \boxed{=}$$

Method 3   Use the **unitary method** by finding 1%:

$$1\% \text{ of } £80 = \frac{80}{100} = £0.80$$
$$35\% \text{ of } £80 = 35 \times £0.80 = £28$$

To express one number as a percentage of another, e.g. £18 as a percentage of £30: write the first as a fraction of the second ($\frac{18}{30}$), change it to a decimal, using a calculator if necessary (0.60), and then convert it to a percentage (60%).

Example 1   Find 18% of £25

Method 1 – using fractions: $18\% \text{ of } £25 = \frac{\overset{9}{\cancel{18}}}{\underset{4}{\cancel{100}}} \times \frac{\overset{1}{\cancel{25}}}{1} = \frac{9}{2} = £4.50$

$18\% = \frac{18}{100} = 0.18$

Method 2 – decimals: $18\% \text{ of } £25 = 0.18 \times £25 = £4.50$

Method 3 – unitary method: $1\% \text{ of } £25 = \frac{25}{100} = £\frac{1}{4} \text{ or } 25p$

$18\% \text{ of } £25 = 18 \times \frac{1}{4} \text{ or } 18 \times 25p = £4.50$

Example 2   What is 5 minutes as a percentage of 1 hour?

$$\frac{5 \text{ min}}{1 \text{ hr}} = \frac{5}{60} \qquad \frac{5}{60} = 0.0833 \qquad 0.0833 \times 100 = 8.3\%$$

Change into the same units

Multiply by 100 to change a decimal into a percentage.

Exercise 2.8

1 Using different methods find the following:
- **a)** 20% of £60
- **b)** 75% of 36 kg
- **c)** 5% of 150 m
- **d)** 17% of £45
- **e)** 23% of 350 ml
- **f)** 65% of 1700 km
- **g)** 3% of £300
- **h)** 5% of 25 kg
- **i)** 8% of 250 ml

2 If I scored 12 out of 15 in a Maths test, what percentage did I score?

3 In English I got 65% of the 40 questions correct. How many questions did I get right?

4 Which is larger, 15% of 30 g or 18% of 20 g?

5 What is 150 g as a percentage of 1 kg?

6 Ann earns £120 per week. She has to pay 22% of this in tax. How much tax does she pay?

7 A pair of shoes are marked "£35". In the sale there is 15% off the marked price.
- **a)** How much will I save in the sale?
- **b)** How much will the shoes cost now?

8 A survey of how the 820 pupils at Great Hall School came to school each day is shown in the pie chart. Work out how many pupils came by each method.

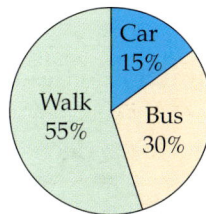

Car 15%
Walk 55%
Bus 30%

9 Mr White had to pay 15% deposit on his new car. If the car cost £8000, how much deposit did he have to pay?

10 Can you find 5 more percentage questions that have an answer of 24?

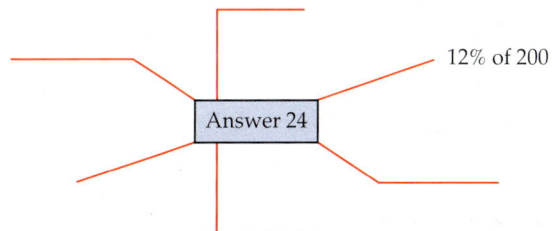

12% of 200

Answer 24

Investigation

11 This is part of the results of a football league.
- **a)** Work out the percentage of wins for each team. Place them in order. Is this the same as the league table?
- **b)** Work out the percentage of games lost for each team. Place them in order. Is this the same as the league table?

	P	W	D	L	Points
Luton	15	10	2	3	32
Bradford	15	9	1	5	28
Huddersfield	14	7	2	5	23
Swindon	14	6	3	5	21

- **c)** Now look at another league. Work out the percentage of games won and lost and see it this is the same order as the table.

Percentage increase and decrease

⊕ Know how to find a percentage increase or decrease

Key words
percentage
increase
percentage
decrease
unitary method

When a price goes up, it increases.
When a price goes down, it decreases.

Examples of **percentage increases** are:
    8% more (108%)   10% extra (110%)   up by 25% (125%)

Examples of **percentage decreases** are:
    5% less (95%)   35% off (65%)   reduced by 12% (88%)

To calculate the result of £240 decreased by 15%:
    Find 85% of £240 by one of these methods:
    Method 1   Use fractions and cancel: $\frac{85}{100} \times \frac{240}{1} = £204$
    Method 2   Use decimals: $0.85 \times £240 = £204$
    Method 3   Use the **unitary method** : 1% of £240 = £2.40,
                                 85% of £240 = 85 × £2.40 = £204
    85% of £240 is £204, which is a decrease of £36.

Example 1   John gets a 4% increase in pay. If he was earning £12 000 a year, how much will he be earning now?

4% increase = 100% + 4% = 104%

$104\% \text{ of } £12\,000 = \dfrac{104}{100} \times \dfrac{12\,000}{1} = £12\,480$

You can use any method to find 104%.

Example 2   Molly's car cost £2500. After one year it is worth 15% less.
    a) How much is it worth now?
    b) How much has the car fallen in value?

a) 15% less = 100% − 15% = 85%

    85% of £2500 = 0.85 × £2500 = £2125

b) £2500 − £2125 = £375

Exercise 2.9

1 What percentage would you use to calculate these percentage increases and decreases?
The first one has been done for you.
    a) 5% more = 100% + 5% = 105%
    b) 5% less   **c)** extra 25%   **d)** 12% off   **e)** down 20%

2 Copy and complete the table

	7% increase	3% decrease
£40		
125 g		
6.5 kg		

3 A packet of biscuits that is usually 150 g is going on special offer. The new pack says "25% extra free". What will be the mass of the new pack?

4 Find the cost of these items in the sale.
   a) £20 jumper with 5% off
   b) £32 trousers with 15% off
   c) £45 tracksuit with 12% off
   d) £66 coat with 30% off

5 Mr Brown increases the size of his lawn by 40%. If his lawn was 90 m², how big is it now?

6 Gary bought a mountain bike for £65. He sold it a month later and made 12% profit. How much did he sell his bike for?

> The original cost of his bike is 100%.

7 Carla borrows £2300 from "Car Loans 4 U" to buy a car. An interest charge of 9% is added on at the beginning of the year. How much does she now owe?

8 The Building Society pays an interest rate of $4\frac{1}{2}$% per year. If I saved £500, what would I get back at the end of the year?

> Write $4\frac{1}{2}$ as a decimal first.

9 The cost of a T.V. was £238 plus VAT at $17\frac{1}{2}$%. What was the full cost of the T.V.?

> VAT stands for Value Added Tax.

10 Ray earned £12 600 per annum before his $3\frac{1}{2}$% pay rise.
   a) What is his new wage per year?
   b) He has to pay 18% tax. How much tax does he pay now?

11 The population of sparrows is decreasing by 8% per year. If there are 200 000 sparrows now,
   a) how many will there be after one year?
   b) how many will there be by the end of 2 years?

> Use your answer to part **a)** for the number of sparrows at the start of the second year.

Investigation

12 This question requires a dice.
Your first throw of the dice gives you a number, use it to find a value from box A.
If the second throw is an even number then it is an increase, if it is odd it is a decrease.
The third throw gives you a percentage from box B.
For example, throws of 1, 4, 3 would give £250 increased by 15%.

Box A	
1	£250
2	800 g
3	620 m
4	2400 km
5	£2750
6	12.5 ℓ

Box B	
1	20%
2	12%
3	15%
4	8%
5	45%
6	86%

Now complete your calculation. Repeat this several times.

Solving equations 1

⊕ Solve equations with the unknown on one side

An **equation** is when two things are **equal**.
An equals sign means that both sides have the same value. For example, $2x + 3 = 13$ is an equation. The letter x is a particular **unknown** number.

You can **solve** equations using inverse operations, or by balancing the equation by doing the same to both sides.

Example 1 Use the balancing method to solve the equation $2x + 3 = 13$.

First, look at the equation to see what has been done to the unknown 'x'.

x has been multiplied by 2 and then 3 has been added.

To solve the equation we get a single x by itself on one side of the equals sign.

To keep the equation balanced we must do the same to both sides.

The inverse of adding 3 is subtracting 3.

The inverse of multiplying by 2 is dividing by 2.

Always check your answer:

$$LHS = 2x + 3$$
$$= 2 \times 5 + 3$$
$$= 10 + 3$$
$$= 13$$
$$= RHS$$

Example 2 Find the value of q in the equation $6 = \frac{3q}{4}$.

q has been multiplied by 3 and then divided by 4.

We carry out the inverse operations in reverse order: multiply by 4 then divide by 3.

Check:

$$RHS = \frac{3q}{4}$$
$$= \frac{3 \times 8}{4}$$
$$= \frac{24}{4}$$
$$= 6$$
$$= LHS$$

1 Copy and complete the following to find the value of t in each equation:

a)

$3t - 5$	$=$	16

| $+\ldots$ | | $+\ldots$ |

| $3t$ | $=$ | $\ldots$ |

| $\div\ldots$ | | $\div\ldots$ |

| t | $=$ | $\ldots$ |

b)

8	$=$	$5t - 2$

| $\ldots$ | | $\ldots$ |

| $\ldots$ | $=$ | $\ldots$ |

| $\ldots$ | | $\ldots$ |

| $\ldots$ | $=$ | $\ldots$ |

c)

$\dfrac{3t}{5}$	$=$	6

| $\times\ldots$ | | $\times\ldots$ |

| $3t$ | $=$ | $\ldots$ |

| $\div\ldots$ | | $\div\ldots$ |

| t | $=$ | $\ldots$ |

d)

$\dfrac{t}{5} + 4$	$=$	14

| $\ldots$ | | $\ldots$ |

| $\ldots$ | $=$ | $\ldots$ |

| $\ldots$ | | $\ldots$ |

| $\ldots$ | $=$ | $\ldots$ |

2 Find the value of the unknown in each of the following equations:
  a) $3a + 1 = 19$ **b)** $4b - 5 = 3$
  c) $10 = 5c + 5$ **d)** $12 = 2d - 10$

> Remember to check your answers.

3 Find the value of x in each of the following equations:
  a) $\dfrac{3x}{4} = 9$ **b)** $\dfrac{2x}{50} = 4$ **c)** $5 = \dfrac{10x}{50}$

4 Find the value of z in each of the following equations:
  a) $2z + 5 = 1$ **b)** $5z - 3 = {}^-23$ **c)** $5 = 3z + 35$

> You may find the value of z is negative!

5 Find the value of y in each of the following equations:

  a) $7y = {}^-21$ **b)** $\dfrac{y}{4} = {}^-5$ **c)** ${}^-20 = 10y$

  d) $\dfrac{10y}{15} = {}^-10$ **e)** $\dfrac{2y}{3} = {}^-22$ **f)** ${}^-3 = \dfrac{3y}{4}$

6 In a magic square the sum of the expressions in each row, column and diagonal is the same.
Find the value of x and use it to rewrite the magic square with numbers instead of algebraic expressions.

11	$3x - 1$	x
$x - 1$	10	$3x + 1$
$3x$	$x + 1$	9

> Do you know what each row, column and diagonal must add up to?

Forming equations 1

◈ Form and solve equations for real-life situations

Equations can help us find unknown values in real-life problems.

We use **algebraic expressions** to write an equation, and then solve it to find the unknown.

Remember, when solving equations we always do the same to both sides of the equation.

Example   Find the value of the unknown angles in the following triangle.

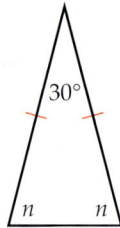

The triangle is isosceles, so the two unknown angles are equal. Label the unknown angles with a letter, n.

$n + n + 30 = 180$

$2n + 30 = 180$ — The angles in a triangle sum to 180°. Write an equation to show this.

$\boxed{-30}$ $\boxed{-30}$

$2n = 150$ — Simplify the equation.

$\boxed{\div 2}$ $\boxed{\div 2}$ — Solve the equation using the balancing method.

$n = 75$ — Make sure you answer the question you were asked.

The two missing angles are both 75°.

Check: LHS $= 2 \times 75 + 30$

$= 150 + 30$

$= 180$

$= $ RHS — Always check your answer.

Exercise 3.2

1 In an arithmagon, the number in the rectangle is the sum of the numbers in the two circles on either side of it.

   a) Write an equation using the base of the arithmagon.
   b) Solve your equation to find the value of x.
   c) Write two more equations using the arithmagon.
   d) Check your value of x by substituting it into these equations.

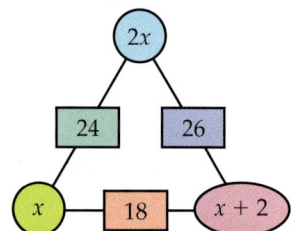

2 A rectangle's width is 5 cm more than its height:

h cm

We say the expression is 'in terms of *h*.

a) Write down an expression for the width of the rectangle.

b) Write down and simplify an expression for the perimeter of the rectangle.

The perimeter of the rectangle is 38 cm.

Form an equation and solve to find the value of *h*.

c) Find the height and width of the rectangle.

3 Three consecutive whole numbers sum to 24.

a) We can represent the smallest number with the letter '*n*'.
   Write an expression for:
   i) the second number   ii) the third number.

Consecutive means next to one another. For example the numbers 2, 3 and 4 are consecutive.

b) Write down and simplify an expression for the sum of the three numbers.

c) Using your answer to part **b)**, form and solve an equation to find the value of *n*.

d) What are the three consecutive numbers?

4 In this trapezium two of the angles are unknown.

a) Write an algebraic expression for the sum of the four angles in the trapezium.

$x°$ $x° - 20°$

$100°$ $110°$

The sum of the angles in any quadrilateral is 360°.

b) Use this and your answers to part **a)** to form an equation.

Simplify your equation as much as possible.

c) Solve your equation to find the value of *x*.

d) Write down the size of the missing angles.

5 Three sisters Kate, Caro and Liz share 25 sweets between them.
Caro has five more than Kate.
Liz has twice as many as Kate.
Kate has '*r*' sweets.

a) Write down an algebraic expression for the number of sweets Caro has.

b) Write down an algebraic expression for the number of sweets Liz has.

c) Form and simplify an equation in terms of *r*.

d) Solve your equation.

e) How many sweets does each sister have?

6 Find the value of the missing angles in each of the following triangles:

a)

b)

7 Glyn buys three bunches of flowers for Carla.
He pays with a £10 note and gets £1.75 change.
Form and solve an algebraic equation to find the cost of a bunch of flowers.

Use *x* to represent the cost of a bunch of flowers.

Solving equations 2

◈ Solve equations with an unknown on both sides

Key words
equation
unknown
solve

In some **equations** the **unknown** value occurs both sides of the equals sign. For example, $6x = 2x + 12$.

To **solve** this type of equation you collect all the unknown values on one side.

It is easiest to collect them on the side that has the largest number of unknown values.

Example   Solve the equation $6x = 2x + 12$.

$$6x = 2x + 12$$

$$-2x \qquad -2x$$

$$4x = 12$$

$$\div 4 \qquad \div 4$$

$$x = 3$$

Check: LHS $= 6x = 6 \times 3 = 18$ RHS $= 2x + 12 = 2 \times 3 + 12 = 18$

The LHS has $6x$, and the RHS has $2x$. We collect the unknown values on the left hand side, by subtracting $2x$ from both sides.

Now solve the equation.

Exercise 3.3

1 Copy and complete the following to find the value of t:

a)
$$3t = 2t + 5$$
$$-2t \qquad -2t$$
$$\ldots = \ldots$$

b)
$$5t = 4t + 7$$
$$-\ldots \qquad -\ldots$$
$$\ldots = \ldots$$

c)
$$5t = 3t + 4$$
$$-3t \qquad -3t$$
$$\ldots = \ldots$$
$$\div \ldots \qquad \div \ldots$$
$$\ldots = \ldots$$

d)
$$2t + 10 = 7t$$
$$\ldots \qquad \ldots$$
$$\ldots = \ldots$$
$$\ldots \qquad \ldots$$
$$\ldots = \ldots$$

2 Find the value of x in each of the following equations:

a) $5x + 3 = 6x$
b) $11x = 10x + 4$
c) $7x = 5x + 6$
d) $7x + 9 = 10x$
e) $4x + 12 = 6x$
f) $6x + 3 = 9x$

See the Example.

3 Copy and complete the following to find the value of p.

a) $4p + 5 \quad = \quad 2p + 13$

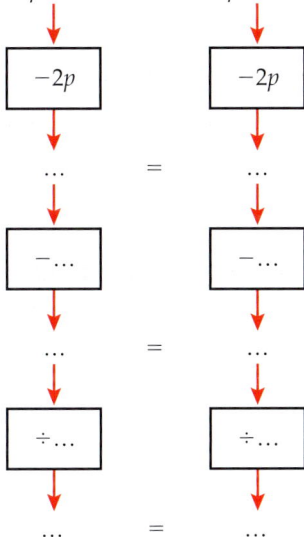

b) $7p + 12 \quad = \quad 10p - 3$

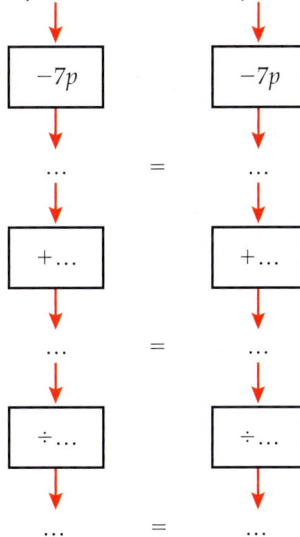

Remember to collect the unknowns on the side of the equation that has the most.

4 Find the value of the unknown in each of the following equations:

a) $2x + 5 = x + 16$
b) $3a + 2 = 2a + 8$
c) $3b + 4 = 6b + 1$
d) $5m - 6 = 3m + 2$
e) $10z - 3 = 12z - 7$

5 Work out the value of the unknown in each of the following equations:

a) $2z - 5 = z$
b) $3y = 2y + 7$
c) $5q = 10q - 15$
d) $7d + 4 = 11d$
e) $b = 2b$

One side of an equation may be equal to zero.

6 Lord Number collects china vegetables. He was given 20 when he was born and one for every birthday.

a) Write down an algebraic expression for the number of china vegetables he owns.

Let his age be represented by x.

Lord Algebra also collects china vegetables. He is given two for every birthday. He is the same age as Lord Number.

b) Write down an algebraic expression for the number of china vegetables he owns.

c) How old will the two Lords be when they have the same number of china vegetables?

The number they have will be equal.

Investigation

7 Explain why the following equation is mathematically impossible:

$x + 3 = x - 3$

What happens when you try to solve the equation?

Write down some more equations that are mathematically impossible.

Forming equations 2

◈ Solve real-life problems by forming and solving equations

Sometimes we can **form equations** to solve real-life problems.

Drawing a diagram can help you see how to represent a problem using **algebra** .

Example A farmer has a length of fencing to make a chicken run. He can make a square chicken run with sides $(x + 4)$ metres long, or a rectangular run, where the short sides are x metres and the long sides are twice the length of the short sides. Which chicken run gives the largest area for the chickens?

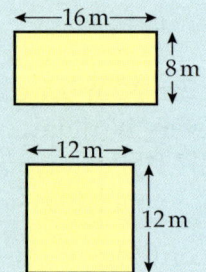

First draw a diagram to represent the problem.

(x + 4) m   2x m

(x + 4) m   x m

For the rectangle, if the shorter side is x metres, then the longer side is twice as long: $2x$ metres.

Perimeter of square: $x + 4 + x + 4 + x + 4 + x + 4 = 4x + 16$

Perimeter of rectangle: $2x + x + 2x + x = 6x$

The length of fencing is the same for both, so the perimeters of the rectangle and square are the same.

Forming an equation:

$6x = 4x + 16$

$2x = 16$ Subtract $4x$ from both sides.

$x = 8$ Divide both sides by 2.

So the chicken runs have these measurements:

The side of the square is 12 m

The area of the square is $12\,m \times 12\,m = 144\,m^2$

The area of the rectangle is $16\,m \times 8\,m = 128\,m^2$

The square run gives the largest area for the chickens.

←16 m→   8 m

←12 m→   12 m

Exercise 3.4

1 The following two shapes have the same perimeter.

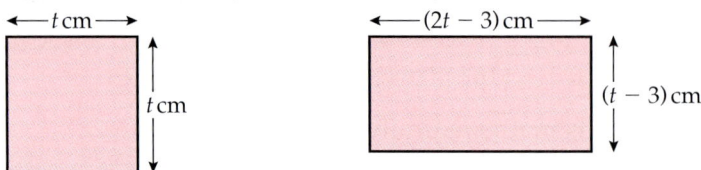

←t cm→   t cm

←(2t − 3) cm→   (t − 3) cm

a) Write down and simplify an algebraic expression for the perimeter of the square.

b) Write down and simplify an algebraic expression for the perimeter of the rectangle.

c) Use the fact that the two perimeters are equal to form an algebraic equation.

d) Solve your equation to find the value of t.

e) Copy the diagrams above, marking in the measurements in cm.

f) Calculate the area of the square.

g) Calculate the area of the rectangle.

h) Which has the larger area?

2 Two painters charge different rates.

	Charge per hour	Call out charge
Mr Rippoff	£50	£20
Mr Workhard	£25	£70

a) One day they both work for 'x' hours. Write down an algebraic expression for the amount in pounds charged by:

i) Mr Rippoff   **ii)** Mr Workhard.

b) Who charges more for 1 hour's work?

c) Who charges more for 5 hours' work?

d) How many hours would they each work for if they charge the same amount?

> Make your two expressions to part **a)** equal and solve the resulting equation.

3 The area of this rectangle is 18 cm.

a) What do you know about the two lengths labelled in the diagram?

b) Use your answer to part **a)** to form and solve an equation to find the value of x.

c) What is the length (in cm) of the rectangle?

d) What is the height of the rectangle?

> Use the area.

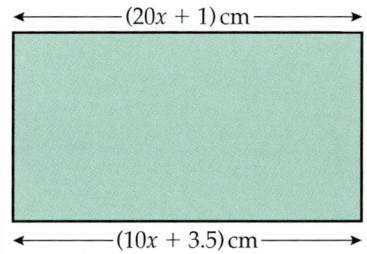

$(20x + 1)$ cm

$(10x + 3.5)$ cm

4 These two flower beds have the same perimeter.

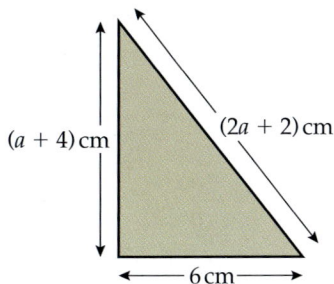

$(a + 4)$ cm $(2a + 2)$ cm   6 cm

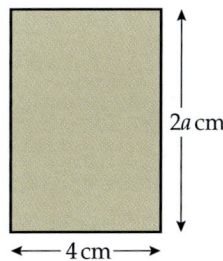

$2a$ cm   4 cm

a) Write down and simplify an algebraic expression for the perimeter of:

i) the triangle   **ii)** the rectangle.

b) Since the perimeters are equal, form and solve an algebraic equation to find the value of a.

c) Calculate the area of the rectangle.

> Area of a triangle: $\frac{1}{2} \times$ base $\times$ height

d) What is the area of the triangle?

Substitution into expressions

◈ Substitute values into algebraic expressions

In algebra we use letters to represent numbers.
Substitution is replacing the letters with numbers.

Look at the **expression** $ab + c$.
If $a = {}^-1$, $b = {}^-3$ and $c = 10$ we can calculate the value of the expression $ab + c$ by replacing the letters with their values.

ab means $a \times b$.

$$ab + c = a \times b + c$$
$$= {}^-1 \times {}^-3 + 10$$
$$= 3 + 10$$
$$= 13$$

Follow the order of operations.
A negative number multiplied by a negative number gives a positive number.

We must remember the order of operations:
Brackets → Indices → Multiplication and Division → Addition and Subtraction.

Example   Find the value of the following expressions when:

$$a = {}^-10, b = {}^-3 \text{ and } c = 2$$

a) $a + b$ **b)** $2b + 3c$

a) $a + b$	$=$	${}^-10 + {}^-3$	
	$=$	${}^-13$	
b) $2b + 3c$	$=$	$2 \times {}^-3 + 3 \times 2$	Follow the order of operations.
	$=$	${}^-6 + 6$	
	$=$	0	A positive number multiplied by a negative number gives a negative number.

Exercise 3.5

1 Find the value of each of the following expressions when $x = 7$ and $y = 12$.

   a) $2x$ **b)** $y + 5$ **c)** $y \div 3$ **d)** $x - 7$

   e) $x + y$ **f)** $2x + 3y$ **g)** $10x - y$ **h)** xy

2 Calculate the value of each of the following expressions when $x = 10$, $y = 2$ and $z = {}^-5$.

   a) $x + y$ **b)** $x + y + z$ **c)** $2x$

   d) $2x + 3y$ **e)** $x - y$ **f)** xyz

3 Work out the value of each of the following expressions when $a = {}^-1$, $b = {}^-3$ and $c = 11$.

   a) $2ab$ **b)** $3a + 4c$ **c)** $5a - 2c$

   d) $5a - bc$ **e)** $2ab + 3bc$ **f)** $3abc - ab - bc$

4 a) Simplify each of the following expressions by collecting like terms.

   i) $2x + 3y - x$

   > You can only add together terms that have EXACTLY the same letters.

   ii) $4xz - 2x + 3xz$

   iii) $3xy + 2yz - 3yz$

   iv) $3xy + 3y - xy$

b) Find the value of each of the expressions in part **a)** when
   $x = ^-10$, $y = ^-20$ and $z = ^-30$

5 When $m = ^-2$, $n = 2$ and $p = ^-1$, each of the expressions in the left hand column has the same value as an expression in the right hand column.
Find the matching pairs:

a)	$2m$	**i)**	$12p$
b)	$m + n$	**ii)**	$n + 7p$
c)	$m + n + p$	**iii)**	$2n + 2m + p$
d)	$3mn$	**iv)**	$4p$
e)	$2m + p$	**v)**	$m + p$
f)	$p - n$	**vi)**	$n + 2p$

Investigations

6 a) In this square grid $m = 0$, $p = ^-1$ and $q = 1$.
Substitute these values into the expressions and draw the grid showing the number values.

$m + 2p + q$	$m - 2p - 2q$	$m + q$
$m - 2p$	m	$m + 2p$
$m - q$	$m + 2q + 2p$	$m - 2p - q$

b) For the grid to be a 'magic square' the sums of the rows, columns and diagonals must be equal.
Is the grid you have drawn for part **a)** a magic square?

c) Choose other sets of values to replace m, p and q. Do you get a magic square each time?

d) By finding algebraic expressions for the sum of each row, column and diagonal, explain your answer to part **c)**.

7 If $a = 5$, $b = 2$, $c = ^-2$ and $d = ^-1$ then we can say:
$$b = cd, \text{ since } cd = c \times d$$
$$= ^-2 \times ^-1$$
$$= 2$$
$$= b$$
Write down as many other facts as you can for the letters a, b, c and d.

Direct proportion

◈ Begin to use graphs to solve problems involving direct proportion

1 ticket costs £5.
2 tickets cost £10
4 tickets cost £20 and so on.

Look back at Lesson 2.7 on direct proportion.

The cost is in **direct proportion** to the number of tickets.

We can draw a graph to show the relationship between two **variables** :

Tickets	1	2	4
Cost	£5	£10	£20

First draw a table to find some points to plot.

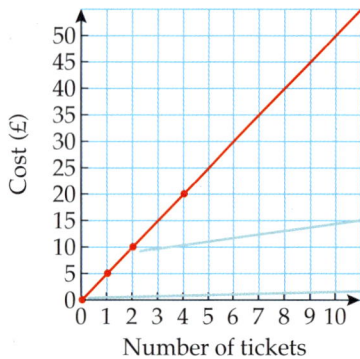

A variable can stand for a range of different values. Here the two variables are 'number of tickets' and 'cost'.

Plot the points (1, 5), (2, 10) (4, 20) and join them with a straight line.

0 tickets cost £0, so the graph passes through the origin.

When two variables are in direct proportion, the graph is a straight line through the origin.

Example   The following table shows how much sugar is needed to make a given number of small cakes:

a) Draw a graph to show the information in the table.

Number of cakes	20	30	45	50
Grams of sugar	40	60	90	100

b) Explain what the graph shows about the relationship between the two variables.

c) Use your graph to work out how many cakes you could make if you had:
   i) 50 g of sugar   **ii)** 96 g of sugar

a)

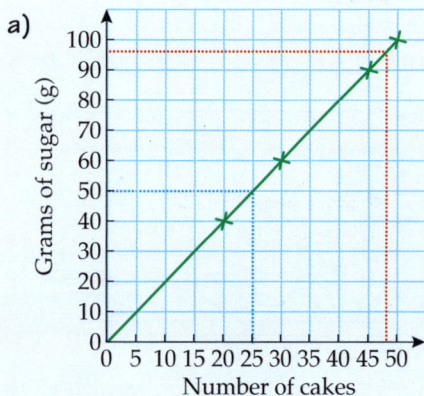

First draw a suitable pair of axes.
Then plot the coordinates given in the table.
Join the points with a straight line.

The variables are 'number of cakes' and 'amount of sugar'.

b) The graph is a straight line through the origin, which shows us that the number of cakes and the amount of sugar are in direct proportion to one another.

c) i) When $y = 50$, $x = 25$
   so you can make 25 cakes with 50 g of sugar.
   See the blue dotted line.

   ii) When $y = 96$, $x = 48$
   so you can make 48 cakes with 96 g of sugar.
   See the red dotted line.

Exercise 3.6

1 Each of the following tables gives values of two variables. For each table:
Plot the points on a graph.
Are the two variables in direct proportion?

a)

x	1	3	5	7	10
y	4	12	20	28	40

See parts **a)** and **b)** of the Example.

The x-axis needs to go up to at least 10, and the y-axis to at least 40.

b)

m	1	4	5	6	12
n	4	13	16	19	37

c)

x	3	6	8	9	10
y	4.5	9	12	13.5	15

d)

z	5	10	15	20	25
q	45	95	145	195	245

2 To make orange squash you mix 2 parts cordial with 5 parts water.
  a) Copy and complete the table to show the quantities:

Cordial (ml)	2	16	20	30	50
Water (ml)	5	...	...	...	...

Plot 'Cordial' along the x-axis, and 'Water' along the y-axis.

  b) Draw a graph to illustrate the information in the table.
  c) Use your graph to work out how much water you need for:

See part **c)** of the Example.

  i) 1 ml   **ii)** 12 ml   **iii)** 40 ml of cordial
  d) Use your graph to work out how much cordial you would require for:
  i) 60 ml   **ii)** 10 ml   **iii)** 115 ml of water.

3 The following two conversion graphs come from a 'Household Manual'.
For each graph, decide whether the variables are in direct proportion.

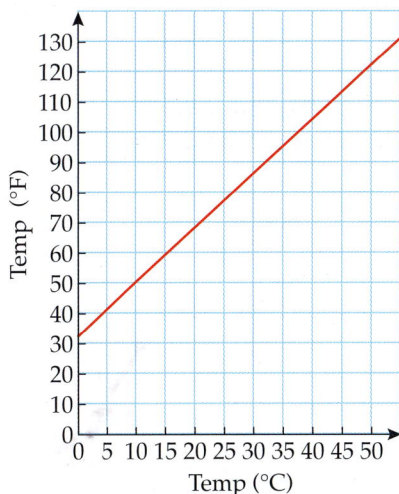

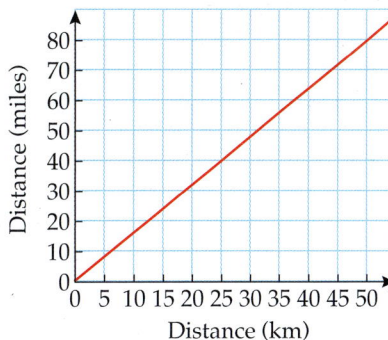

Angles

◆ Recognise alternate and corresponding angles

Remember, **parallel** lines are straight lines which never meet or cross.

The arrows show that the lines are parallel.

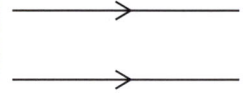

Alternate angles on parallel lines are equal. In this diagram, the **alternate** angles are on *alternate* sides of the red line.

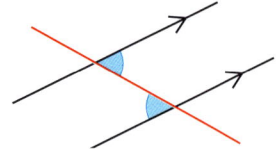

Corresponding angles on parallel lines are equal. In this diagram, the **corresponding** angles are on the *same* side of the red line.

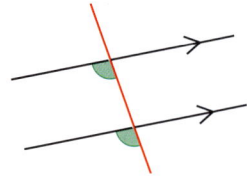

Remember, **vertically opposite** angles are also equal.

They are called **vertically opposite** angles because their vertices are opposite each other.

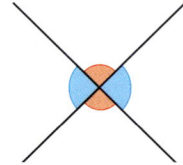

Example 1 Calculate the size of the angles marked a and b in this diagram.

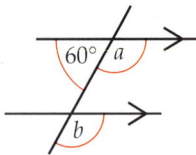

Give reasons for your answers.

$a = 120°$ because $60° + a = 180°$ (angles on a straight line add up to $180°$)

$b = 120°$ because it is the **corresponding** angle to a.

Example 2 Calculate the size of the angles marked c and d in this diagram.

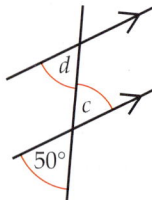

Give reasons for your answers.

$c = 50°$ because it is **vertically opposite** the $50°$ given.

$d = 50°$ because it is the **alternate** angle to c.

Exercise 4.1

1 Measure the size of the shaded angles using a protractor. What do you notice?

a)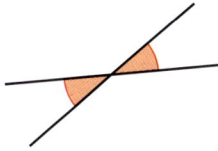
b)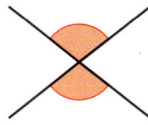
c)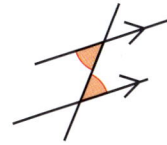

d)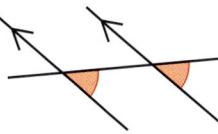
e)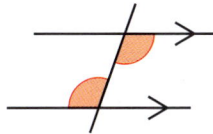
f)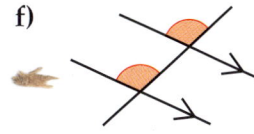

2 Calculate the size of the lettered angles. Give reasons for your answers.

a)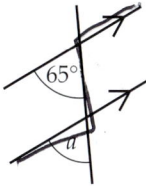
b)
c)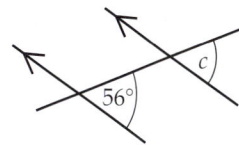

3 Find the size of the angles marked x. State any angle facts you use.

a)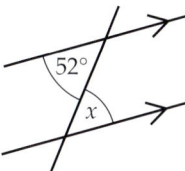
b)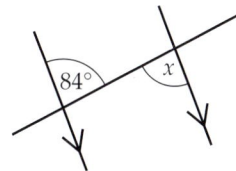
c)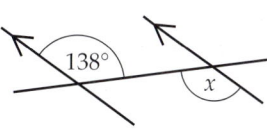

4 Work out the size of the lettered angles. Give reasons for your answers.

a)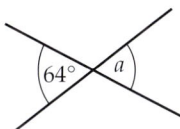
b)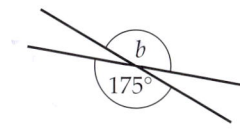
c)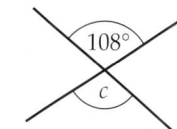

5 Calculate the size of the angles marked x and y. State any angle facts you use.

a)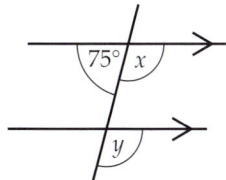
b)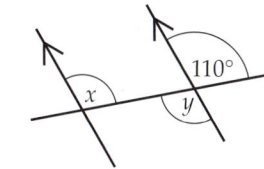
c)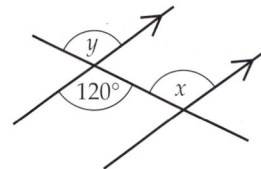

Investigation

6 **a)** Copy this diagram.
　　b) Mark all the angles that are equal to a.
　　c) Mark all the angles that are equal to b.
　　d) What do you notice?
　　e) What do you notice about the pattern of angles in a parallelogram?

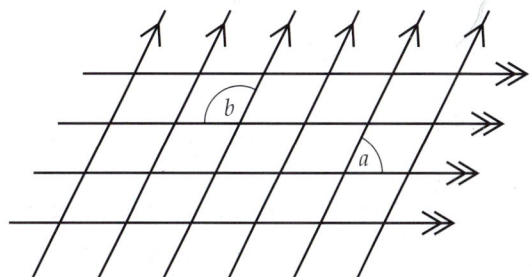

Calculating angles

◈ Know and use the fact that the sum of the angles in a triangle is 180°
◈ Know and use the fact that the sum of the angles in a quadrilateral is 360°
◈ Understand that the exterior angle of a triangle is equal to the sum of the two interior opposite angles

The sum of the angles in any triangle is 180°:

$a + b + c = 180°$

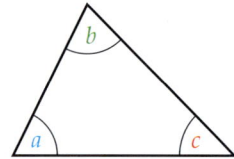

An **interior** angle is inside the shape.

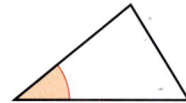

An **exterior** angle is outside the shape. It is made by extending one of the lines of the side of the shape.

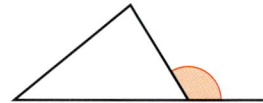

An exterior angle of a triangle is equal to the sum of the two interior opposite angles.
$c + d = 180°$ (angles on a straight line)
$a + b + c = 180°$ (angles in a triangle)
so $a + b = d$.

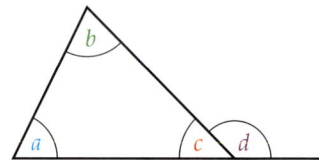

Example   Calculate the size of the lettered angles, giving reasons for your answer.

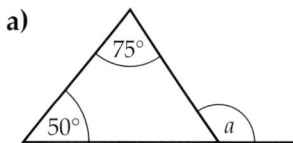

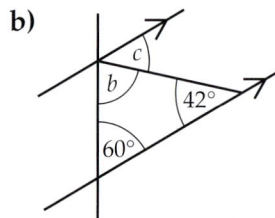

a)

75°
50°   a

b)

c
b
42°
60°

a) $a = 50° + 75° = 125°$ because the exterior angle
is equal to the sum of the interior opposite
angles.

b) $b = 78°$ because angles of a triangle sum to 180°

$c = 42°$ because it is alternate to 42°

Remember the lines with the arrows are parallel so alternate angles are equal.

Exercise 4.2

1 Calculate the size of the lettered angles. Give reasons for your answers.

a)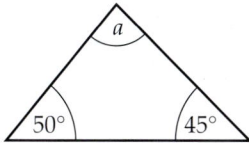

b)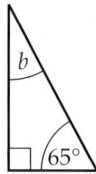

c)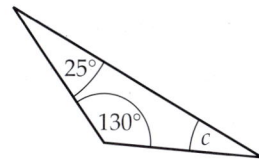

2 Work out the size of the lettered angles. Give reasons for your answers.

a)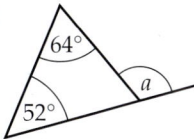

b)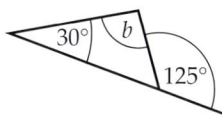

c)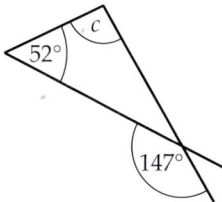

d)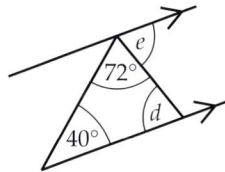

Look at the triangle then the parallel lines.

3 The diagram shows a large blue triangle with a line drawn, inside the triangle, parallel to the base.

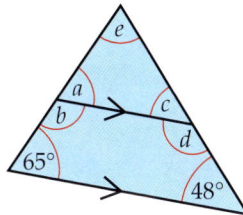

a) Find the size of the angle labelled *e*.

Look at the big triangle first.

b) What is the size of the angles labelled *a* and *c*?

Use the parallel lines.

c) Calculate the angles labelled *b* and *d*.

Investigation

4 Draw two straight lines AB and CD.
Mark a point O between them.
Draw a line through O that crosses the two lines.
Mark the two angles, underneath the line, as *x* and *y*.
Measure the size of *x* and *y* with a protractor.
Draw some more lines through O. Each time
measure the angles underneath the line and record
your results in a table.
What do you notice? Can you explain why this happens?

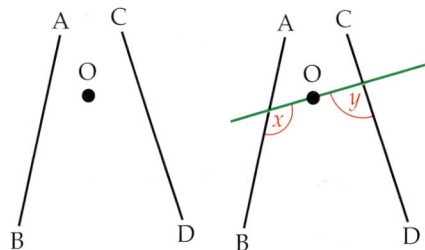

Extend AB and CD so they meet.

Quadrilaterals

⊕ Recognise and classify quadrilaterals by their geometric properties

⊕ Know and use the fact that the sum of the angles in a quadrilateral is 360°

Key words
parallelogram
rhombus
isosceles trapezium
kite
arrowhead or delta

A quadrilateral is a four-sided shape. There are many different quadrilaterals. Some have special names because they have particular geometric properties.

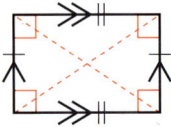

Rectangle
- Four right angles.
- Opposite sides are equal and parallel.
- Diagonals bisect each other.

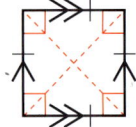

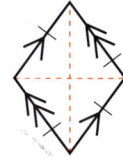

Square
- A rectangle with all four sides the same length.
- Diagonals bisect each other at right angles.

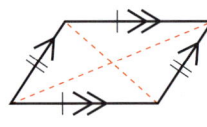

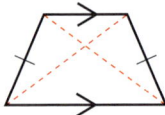

Parallelogram
- Opposite sides are equal and parallel.
- Diagonals bisect each other.

Rhombus
- A parallelogram with all four sides the same length.
- Diagonals bisect each other at right angles.

Isosceles trapezium
- A trapezium with two opposite non-parallel sides that are equal.
- Both diagonals are the same length.

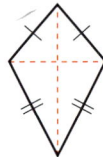

Kite
- Two pairs of adjacent sides are the same length.
- Diagonals cross at right angles.

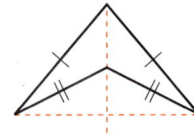

Arrowhead or Delta
- Two pairs of adjacent sides are equal.
- Diagonals cross at right angles outside the shape.

All quadrilaterals can be split into two triangles.
The sum of the angles in any quadrilateral is $2 \times 180° = 360°$.

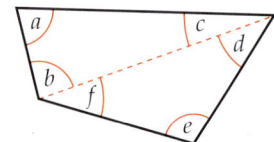

$a + b + c + d + e + f = 360°$

Example 1   Name this shape, using its geometric properties to explain your answer. You will need to measure lines and angles.

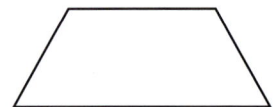

The shape is an isosceles trapezium because the two non-parallel sides are equal and both diagonals are the same length.

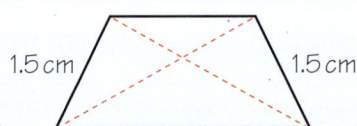

1.5 cm   1.5 cm

Example 2   Calculate the size of the missing angle of this quadrilateral.

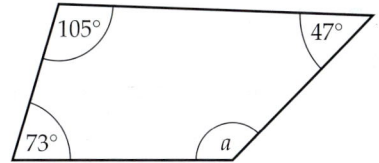

Angle $a = 360° − 47° − 105° − 73° = 135°$

because angles of a quadrilateral add up to $360°$

Exercise 4.3

1 Name each shape, using its geometric properties to explain your answers. You will need to measure lines and angles.

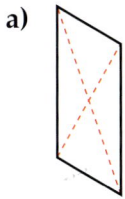

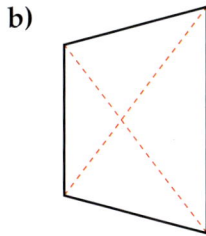

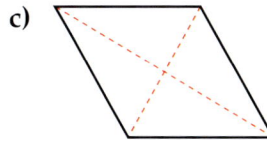

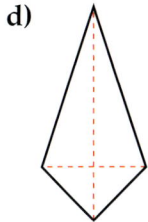

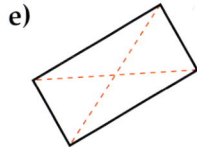

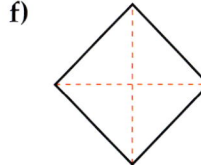

a)

b)

c)

d)

e)

f)

2 Calculate the size of the lettered angles. Give reasons for your answers.

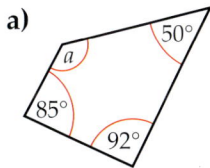

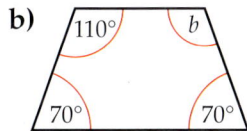

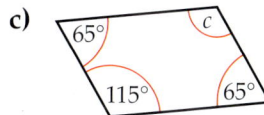

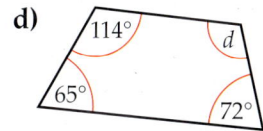

a)
50°
a
85°
92°

b)
110°
b
70°
70°

c)
65°
c
115°
65°

d)
114°
d
65°
72°

3 Find the size of the lettered angles. Give reasons for your answers.

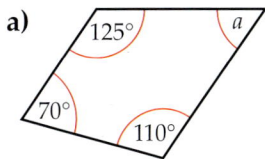

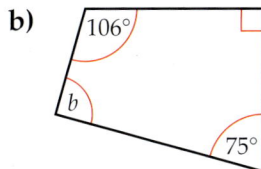

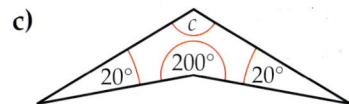

a)
125°
a
70°
110°

b)
106°
b
75°

c)
c
20°   200°   20°

Angle problems

⊕ Solve geometrical problems using side and angle properties of special triangles and quadrilaterals

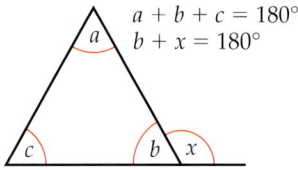

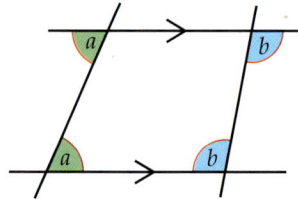

Key words
alternate
corresponding
vertically opposite

$a + b + c = 180°$
$b + x = 180°$

Angles in a triangle add up to 180°.
Angles on a straight line add up to 180°.

Alternate angles are equal.

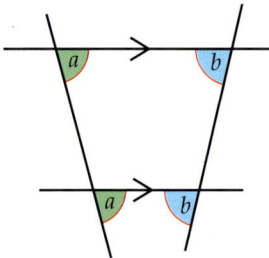

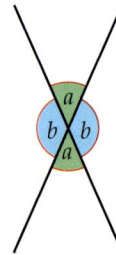

Corresponding angles are equal.

Vertically opposite angles are equal.

We can use this knowledge to find the size of missing angles.

Example Calculate the size of the lettered angles in this diagram.

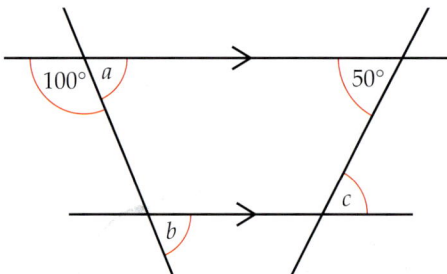

Give reasons for your answers.

$a = 80°$ because $100° + a = 180°$ ———— Angles on a straight line add up to 180°.
$b = 80°$ because it is the corresponding angle to a
$c = 50°$ because it is the alternate angle to 50°

Exercise 4.4

1 Calculate the size of the lettered angles. Give reasons for your answers.

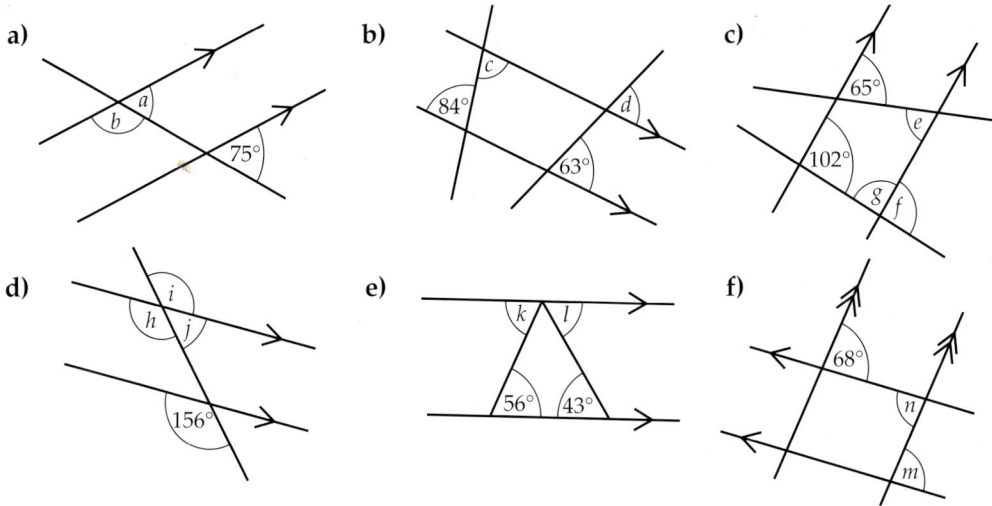

a)

b)

c)

d)

e)

f)

2 Find the size of the lettered angles. Give reasons for your answers and write down each step of your working.

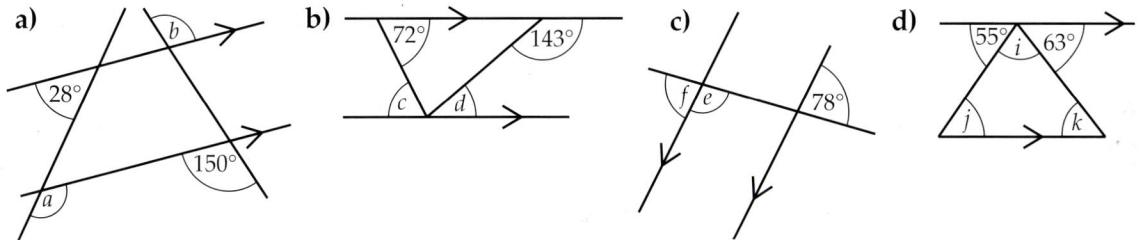

a)

b)

c)

d)

3 Work out the size of the lettered angles, giving reasons for your answers.

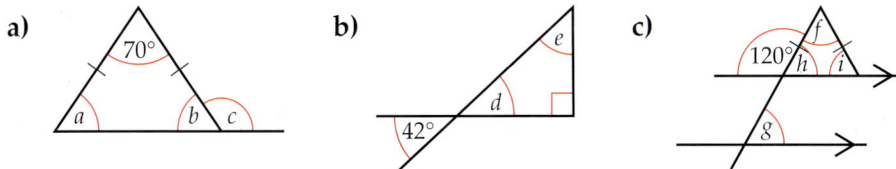

a)

b)

c)

> Isosceles triangles have base angles that are equal.

Investigation

4 The angle at the vertex of a regular pentagon is 108°. Two diagonals are drawn to the same vertex to make three triangles.

> Regular polygons have equal sides and equal angles.

a) Calculate the sizes of the angles in each triangle.

b) The middle triangle and one of the other triangles are placed together like this:

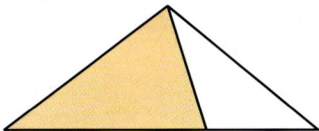

> These triangles are all isosceles.

> Can any of the angles from part **a)** be combined to make a straight line?

Explain why the triangles fit together to make a new triangle. What are its angles?

c) Investigate the other shapes you can make by putting the three triangles together.

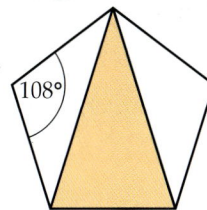

Construction

⊕ Construct a bisector of an angle, using a ruler and compasses
⊕ Construct the mid-point and perpendicular bisector of a line
   segment, using a ruler and compasses

Key words
bisector
compasses
equidistant
perpendicular bisector
mid-point

The **bisector** of an angle is a line that divides the angle into two equal parts. You can construct the bisector of an angle using **compasses**.

In this diagram, BD is the bisector of the angle ABC.
Every point on the line BD is **equidistant** from the lines BA and BC.

Equidistant means equal distance.

The **perpendicular bisector** of a line segment divides the line segment into two equal parts at right angles.

In this diagram, BD is the perpendicular bisector of AC. It crosses AC at the **mid-point** (M) of the line. Every point on the line BD is equidistant from both A and C. If you join ABCD, a rhombus is formed.

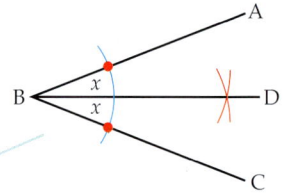

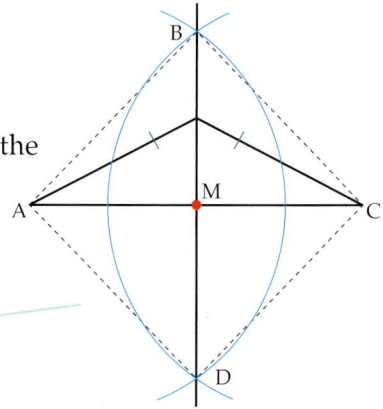

Example 1   Construct the bisector of ∠ABC.

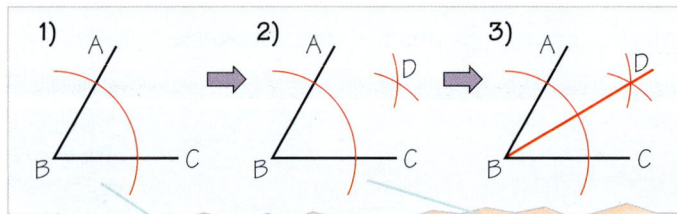

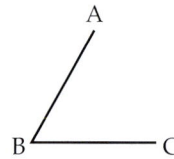

1) Open the compasses and put the point on B. Draw an **arc** that intersects with AB and BC.

An **arc** is part of a circle. You can draw arcs with compasses.

2) Do not change the opening of the compasses. Put the point on the intersection of the **arc** with AB and draw a new **arc**. Do the same thing with BC. Draw the new arcs to intersect at D.

3) Join BD.

Example 2   The line segment PQ is 2.5 cm long. Construct the perpendicular bisector of PQ.

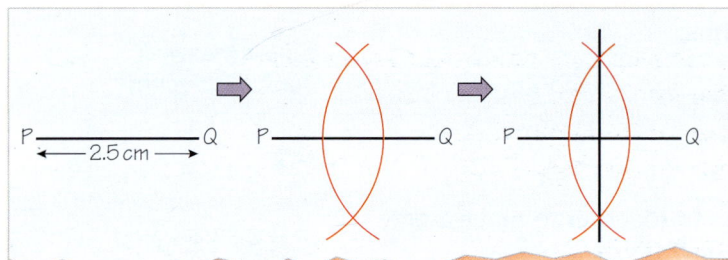

Draw a line PQ of 2.5 cm. Open up the compasses to over half the length of PQ.

Place the point at P and draw an **arc**. Keep the opening of the compasses the same and repeat at Q. Join the points where the arcs intersect.

Exercise 4.5 .... Construction

1 Trace each angle and construct the angle bisector for each.

a)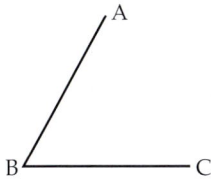

b)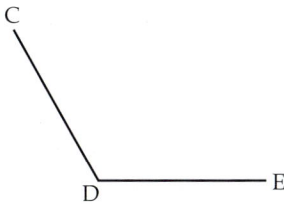

c)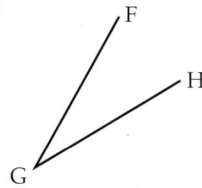

2 Trace each line and construct the perpendicular bisector of each. Label the mid-point. Measure each half of the line to check your accuracy.

a)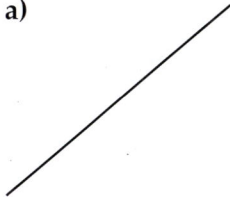

b)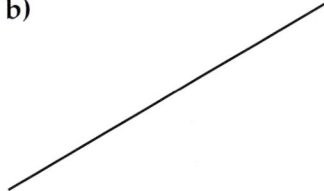

c)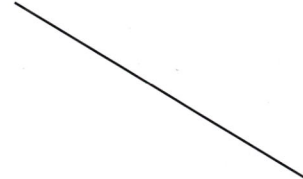

3 Draw any acute angle.
  Construct the angle bisector using only a ruler and compasses.

> Look back at Example 1.

4 Draw any obtuse angle.
  Construct the angle bisector using only a ruler and compasses.
  Check it is correct by measuring the two angles and making sure they are the same.

> Remember an obtuse angle is greater than 90°.

5 Draw a line segment 10 cm in length.
  Construct the perpendicular bisector of the line using only a ruler and compasses.
  Mark the mid-point (M) of the line.

6 Trace this triangle.

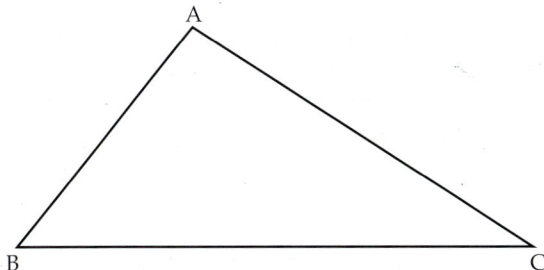

  Make sure the angle bisectors are long enough to cross each other.
  a) Construct the angle bisector for the angle ABC.
  b) Construct the angle bisector for the angle BCA.
  c) Construct the angle bisector for the angle CAB.
  What do you notice?
  Now try it with a triangle of your own.

Perpendiculars

⊕ **Use a ruler and compasses to construct the perpendicular from a point to a line and from a point on a line**

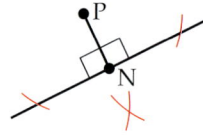

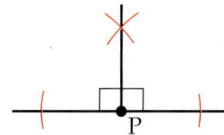

We can use a ruler and compasses to:

• **construct** the **perpendicular** from a point **to** a line

• construct the perpendicular from a point **on** a line

An **arc** is part of a circle. You can draw arcs with your compasses.

Example 1   Make a copy of the diagram.
Using only a ruler and compasses draw
a perpendicular from the point P on the line.

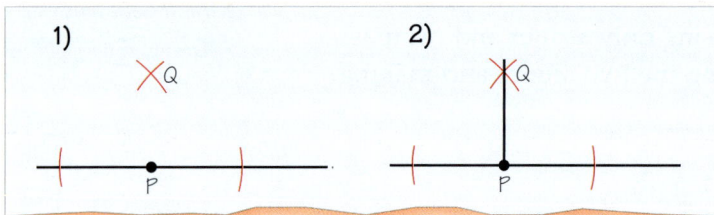

1)

2)

1) Using compasses, draw two **arcs** from P to make two intersections on the line. From the two intersections, draw two **arcs** that intersect and label the intersection Q.
2) Place a ruler from P to Q and join them with a straight line.

Example 2   Make a copy of the diagram.
Using only a ruler and compasses draw
a perpendicular from the point A to the line.

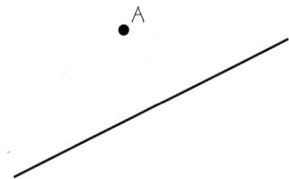

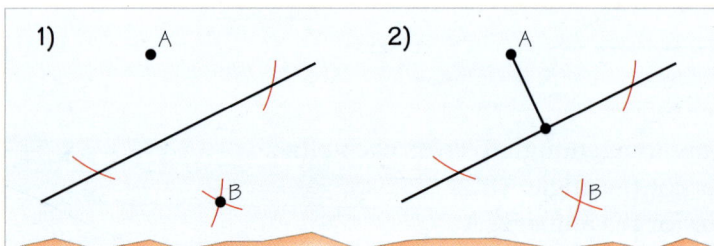

1)

2)

1) Using compasses, draw two **arcs** from the point A that intersect with the line. From the two intersections, draw two more **arcs** that intersect and label the intersection B.
2) Place a ruler from A to B and join A to the straight line.

Exercise 4.6

1 Make a copy of the diagram. Using a ruler and compasses, construct a perpendicular from the point D on the line.

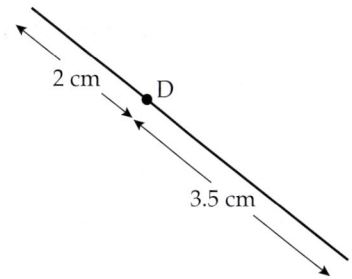

2 cm

D

3.5 cm

2 Make a copy of the diagram. Using a ruler and compasses, construct a perpendicular from the point E to the line.

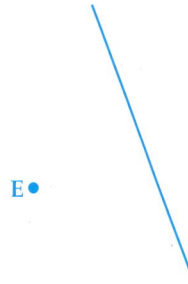

E •

3 Draw a line 6 cm in length and mark a point as shown on the diagram. Construct the perpendicular from the point to the line.

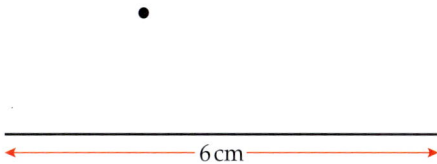

•

←————— 6 cm —————→

4 Draw a line 7 cm in length and mark a point 3 cm from one end as shown on the diagram. Construct the perpendicular from the point on the line.

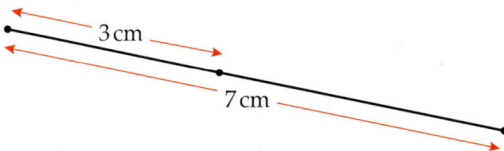

3 cm

7 cm

5 Grace is in the park and walks directly to the path.
Copy the diagram and construct the perpendicular from Grace to the path, using a ruler and compasses.

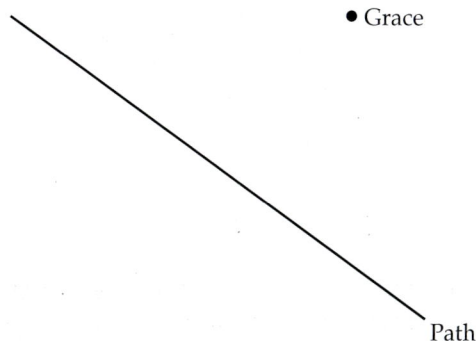

• Grace

Path

Drawing triangles

Key words
construct
SSS
sketch
hypotenuse
RHS

⊕ Construct a triangle given three sides (SSS)

⊕ Construct a triangle given the hypotenuse, one side and a right-angle (RHS)

We can **construct** a triangle using a ruler and compasses, if we know the lengths of the three sides **(SSS)** :

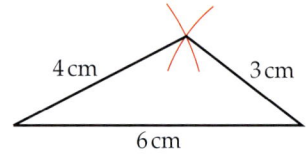

4 cm   3 cm
6 cm

A **sketch** is a rough diagram that helps us to visualise the shape.

We can also construct a triangle if we know it has a right angle and we know the length of the **hypotenuse** and one of the other sides **(RHS)** .

Hypotenuse is the name given to the longest side of a right-angled triangle.

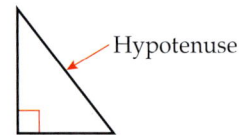

Hypotenuse

Example 1   Construct a triangle DEF with the following (SSS) information: DE = 2 cm, EF = 3 cm and FD = 4 cm.

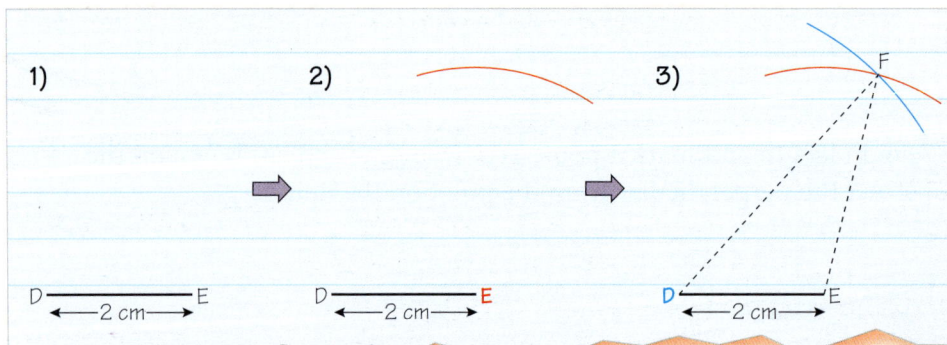

1)

D ←— 2 cm —→ E

2)

D ←— 2 cm —→ E

3)

F

D ←— 2 cm —→ E

1) Draw a base line DE of 2 cm.

2) Open the compasses out to 3 cm and place the point at E. Draw an arc.

3) Open the compasses out to 4 cm and place the point at D. Draw an arc to intersect with the other arc. Join D and E to the point where the arcs intersect, F.

Example 2   Construct a right-angled triangle with one side 5 cm and hypotenuse 8 cm.

Draw a line 5 cm long and draw a perpendicular line from A.

A   5 cm   B

C
8 cm
A   5 cm   B

Open compasses to 8 cm and draw an arc from B to cross the perpendicular from A.

Label the point C and join to B to form the triangle.

Exercise 4.7 ....

1 Draw these triangles sketched below accurately:

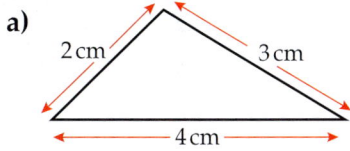

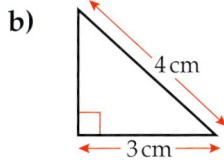

a)

2 cm   3 cm   4 cm

b)

4 cm   3 cm

2 Draw the shapes sketched below accurately:

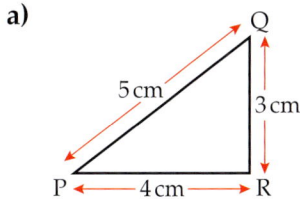

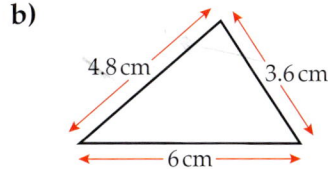

a)

Q   5 cm   3 cm   P   4 cm   R

b)

4.8 cm   3.6 cm   6 cm

3 Draw the shapes sketched below accurately:

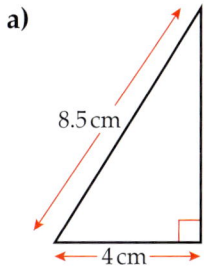

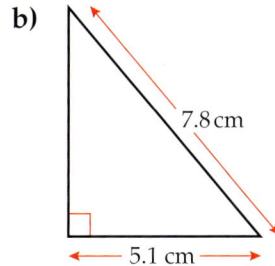

a)

8.5 cm   4 cm

b)

7.8 cm   5.1 cm

4 Construct triangles with the following SSS information then measure and write down the size of the three angles:

   a) 5 cm, 10 cm, 7 cm   **b)** 8 cm, 7 cm, 7 cm   **c)** 6 cm, 5 cm, 3.5 cm.

5 Construct the triangles with the following RHS information:

   a) a right-angle, hypotenuse 5 cm, a side 3 cm
   b) a right-angle, hypotenuse 12 cm, a side 7 cm
   c) a right-angle, a side 8 cm, hypotenuse 10 cm

Investigation

6 Can you successfully draw a triangle with sides 5 cm, 4 cm and 10 cm?

Can you draw a triangle with sides 5 cm, 4 cm and 8.5 cm?

If a triangle had sides with lengths 6 cm and 2 cm, what are some of the lengths the third side cannot be?

Exploring constructions

⊕ Construct triangles and quadrilaterals using a ruler, compasses and protractor

Key words
construct
triangle
included angle
included side
hypotenuse
quadrilateral

We can **construct** any **triangle** if we know enough information about its sides and angles, using a ruler and protractor or compasses.

We need to know either:

the lengths of two sides and the size of the **included angle** (SAS)

the size of two angles and the length of the **included side** (ASA)

the length of all three sides of the triangle (SSS)

the triangle has a right-angle and the length of two sides, one of which is the **hypotenuse** (RHS).

A **quadrilateral** can be drawn with information about its sides and angles or by joining two triangles.

Example   Construct the quadrilateral shown in the diagram.

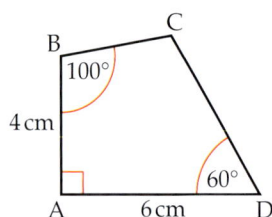

Draw the line AD of 6 cm, and using compasses construct a perpendicular at A.	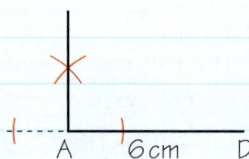
Mark the vertex B, 4 cm from A. Using a protractor, measure an angle of 100° and draw a line a few centimetres in length.	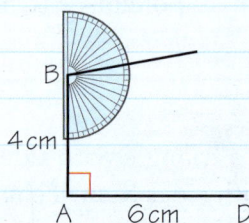
At the vertex D measure an angle of 60° and draw a line that intersects the line from B. Label the vertex C.	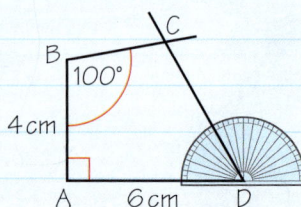

1 Construct these quadrilaterals:

a)

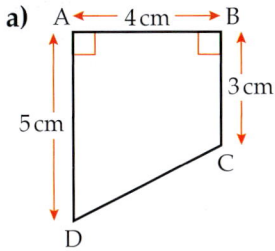

b)

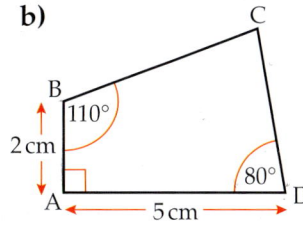

2 Construct and name these quadrilaterals:

a)

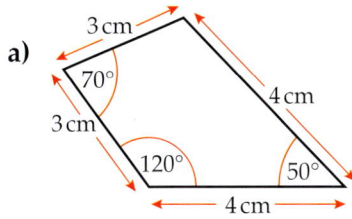

b)

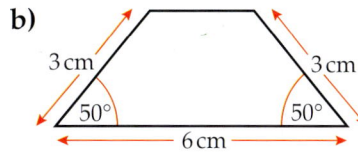

3 Construct the quadrilaterals shown in these diagrams:

a)

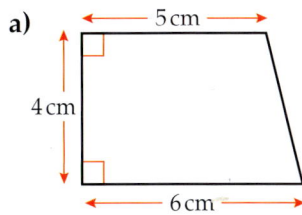

b)

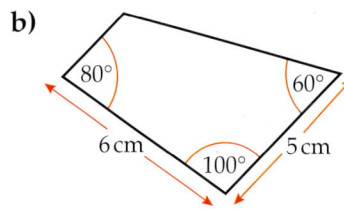

4 Construct the following triangles:

a)

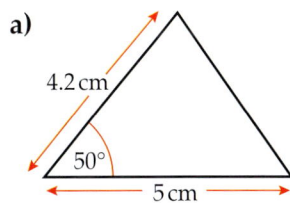

b)

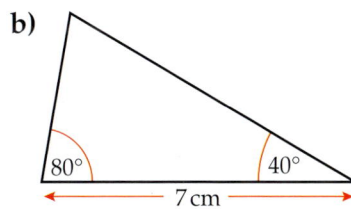

c)

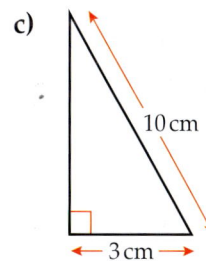

Measure the other sides and angles.

5 Construct this quadrilateral by joining two triangles:

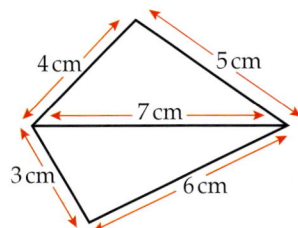

Loci

- Understand that a locus describes the path of a moving point
- Know how to construct a locus

Key words
locus
path
equidistant
perpendicular bisector
bisector

A **locus** describes the position of points that obey a certain rule.
An example of a locus is the **path** traced out by a moving point.

The locus of points that are **equidistant** from a fixed point O
is a circle shape.

Equidistant means equal distance.

You can use compasses to construct this locus.

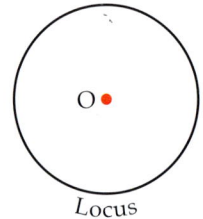

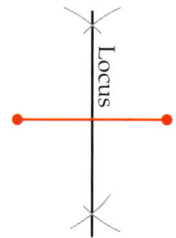

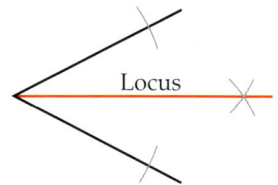

Locus

The locus of the points that are equidistant from two fixed points is the
perpendicular bisector of the line joining the points.
You can use compasses to construct this locus.

Locus

The locus of the points that are equidistant from two intersecting
straight lines is the **bisector** of the angle between the two lines.
You can use compasses to construct this locus.

Locus

Example 1 Draw the locus of the points
2 metres from a fixed point.
Use a scale of 1 cm to 1 m.

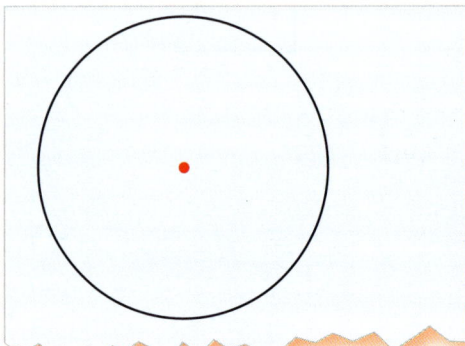

Example 2 Mark two points 5 cm apart.
Draw the locus of the points
equidistant from the points
you have drawn.

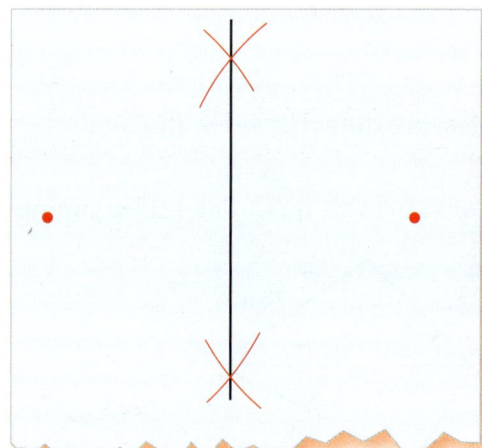

Use compasses for these constructions.

Exercise 4.9 ....

1 Mark a point with a pencil on a plain sheet of paper.
Draw the locus of the points 4 cm from your point.

2 Mark two points 7 cm apart. Draw the locus of the points equidistant from the points you have drawn.

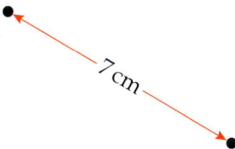

7 cm

3 Trace the diagram showing two points A and B.

•
A

•
B

a) Draw the locus of the points 3 cm from A.

b) Draw the locus of the points 4 cm from B.

What do you notice?

4 Trace the diagram showing the position of two castles. Draw the locus of all the points that are equidistant from the two castles.

Castle 1
•

•
Castle 2

5 Trace the diagram which shows the flight path of two planes.
Find the locus of the points equidistant from both planes.

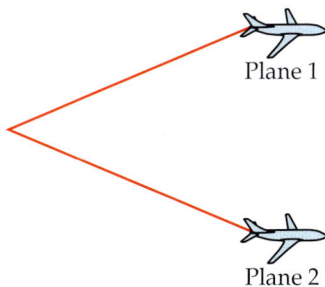

Plane 1

Plane 2

Planning an investigation 1

◈ Decide which data to collect and where to collect it from

An investigation is planned around the data handling cycle.

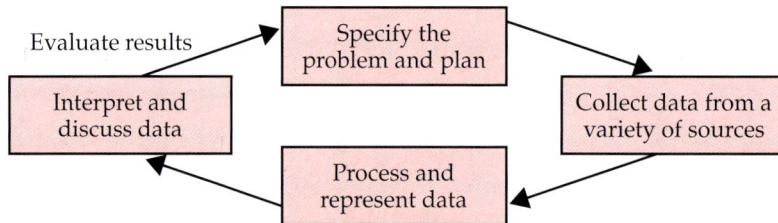

Most investigations start with choosing a problem to investigate, then planning it, including designing a data collection sheet.

The data will be from either a **primary source** , which is data collected by yourself, e.g. by using a questionnaire, or from a **secondary source** , where the data has already been collected, e.g. from the internet or a book.

When planning an investigation you should think of things such as where and how to collect the data, who to collect the data from and if any special equipment is needed. The **sample size** is the number of people asked or the number of times an investigation is carried out. The sample size is important. A sample size that is too small may give inaccurate results but a sample size that is too big may make too much data and be difficult to make sense of.

It is a good idea to do a trial with your data collection sheet to get a small amount of data. This will make it easier to spot any problems so your questions can be changed.

Example   Sharon is planning an investigation about how accurate pupils are at estimating angles. She will show pupils a drawing of an angle and ask them to estimate its size in degrees.

a) What does she need to take into consideration when planning her investigation?

b) Design a data collection sheet for her investigation.

a) Who she will ask: pupils in her school, of different ages and both boys and girls.

How many people she will ask: between 50 and 80.

What equipment she will need: an angle measurer to accurately draw the angle.

Where to carry out the investigation: in different places around school so a variety of pupils are asked.

b) A possible data collection sheet:

Name	Age	Class	Male or female	Size of angle

Exercise 5.1

1 Where could information about the following be found?

Questionnaire, experiment, survey, newspaper, other secondary sources?

   a) The length and cost of journeys to town centres using different types of public transport.

   b) Types of birds in different parts of the country.

   c) The cost of buying new cars.

   d) People's attitudes towards building a new supermarket in their area.

   e) The temperature in different towns yesterday.

   f) What pupils in the school think about school uniform.

   g) The number of Euros to £ sterling.

2 For each part of **Q1** would data be from a primary or a secondary source?

3 Sid works in a sports shop. He is writing a questionnaire to find out about his 'average' customer. This is his questionnaire

   1. How old are you?

   2. How often do you visit the shop?
      Often   sometimes   never

   3. How much did you spend at the shop today?
      £0–£10   £10–£30   £30+

Sid trials his questionnaire on 10 people. Six people refused to answer the first question and most people were confused about how to answer the other two.
For each of the three questions:

   a) Write down any problems that Sid may have had when asking the questions.

   b) Improve the question and/or the tick boxes.

4 Plan an investigation for one of the following hypotheses or questions:
- some cars depreciate (lose their value) faster than others
- more goals are scored in a football game at home compared to away
- there is a connection between the pulse rate before and after exercise
- what is the 'average' spectator at the local sports club?

Include in your plan:
Who to ask (if appropriate)   The sample size
Where and how to collect the data   Any special equipment needed

Think of different questions you could ask a spectator.

Investigation

5 Requires newspapers.
Look through a newspaper. Look for data that could be used in a statistical investigation.
Make a list of the data you find. Try to suggest how each type of data could be used in a statistical investigation.

Processing data 1

⊕ Calculate statistics, recognising when it is appropriate to use which average

⊕ Use stem-and-leaf diagrams

Key words
mode
median
mean
range
stem-and-leaf

Mode : category or outcome with the highest frequency

Median : middle item of data once data has been ordered

Mean : $\dfrac{\text{sum of all data}}{\text{number of items of data}}$

Range : the highest value minus the smallest value. (The range is not an average but shows the spread of data.)

The mean can be found using different ways: adding up each individual value, using a frequency table or using an assumed mean. An assumed mean is where a value is chosen as a possible mean and the mean differences from this value is added to it.

A **stem-and-leaf** diagram can be used to find averages and organise the data.

Example 1 Ian counts the number of strawberries in eight different punnets.

9   11   12   11   11   12   12   10

Calculate the mean number of strawberries in a punnet
a) by adding each individual number of strawberries
b) using an assumed mean of 10 strawberries.

a) Total = 9 + 11 + 12 + 11 + 11 + 12 + 12 + 10 = 88

Mean = $\frac{88}{8}$ = 11 strawberries

b)
Number of strawberries	9	11	12	11	11	12	12	10
Number of strawberries − 10	⁻1	1	2	1	1	2	2	0

Mean = assumed mean + mean of differences

$= 10 + \dfrac{(^-1+1+2+1+1+2+2+0)}{8} = 10 + \dfrac{8}{8} = 10 + 1 = 11$

Example 2 The cost of each punnet in pence is shown here.

68   75   89   75   79   95   89   75

Use a stem-and-leaf diagram to calculate the range, mode and median price.

6	8
7	5 5 5 9
8	9 9
9	5

key: stem=tens   leaf=units

You must include a key.

This represents a punnet sold at 95p.

Range = 95p − 68p = 27p

Mode = 75p

Median is between 75p and 79p = 77p

There are 8 items of data. The middle value is between the 4th and 5th items.

Exercise 5.2

1 The ages of a family group are 3, 3, 10, 21, 25, 26, 29, 71.
   a) Draw a stem-and-leaf diagram for this data.
   b) Calculate the range, mode, median and mean age.
   c) Which of the three averages is not a suitable representation of the age of the family group?

2 **a)** Copy and complete the frequency table to find the mean average amount of sunshine during 1 week

Number of hours of sunshine	Number of days	Number of hours of sunshine × Number of days
6	1	
8	4	
9	2	
	Total =	Total =

3 Calculate the mean for Example 1 using an assumed mean of 12.

> Copy out the table again, using 'mean number of strawberries = 12' instead of 10.

4 Kate looks at the cost of buying a particular CD from different shops.

£12   £15   £13   £12   £10   £10   £12

Calculate the mean,
   a) by adding each individual price first   **b)** using a frequency table
   c) using an assumed mean of £11   **d)** using an assumed mean of £13.

5 The marks of 19 pupils in a maths test are shown in this stem-and-leaf diagram

```
3 | 6                    Key: stem = tens   leaf = units
4 | 0  5  5
5 | 1
6 | 3  4  6  8
7 | 2  3  5  6  8  9
8 | 0  4  6  7
```

   a) Calculate the range, mode and median mark.
   b) Which average best represents how well the class did in the test?

Investigation

6 Requires newspapers.

> Collect data from two different newspapers and find the averages and the range for comparison.

   a) Is there a difference in the lengths of the answers to the crossword in two different types of newspaper? Draw a stem-and-leaf diagram for this data.
   b) Collect data about temperatures around the world yesterday. Draw a stem-and-leaf diagram for these temperatures. Group your data according to where in the world the temperatures were taken (e.g. hemisphere or continent). Do the average temperatures for each group tell you something?

Working with data

- Recognise discrete and continuous data
- Group data into class intervals
- Use the model class for grouped data

Key words
discrete
continuous
class interval
modal class
modal group

Data which contains numbers will either be **discrete** or **continuous**.

Discrete data is usually counted and recorded as whole numbers, with a limited number of values, for example, money spent or number of cars. A **class interval** or group of 4–6 cars will only include 4, 5 or 6 cars. It cannot have a value of 4.1 cars.

Continuous data is usually measured and may not be totally accurate e.g. height or speed. A class interval of 1.3 m ≤ height < 1.4 m includes values such as 1.3 m, 1.307 m, 1.39 m. It does not include 1.4 m, which would be recorded in the class interval of 1.4 m ≤ height < 1.5.

The class with the highest frequency is the **modal class** or **modal group**.

Example 1   Jake is collecting data about countries.

	Population (millions)	Area (km²)	Height of highest mountain (m)	Continent	Currency	Number of airports
United Kingdom	60	245 000	1343	Europe	£ sterling	470

Group the information into discrete data, continuous data or 'other'.

Population and number of airports are discrete. Area and height of highest mountain are continuous. Currency and continent are 'other'.

Example 2   Melissa is investigating the length of daisies and the number of petals each flower has.

Length (cm)	6.3	6.2	3.9	5.8	3.0	6.6	8.1	7.3	10.9	4.3	2.9	5.1	9.7	6.2
Number of petals	24	21	18	17	25	13	20	15	22	19	21	16	24	20

a) Is the data discrete or continuous?
b) Group the data into equal class intervals.
c) Write down the modal class for each set of data.

a) Length is continuous, number of petals is discrete.

b)

Length (cm)	2 ≤ length < 4	4 ≤ length < 6	6 ≤ length < 8	8 ≤ length < 10	10 ≤ length < 12
Frequency	3	3	5	2	1

Number of petals	12–15	16–19	20–23	24–27
Frequency	2	4	5	3

c) Modal class is 6 ≤ length < 8 cm.   Modal class is 20–23 petals

Exercise 5.3

1 Is the following continuous data, discrete data or 'other'?
  a) Time taken to travel to school.   **b)** Cost of bus fare to school.
  c) Number of people on the bus.   **d)** Colour of the bus.

2 The data below shows the number of runs per match achieved by a school cricket team, over a year.

Number of runs	80–89	90–99	100–109	110–119	120–129	130–139	140–149	150–159
Frequency	1	3	2	5	2	5	7	3

Regroup the data using class intervals of
  a) 80–99, 100–119 etc.   **b)** 80–109, 110–139 etc.   **c)** 80–119, 120–159 etc.
Each time identify the modal class.

  d) Which grouping do you think is best for this data? Explain why.

3 This stem-and-leaf diagram shows the time taken for a group of students to run 100 m.

```
13 | 2   2   6   7            key: stem=seconds   leaf=tenth of a second
14 | 0   1   1   5   9
15 | 1   3   6   7 ─────────────────────── This represents a time of 15.7 seconds.
16 | 5   9
17 | 2   4   5   8
```

  a) Using a first class interval of $13 \leqslant$ time < 14 seconds, group this data into a frequency table.
  b) What is the modal class for the data?

4 The time taken for swimmers to swim the English channel in 2001 are

```
 8 | 32                   key: stem = hours   leaf = minutes
 9 | 30   51
10 | 14   37   54
11 | 08   22   56   56
12 | 05   33   49
13 | 10   31   41 ─────────────────────── This shows a time of 13:41.
14 | 00   24
15 | 18
16 | 29   54
17 | 36
18 | 04
```

  a) Group the data into equal class intervals.   A class width of 2 hours could be used.
  b) What is the modal class of your grouping?

Investigation

5 Think about different sports and how their results are recorded.
  For example when running the 100 m the data is continuous, but the number of goals scored in a football match is discrete.
  Make a list of five sports that use discrete data and five that use continuous data.

Pie charts

⊕ Draw pie charts by hand and using ICT

A **pie chart** is usually used for data that is not about number. It shows the categories when the whole of something is divided.

In order to draw a pie chart by hand, the percentage size of each **sector** (piece) needs to be known. A computer may also be used to draw pie charts.

A pie chart should not have just two sectors or have too many sectors.

Example   Helen is carrying out a survey about where pupils do their homework.

Where homework is done	Home	School library	Homework club
Number of pupils	24	6	10

Calculate the percentages for each category and draw a pie chart.

Where homework is done	Home	School library	Homework club
Number of pupils	24	6	10
Percentage	$\frac{24}{40} \times 100\% = 60\%$	$\frac{6}{40} \times 100\% = 15\%$	$\frac{10}{40} \times 100\% = 25\%$

Where pupils do their homework

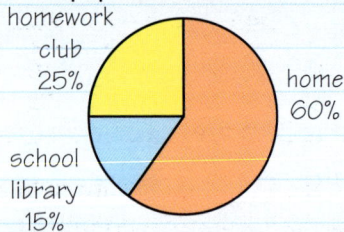

When you draw a pie chart by hand, each time a new sector is drawn, turn the pie chart scale to 0%.
There should be no gaps when you have finished your pie chart.

	A	B
1	home	60
2	school library	15

When using ICT, put your data into the Excel cells like this. Use the chart wizard to make a pie chart.

Exercise 5.4

1 Mohammed carries out a survey asking if school uniform should be kept at his school.

Should school uniform be kept?	Yes	No	Don't know
Percentage	60%	10%	30%

As the data is already in percentages you do not need to make any calculations.

Draw a pie chart for his data.

2 Using a computer, or by hand, draw a pie chart showing the area of the world by continent.

Continent	Asia	Africa	North America	South America	Antarctica	Australasia	Europe
Percentage	29%	20%	16%	12%	10%	6%	7%

3 a) Using a computer, or by hand, draw a pie chart to show the favourite evening activity of a group of pupils.

Place	Cinema	Bowling	Disco	Playing sport
Percentage	10%	30%	20%	40%

b) If three pupils like to go to the cinema, how many like playing sport?

c) How many pupils were asked in total?

4 Phil asks the people at his youth club about their favourite take-away food.

a) Draw a pie chart for this information.

Favourite food	Indian	Pizza	Fish & chips	Chinese	Other
Percentage	25%	10%	20%	30%	15%

b) What is the only average that can be found from your diagram?

5 Lata surveys the number of cars parked at each of the 50 houses in her road.

a) Copy and complete the table.   **b)** Draw a pie chart to represent her data.

Number of cars	0	1	2 or more
Number of houses	5	25	20
Percentage	$\frac{5}{50} \times 100 =$		

> Use the Example to help you.

6 Ravi surveys traffic passing his school. He counts 200 vehicles.

a) Copy and complete the table.   **b)** Draw a pie chart for his survey.

Type of vehicle	Car	Lorry	Taxi	Bus
Frequency	120	40	30	10
Percentage				

7 The number of people living in all of the houses in the United Kingdom is shown below. Copy and complete the table and draw a pie chart. You may wish to use a computer.

Number of people in a household	1	2	3	4	5+
Number of households (millions)	6.9	8.3	3.8	3.4	1.7
Percentage (1 decimal place)	$\frac{6.9}{24.1} \times 100 =$				

8 Formula One racing is the most expensive sport in the world. This is how an average team spends its money.

Item	Car	Spare parts	Servicing	Salaries	Entertainment
Cost (£ millions)	20	5	4	10	1
Percentage					

a) Copy and complete the table.   **b)** Draw a pie chart to show the costs.

Investigation

9 Draw a pie chart showing the colour of hair for the pupils in your class.

> You will need to decide which colours you will record. You may need an 'other' category.

Drawing diagrams

⊕ Construct diagrams to represent data, on paper and using ICT

⊕ Choose the most appropriate diagram for a set of data

A **frequency diagram** should be drawn for grouped, continuous data.

The bars will touch and the numbers on the *x*-axis are written where two bars touch.

A **pie chart** is usually drawn when the data is not about number.

A **bar chart** or **bar-line graph** is used for discrete data, either grouped or ungrouped.

A computer is useful for drawing the different types of diagrams.

Example 1   Jem records the speed of cars on a road near his school.

Speed, S (miles per hour)	$15 \leqslant S < 20$	$20 \leqslant S < 25$	$25 \leqslant S < 30$	$30 \leqslant S < 35$	$35 \leqslant S < 40$
Number of cars	11	15	26	20	32

Draw a frequency diagram for this data.

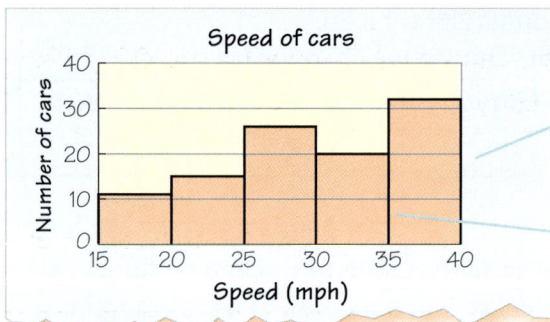

This shows the speed of 32 cars was between 35 and 40 miles per hour, including 35 mph but not 40 mph.

The bars are touching and the numbers are written where the bars touch.

Example 2   The number of emails received in a day by members of a school is shown:

No. of emails	0–9	10–19	20–29	30–39	40+
Frequency	156	195	169	104	26

a) Show this data using a bar chart.

b) Would a different diagram be better for showing this data?

a)

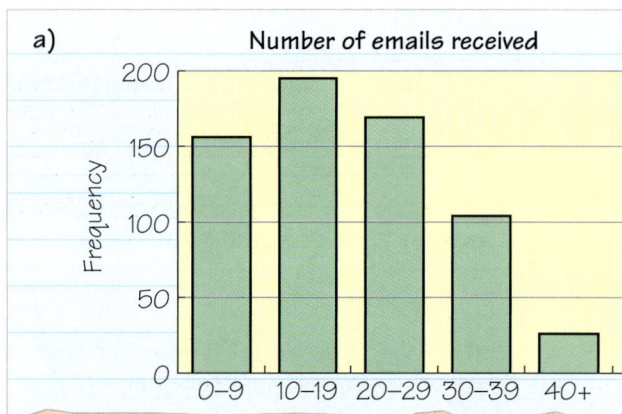

b) A pie chart would be better as it would be easier to compare the groups by eye.

Exercise 5.5

Draw the diagrams in this exercise by hand, or using a computer.

1 Draw a frequency diagram to show how long a class of students spent on homework.

Time (minutes)	0 ≤ time < 10	10 ≤ time < 20	20 ≤ time < 30	30 ≤ time < 40	40 ≤ time < 50
Number of students	1	5	9	13	2

2 Draw a frequency diagram to show the average number of hours of daylight in a year.

Hours of daylight	8 ≤ hours < 10	10 ≤ hours < 12	12 ≤ hours < 14	14 ≤ hours < 16	16 ≤ hours < 18	18 ≤ hours < 20
Number of weeks	9	10	9	7	11	6

3 Rupa measures the amount of rainfall each day during November.

```
0 | 0  0  0  0  6  8      key: stem=cm    leaf=mm
1 | 0  1  1  2  7  9
2 | 8
3 | 6  7  7  9
4 | 0  2  3  8  ———————————————   This represents 4.8 cm of rain.
5 | 1  2  3  3  4  5  6
6 | 3  5
```

a) Draw a frequency table for this data with a first class interval of 0 ≤ rainfall < 1 cm.
b) Draw a suitable diagram for the data in these groups.
c) What is the modal amount of rainfall from the stem-and-leaf diagram?
d) What is the modal class from the frequency table?

4 The average amount of council tax paid by a household in England for each county in 2002 was:

Amount	£700–£749	£750–£799	£800–£849	£850–£899	£900–£949	£950+
Number of counties	15	13	6	3	3	2
Percentage	36%	31%	14%	7%	7%	5%

Draw   **a)** a bar chart   **b)** a pie chart for this data.

5 Draw a suitable diagram for each of the 2 sets of data in Example 2 in Lesson 5.3.

6 The longest 125 throws as at January 2004 for the women's javelin are:

Distance (D) in metres	58 ≤ D < 60	60 ≤ D < 62	62 ≤ D < 64	64 ≤ D < 66	66 ≤ D < 68	68 ≤ D < 70	70 ≤ D < 72
Frequency	5	24	14	37	36	8	1

a) What does 58 ≤ D < 60 mean in words?
b) Write down three possible distances that could be in this interval

Use Example 1 to help you.

c) Draw a suitable diagram for this data.
d) What is the modal class?

Interpreting information

◈ Interpret tables, graphs and diagrams for discrete and continuous data

◈ Compare two distributions using the range and one or more of the mode, median and mean

---

Once diagrams have been drawn and averages calculated it is important that these are **interpreted** or made sense of in some way.

If an investigation is exploring a particular question or **hypothesis** , this should be talked about.

Example   A teacher believes that pupils do not like attending his class.
He records the number of pupils absent from his class during a period of 20 days.

Use the diagram to calculate the mean, mode, median and range.

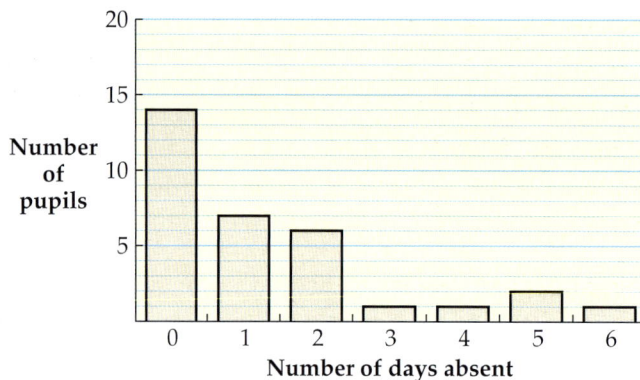

Mean: $\dfrac{14 \times 0 + 7 \times 1 + 6 \times 2 + 1 \times 3 + 1 \times 4 + 2 \times 5 + 1 \times 6}{32} = \dfrac{7 + 12 + 3 + 4 + 10 + 6}{32}$

$= \dfrac{42}{32}$

Total number of pupils in the class.

$= 1.3125$ days

Mode $= 0$ days

Median $= 16.5$th value — This is the $\dfrac{(32 + 1)}{2}$th value.

This in found in the '1 day absent' group

Range $= 6 - 0 = 6$ days

The median for absent days from the teacher's class was 1 day.

Most pupils attend most of the classes. It is likely that most of the absent students had a day off because they were sick.

Exercise 5.6

1 DVD's can be hired on some long train journeys.
The time of journey in minutes between stations is shown in this two-way table.

A two-way table sorts data into different categories.

Paddington			
104	Taunton		
131	27	Exeter	
193	89	62	Plymouth

Film	length of film
Pirates of the Pacific	137 minutes
Brian Almighty	101 minutes
Harry Trotter	154 minutes
The Invincibles	104 minutes

This shows that it takes 193 minutes to travel from Paddington to Plymouth.

a) Helen travels from Paddington to Taunton. Which films can she watch all of?

b) Liam travels from Plymouth to Paddington. He chooses Harry Trotter. How much time does he have left of his journey after watching the film?

c) On which journeys is it not possible to watch a film to the end?

2 Melanie draws a two-way table to show the number of boys and girls in each family in her form group.

a) How many families have 2 girls and 3 boys?

b) How many families have 0 boys?

c) How many pupils are in her form group?

d) How many families have the same number of boys as girls?

e) What is this as a fraction?

Number of girls

		0	1	2
Number of boys	0	0	1	1
	1	3	7	3
	2	2	5	2
	3	4	1	1

3 A school nurse is collecting information about eating patterns. She asks a group of children how many portions of chips they each eat per week.
From the diagram, calculate the mean, median, mode and range for the number of portions of chips eaten per week.

Number of portions of chips eaten per week

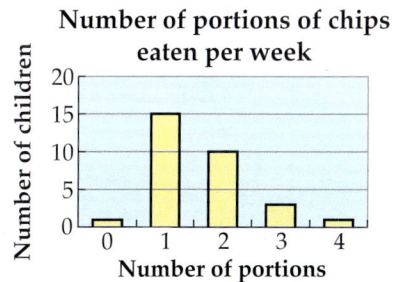

Investigation

4 **Requires the internet or a map.**
The diagram shows line graphs for the average number of hours of daylight each month for three different places in the world.

a) Write a sentence about the amount of daylight over the year for each place.

b) Can you explain why each place has different amounts of daylight?

Average number of hours of daylight each month

— South Pole
— Quito
— Chicago

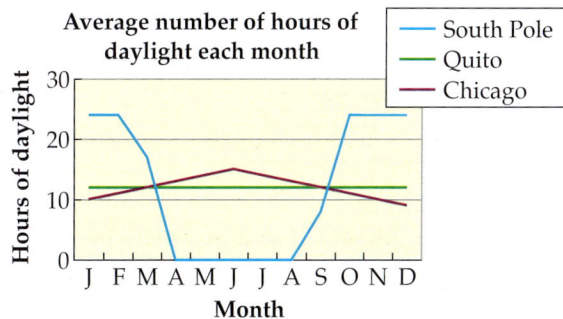

Using a map or the internet, find where the three places are.

This is a set of revision questions covering Units 1–5. If you have a problem with a question, look back at the lesson shown in the box to refresh your memory.

Questions 1–20 are non-calculator questions.

1 By looking at the pattern of differences between terms, write down the next three terms for each of the sequences below.

    a) 10, 17, 24, 31, …   **b)** 67, 64, 61, 58, …   **c)** 3, 5, 9, 15, 23, …

Lesson 1.1

2 Tom has n pence. Aaron has 5 pence more.

    a) Write an expression for the amount in pence Aaron has.

Together the boys have 27p.

    b) Write an equation to show this.

    c) Simplify your equation and use it to find out how much money each boy has.

Lesson 3.2

3 Find the value of:

    a) $^-3 \times {}^-5$ **b)** $^+6 \times {}^-4$ **c)** $^-10 \div {}^+2$

    d) $^+8 \div {}^+2$ **e)** $^+5 \times {}^-4 \times {}^-6$ **f)** $^-4 \times {}^+5 \div {}^+2$

Lesson 2.1

4 Calculate the size of the lettered angles. Give reasons for your answers.

Lesson 4.1
Lesson 4.2

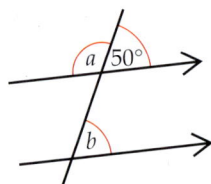

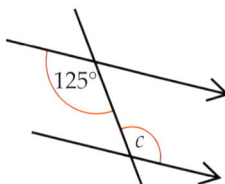

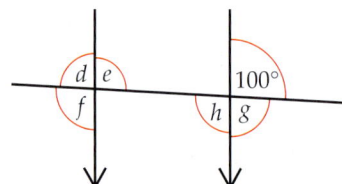

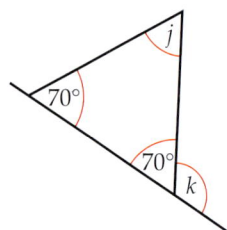

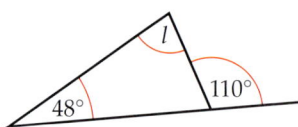

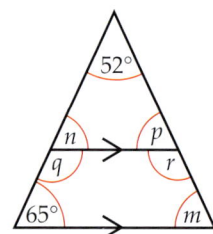

5 Zac thinks that most goals in the premier league are scored in the second half. He plans to do an investigation to find out if this is true.
What will he need to consider when planning his investigation?

Lesson 5.1

What does he need to know?
Who will he look at?
Where will he get the data?

6 The general term of a sequence is $T(n) = 3n - 2$. Find:

    a) the first term   **b)** the 100th term   **c)** the term-to-term rule

Lesson 1.2

7 **a)** Write these fractions from smallest to biggest.

Lesson 2.2
Lesson 2.5

$\frac{3}{8}$ $\frac{7}{24}$ $\frac{5}{12}$ $\frac{1}{3}$

b) Place these lengths in order from shortest to longest.

Change them into equivalent fractions with a common denominator.

7.39 m   7.4 m   7.408 m   7.42 m   7.309 m

8 Find the value of the unknown in each of the following equations.

Lesson 3.1
Lesson 3.3

a) $5a - 7 = 18$

b) $\frac{7x}{5} = 14$

c) $5a = 3a + 8$

d) $3x + 3 = 2x + 7$

9 Write these ratios in their simplest form.

Lesson 2.6

a) $25 : 20$

b) $6 : 12 : 15$

c) $15 \text{ min} : 1 \text{ hour}$

10 A class are investigating hand span and shoe size. Their results are:

Lesson 5.3

Hand span (cm)	9.9	14.5	12.5	16.2	18.9	13.8	19.4	14.3	16.5	17.3	21.3	15.6
Shoe size	3	5	4	6	7	4	8	6	7	5	8	6

a) Which of the data is discrete and which is continuous? Explain how you know.

b) Group each set of data into class intervals, e.g. Hand span $5 \leqslant S < 10$, $10 \leqslant S < 15$, Shoe size 3–4, 5–6, etc.

c) What is the modal class for each set of data?

11 A sequence of numbers starts 3, 8, 13, 18, 23 …

Lesson 1.3

a) What is the difference between consecutive terms?

b) What number will come before the n in the general term?

c) Copy and complete the general term of the sequence.

$T(n) = \_\_ n - \_\_$ It might help to use a table showing multiples.

12 Yasmin eats $\frac{2}{5}$ of a chocolate bar and Ian eats $\frac{1}{4}$.

Lesson 2.3

a) How much did they eat altogether?

b) If they had $1\frac{1}{2}$ chocolate bars to begin with, how much is left?

13 Trace this triangle.

Lesson 4.5

a) Construct the perpendicular bisector of the line AB. Measure each half of the line to check your accuracy.

b) Construct the bisector of the angle at A.

c) Measure the angle at x.

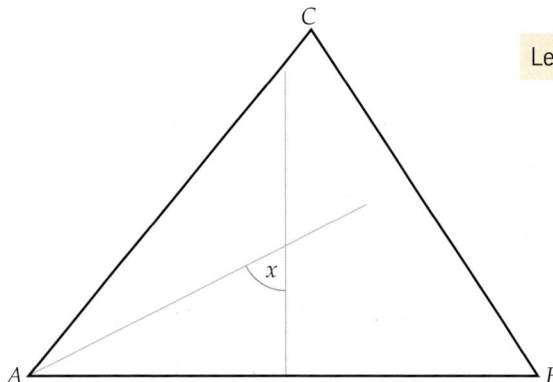

14 To raise money for charity, Year 9 had a doughnut-eating contest. They timed each person and the results were:

Lesson 5.3

Time, t (secs)	$5 \leqslant t < 10$	$10 \leqslant t < 15$	$15 \leqslant t < 20$	$20 \leqslant t < 25$	$25 \leqslant t < 30$	$30 \leqslant t < 35$
Frequency	3	6	9	12	24	6

a) Explain in words what $10 \leqslant t < 15$ means.
b) Draw a suitable diagram for this data.
c) What is the modal class?

15 Using three pairs of number lines from 0 to 10, complete separate mapping diagrams to show each of the following functions.

Lesson 1.4

a) $x \to 3x$ b) $x \to 2x - 2$ c) $x \to x \div 2$

16 Work out: a) $\frac{3}{5}$ of £65   b) $7 \div \frac{1}{3}$

Lesson 2.4

17 a) Name the following quadrilaterals. Explain your answer using their geometric properties.

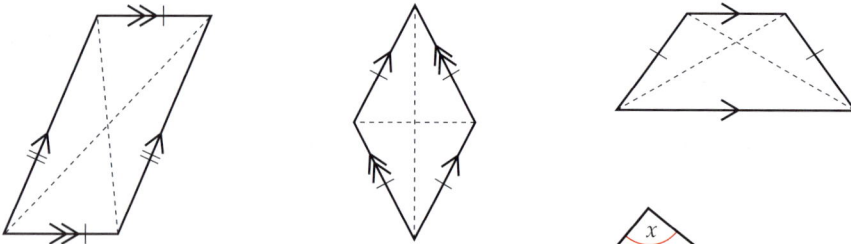

Lesson 4.3

b) What is the size of the missing angle? Explain how you know.

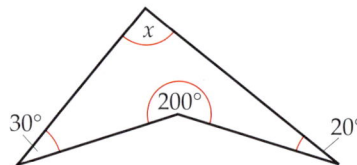

18 Find the value of each of the following expressions when $a = 3$, $b = {}^-2$ and $c = 5$.

Lesson 3.5

a) $2a + 2c$ b) $3a + 2b$ c) $2c - 3a$
d) $a - b$ e) ac f) $bc + a$

19 Find the missing functions in this function machine. It might help to use a table showing inputs, outputs and multiples.

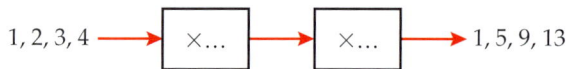

Lesson 1.5

$1, 2, 3, 4 \longrightarrow \boxed{\times \ldots} \longrightarrow \boxed{\times \ldots} \longrightarrow 1, 5, 9, 13$

The difference between consecutive terms of the output sequence tells you which multiples to compare.

20 The prisoner at the tower door (P) can make his escape by running to the path AB or the road CD. By constructing perpendiculars to both, find which one is the closest.

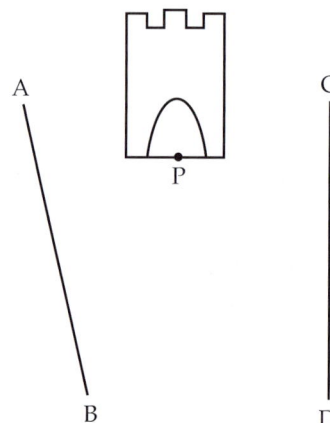

Lesson 4.6

You will need to trace the lines and the point P.

21 To make a cake you mix 10 g of sugar in every 30 g of flour.

Lesson 1.6
Lesson 3.6

   a) Copy and complete the table.

   b) Draw a graph to illustrate this information.

Sugar (g)	0	10	50	100	150	200
Flour (g)	0	30	150			

   (Plot sugar along the x-axis and flour up the y-axis)

   c) Is the relationship between sugar and flour in direct proportion? Explain how your graph shows this.

   d) Copy and complete the equation connecting flour (F) and sugar (S)

   $$F = \_\_ S$$

22 At Rent-a-car it costs £25 per day, plus an additional £50, to hire a car.

Lesson 3.4

   a) Copy and complete this equation to show the cost of hiring a car.

   Cost = £50 + ___ d   (where d stands for the number of days)

   At Cars-4-U it costs £15 per day, plus an additional £100, to hire a car.

   b) Write an equation to show the cost of hiring a car from Cars-4-U.

   c) How much would each company charge to hire a car for
   (i) 3 days   **(ii)** 8 days?

   d) The cost of hiring a car from both firms is the same for a particular number of days. How many days is this?

   > This will be when both equations are equal to each other.

23 To make spaghetti bolognese for 8 people, I use 800 g spaghetti, 600 g minced meat and 520 g of tomatoes. How much of each ingredient will I need to make enough for 5 people?

Lesson 2.7

24 **a)** Which is bigger: 21% of 70 litres or 18% of 80 litres?

   b) A salesman earned £25 000 per year. He is given a salary increase of 4%. How much will he earn now?

Lesson 2.8
Lesson 2.9

25 Construct the following as accurately as you can. Measure the unknown angles marked x.

Lesson 4.7
Lesson 4.8

a)

b)

c)

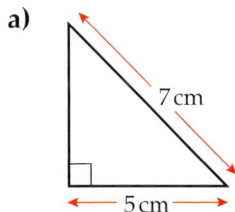

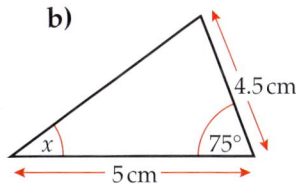

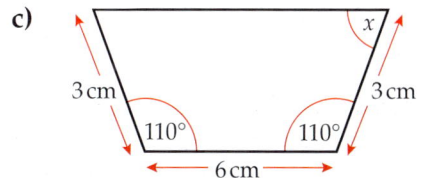

26 Some pupils were asked which their favourite lesson was. The results were:

Lesson 2.8
Lesson 5.4

Lesson	Art	English	P.E.	Maths	Geography
Frequency	11	9	13	10	7

   a) Work out the percentage for each lesson.

   b) Draw a pie chart of the results.

27 **a)** Mark a point A on the left hand side of your paper. Draw the locus of points 3 cm from A.

Lesson 4.9

   b) On your paper now mark a point B 9 cm away from A. Draw the locus of points equidistant from A and B.

Mid-points

⊕ Find the mid-point of a line segment connecting two coordinates

Key words
coordinates
mid-point
line segment

Look at this diagram.
The **coordinates** of A are (3, 2) and the coordinates of B are (7, 2).
The **mid-point** of the **line segment** AB is halfway between the end points A and B.
The mid-point, M, has coordinates (5, 2).

In this diagram the line segment CD is a diagonal line.
The x-coordinate of the mid-point, M, is the distance of C from the y-axis plus half the horizontal distance between C and D:
$2 + (\frac{1}{2} \times 8) = 6$
The y-coordinate of the mid-point, M, is the distance of D from the x-axis plus half the vertical distance between C and D: $3 + (\frac{1}{2} \times 4) = 5$
The coordinates of M are therefore (6, 5).
The coordinates of the mid-point can also be calculated from the mean of the x-coordinates and the mean of the y-coordinates:
$\dfrac{2 + 10}{2} = 6$ and $\dfrac{7 + 3}{2} = 5$

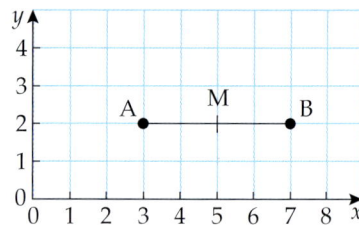

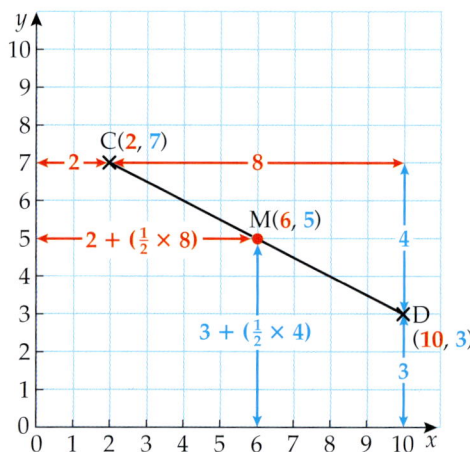

Example Find the coordinates of the mid-points of lines joining the following pairs of points by plotting the points and drawing the lines.
Check your results by calculation.

a) (3, 4) and (7, 4)   b) (4, 2) and (4, ⁻3)   c) (3, ⁻2) and (7, 5)

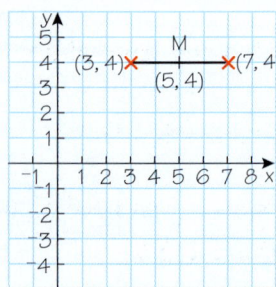

$x\text{-coordinate} = \dfrac{3 + 7}{2}$

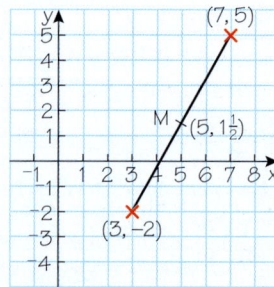

$= 5$

$y\text{-coordinate} = \dfrac{4 + 4}{2}$

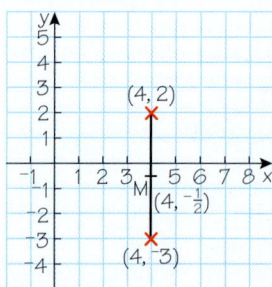

$= 4$

Coordinates = (5, 4)

$x\text{-coordinate} = \dfrac{4 + 4}{2}$

$= 4$

$y\text{-coordinate} = \dfrac{2 + {}^-3}{2}$

$= {}^-\dfrac{1}{2}$

Coordinates = (4, ⁻$\frac{1}{2}$)

$x\text{-coordinate} = \dfrac{3 + 7}{2}$

$= 5$

$y\text{-coordinate} = \dfrac{{}^-2 + 5}{2}$

$= 1\frac{1}{2}$

Coordinates = (5, 1$\frac{1}{2}$)

Find the mean of the x-coordinate.

Find the mean of the y-coordinate.

Exercise 6.1

1 Find the coordinates of the mid-points of lines joining the following pairs of points by plotting the points and drawing the lines.

a)
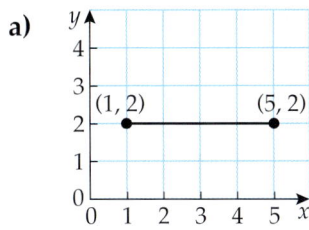

b)
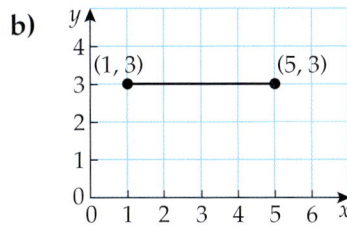

c)
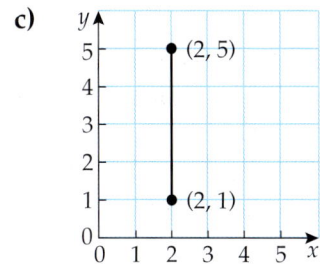

d)
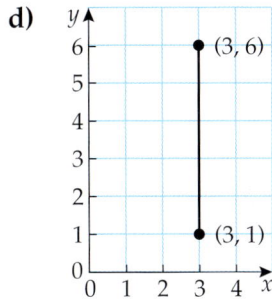

e)
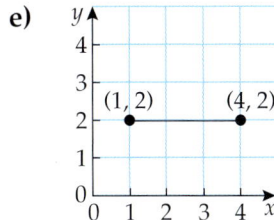

2 Find the coordinates of the mid-points of lines joining the following pairs of points by plotting the points and drawing the lines.

a)
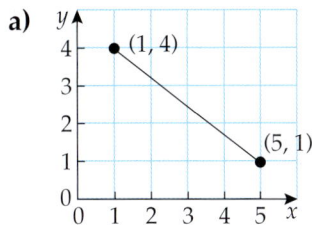

b)
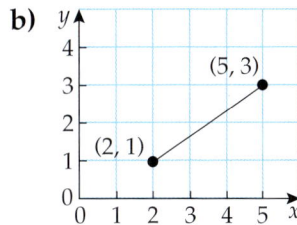

c)
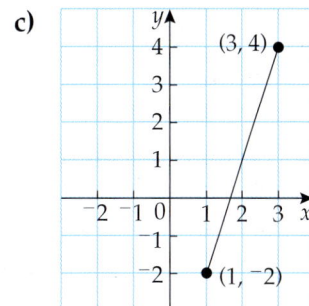

3 Work out the coordinates of the mid-points of lines joining the following pairs of points by plotting the points and drawing the lines.
   a) (6, 2) and (6, 8)
   b) (5, 3) and (9, 3)
   c) (⁻2, 7) and (⁻2, ⁻1)

4 Calculate the coordinates of the mid-points of lines joining the following pairs of points.
   a) (3, 10) and (9, 6)
   b) (12, 5) and (4, 13)
   c) (8, 11) and (12, 7)

Investigation

5 On a coordinate grid, plot the points (1, 1), (2, 3), (6, 3) and (7, 1).
   Join the points to make an isosceles trapezium.
   Join up the mid-points of each side of the trapezium. Name the shape that is made.
   Investigate joining the mid-points of other quadrilaterals. What do you notice?

Metric equivalents

◈ Know rough metric equivalents for imperial measures in daily use

Since 1971, **metric** units have replaced **imperial** units in most contexts in the UK. However, lots of people still use imperial units.

Here are some metric equivalents that you are expected to know:

8 km ≈ 5 miles	1 kg ≈ 2.2 pounds (lb)	1 gallon ≈ 4.5 litres
1 m ≈ 3 feet (ft)	1 ounce (oz) ≈ 30 g	1 litre is just less than 2 pints

The sign ≈ means 'approximately equal to' or 'about the same as'.

Example 1   Convert the following imperial measurements into the approximate metric equivalents:

   a) 15 miles   **b)** 8 pints   **c)** 9 feet   **d)** 13.2 pounds

a) 15 ÷ 5 = 3   15 miles ≈ 24 km

5 miles ≈ 8 km so divide by 5 and multiply by 8.

b) 8 ÷ 2 = 4

   8 pints ≈ 4 ℓ

2 pints ≈ 1 litre so divide by 2.

c) 9 ÷ 3 = 3

   9 feet ≈ 3 m

3 feet ≈ 1 m so divide by 3.

d) 13.2 ÷ 2.2 = 6

   13.2 pounds ≈ 6 kg

2.2 lb ≈ 1 kg so divide by 2.2.

Example 2   Convert the following metric units into the approximate imperial equivalents:

   a) 80 km   **b)** 5 litres   **c)** 4 metres   **d)** 3 kg

a) 80 ÷ 8 = 10, 10 × 5 = 50

   80 km ≈ 50 miles

Every 8 km is equal to 5 miles, so divide by 8, then multiply by 5.

b) 5 × 2 = 10

   5 ℓ ≈ 10 pints

1 litre is about 2 pints so multiply by 2.

c) 4 × 3 = 12

   4 m ≈ 12 ft

1 metre is about 3 feet so multiply by 3.

d) 3 × 2.2 = 6.6

   3 kg ≈ 6.6 lb

1 kg is about 2.2 lb so multiply by 2.2.

Exercise 6.2

1 Convert the following metric lengths into approximate imperial equivalents:

a) 40 km
b) 120 km
c) 10 m
d) 100 m
e) 2.5 m

> 8 km ≈ 5 miles,
> 1 m ≈ 3 feet.

2 Change these imperial lengths into approximate metric equivalents:

a) 30 miles
b) 100 miles
c) 6 feet
d) 15 feet
e) 21 feet

3 Convert the following metric measures into approximate imperial equivalents:

a) i) 10 kg
   ii) 120 g
   iii) 5 kg
   iv) 12 kg
   v) 300 g

b) i) 100 ℓ
   ii) 20 ℓ
   iii) 5 ℓ
   iv) 2.5 ℓ

> 1 kg ≈ 2.2 pounds.
>
> 1 ℓ is about 2 pints.

4 Change these imperial measures into approximate metric equivalents:

a) i) 22 lb
   ii) 50 lb
   iii) 6 lb
   iv) 14 lb

b) i) 4 pints
   ii) 10 pints
   iii) 3 gallons
   iv) 2 gallons

> 2.2 lb ≈ 1 kg.
>
> 2 pints is about
> 1 ℓ, 1 gallon is
> about 4.5 ℓ.

5 An African elephant is 24 feet long. How long is this in metres?

6 African elephants consume between 300 and 600 pounds of food in a day. How much is this in kilograms?

Investigation

7 a) Measure the length of your pencil in both inches and centimetres. Calculate the number of centimetres to an inch by dividing your inch measurement by your centimetre measurement.

b) Measure another three lengths of your choice in both inches and centimetres. Each time, calculate the number of centimetres to an inch. What do you notice?

⬦ Be able to find areas of compound shapes

Key words
area
formula
base
perpendicular
  height

We can calculate the **area** of a rectangle by multiplying the length by the width. The **formula** is
Area = length × width

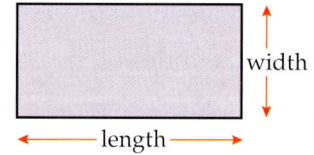

The formula for calculating the area of a triangle is
Area = $\frac{1}{2}$ (**base** × **perpendicular height**)

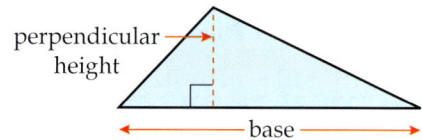

This shape is made up from two rectangles.

The area is found by calculating the area of the two rectangles and then adding them together.

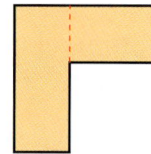

To find the area of this shape we first show how it can be split into a rectangle and a triangle.
Then we find the area of each part and add them together.

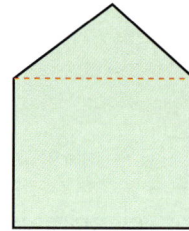

Example   Calculate the area of this shape.

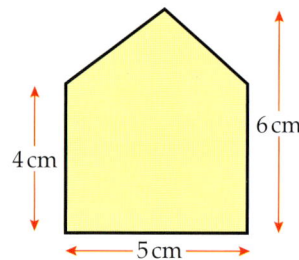

Area of rectangle = 5 cm × 4 cm = 20 cm².

Area of triangle = $\frac{1}{2}$(5 cm × 2 cm) = 5 cm².

Total area = 20 cm² + 5 cm² = 25 cm².

1 Calculate the areas of these rectangles:

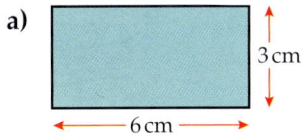

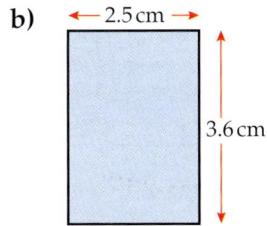

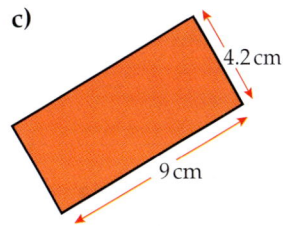

a)

3 cm
6 cm

b)

2.5 cm
3.6 cm

c)

4.2 cm
9 cm

2 Find the areas of these triangles:

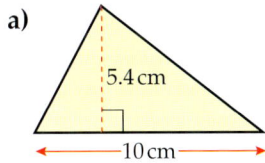

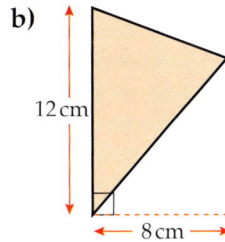

a)

5.4 cm
10 cm

b)

12 cm
8 cm

3 Calculate the areas of these shapes:

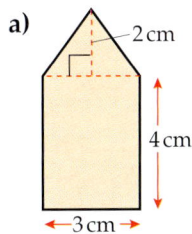

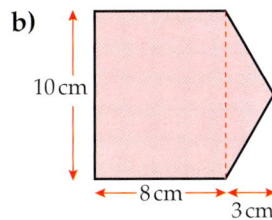

a)

2 cm
4 cm
3 cm

b)

10 cm
8 cm
3 cm

4 Find the areas of these shapes:

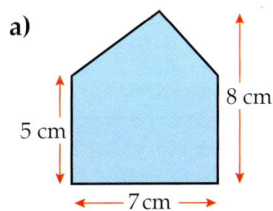

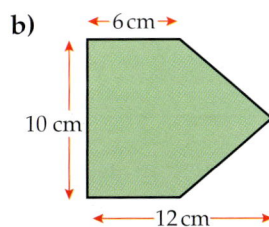

a)

8 cm
5 cm
7 cm

b)

6 cm
10 cm
12 cm

5 The diagram shows the sail of a barge.
Calculate the area of the sail.

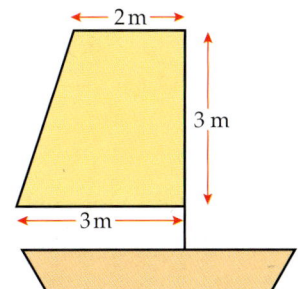

2 m
3 m
3 m

6 a) Using 1 cm square paper draw a rectangle that has an area of 20 cm².
  b) Using 1 cm square paper draw a triangle that has an area of 20 cm².
  c) Using 1 cm square paper draw a rectangle with a triangle joined to one side that has a total area of 40 cm².
  d) Using 1 cm square paper draw a rectangle with a triangle joined to one side that has a total area of 20 cm².

More areas

- ◈ Understand and use the formula for finding the area of a parallelogram
- ◈ Understand and use the formula for finding the area of a trapezium

Key words
area
formula
base
perpendicular
  height

We can calculate the **area** of a parallelogram by doubling the area for a non right-angled triangle.

The **formula** is: Area of parallelogram $= 2 \times$ area of triangle

$$= 2 \times \tfrac{1}{2} \times \textbf{base} \times \textbf{(perpendicular) height}$$

$$= \text{base} \times \text{(perpendicular) height}.$$

perpendicular height

base

These triangles have the same area.

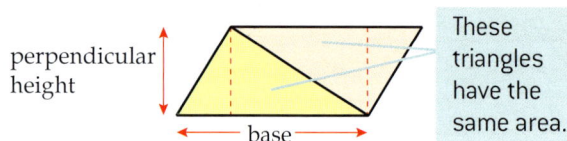

Look at this trapezium.

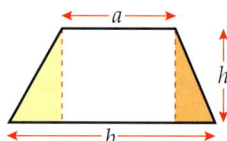

We can put two of them together to make a parallelogram.
The area of the trapezium is half the area of the parallelogram.

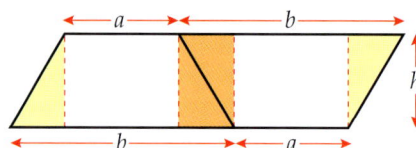

The base of this parallelogram is $a + b$.

The formula for the area of a parallelogram is base $\times$ (perpendicular) height, so the area of the trapezium is $\tfrac{1}{2} \times$ base $\times$ (perpendicular) height $= \tfrac{1}{2}(a+b)h$.

You can use this formula to find the area of any trapezium where a and b are the lengths of the parallel sides and h is the height.

Example   Calculate the area of the parallelogram and the trapezium.

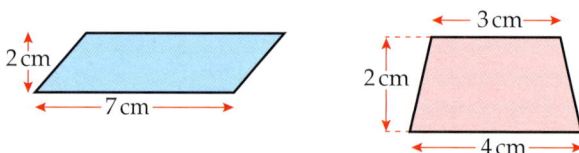

2 cm
7 cm

3 cm
2 cm
4 cm

Area of parallelogram $= 7 \times 2 = 14$ cm^2.

Area of trapezium $= \tfrac{1}{2}(4 + 3) \times 2 = 7$ cm^2.

Notice that the area of the trapezium is $\tfrac{1}{2}$ the area of the parallelogram.

By placing two of the trapezia together they make the parallelogram.

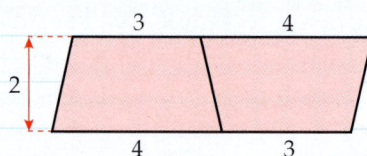

3   4
2
4   3

Exercise 6.4

1 Calculate the area of each of these parallelograms:

> Area = base × height

a)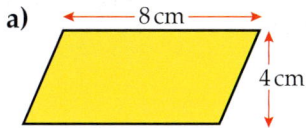

b)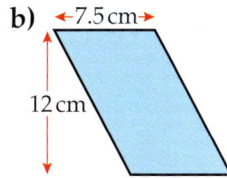

c)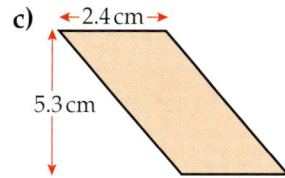

2 Find the area of each of these trapezia:

> Area = $\frac{1}{2}(a + b) \times h$. Where is the base?

a)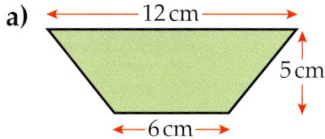

b)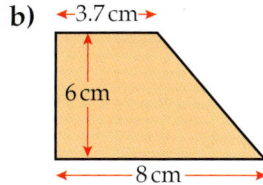

c)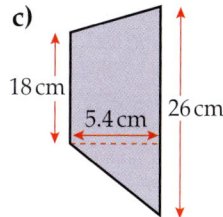

3 Work out the area of these shapes:

a)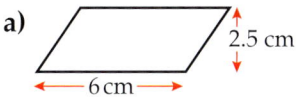

b)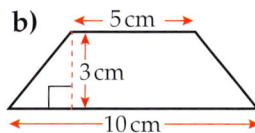

c)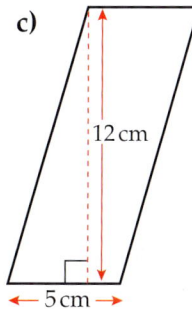

d)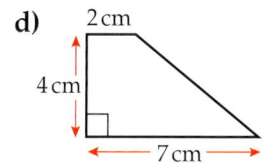

4 Megan and Grace divide this shape up in different ways.

  a) Calculate the area using Grace's suggestion.

  b) Calculate the area using Megan's suggestion.

  c) State which method you think is best and why it is best.

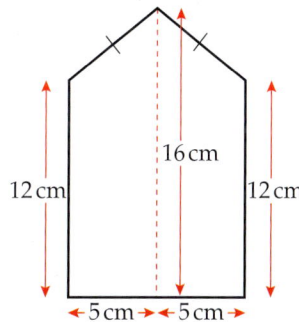

Megan

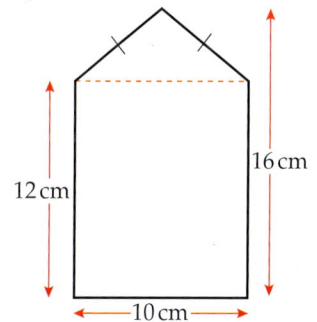

Grace

---

5 The area of this trapezium is 100 cm². Investigate what values a, b and h could be.

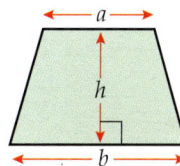

For example, this trapezium has h = 10 cm, a = 8 cm and b = 12 cm
Area = $\frac{1}{2} \times (12 + 8) \times 10 = \frac{1}{2} \times 20 \times 10 = 100$ cm².

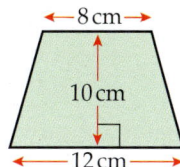

Try heights like 4 cm, 20 cm and 25 cm.

Volume 1

◈ Know and use the formula for the volume of a cuboid

Key words
volume
cuboid
cross-section
formula

You can think of the **volume** of a **cuboid** as the number of cubes inside the shape.

There are $3 \times 3 = 9$ cubes in each 'slice'.

The 'slice' is called the **cross-section** of the cuboid.

There are 2 'slices', each containing 9 cubes, so the total number of cubes is $2 \times 9 = 18$ cubes.

A shorter way to write this is Volume $= 3 \times 3 \times 2 = 18$.

The volume of any cuboid can be found by multiplying the width (w) by the length (l) and the height (h).

The **formula** can be written:
Volume $= w \times l \times h$ or just $V = wlh$.

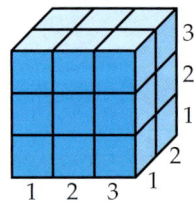

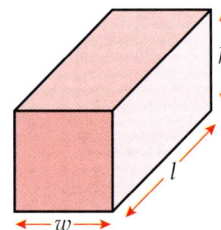

Example 1   Calculate the volume of this CD box.

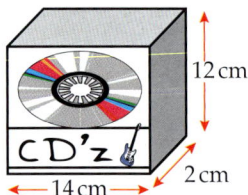

Volume $= w \times l \times h$

$= 14 \text{ cm} \times 2 \text{ cm} \times 12 \text{ cm} = 336 \text{ cm}^3$.

The numbers 14, 2 and 12 are the **w**idth, **l**ength and **h**eight of the cuboid, the numbers have been substituted for the letters in the formula, $w = 14, l = 2, h = 12$.

Example 2   Work out the volume of this cuboid.

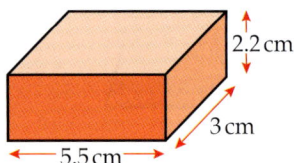

Volume $= w \times l \times h$

$= 5.5 \text{ cm} \times 3 \text{ cm} \times 2.2 \text{ cm} = 36.3 \text{ cm}^3$.

$w = 5.5, l = 3, h = 2.2$

Exercise 6.5

1 Work out the volume of each of these cuboids by counting the cubes.

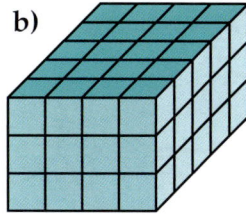

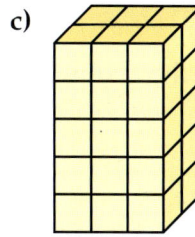

a)

b)

c)

2 Joy is packing a large trolley at Bristo's supermarket.
   a) She can pack 15 boxes on the bottom layer and can get 4 layers into the trolley.
   How many boxes can Joy pack in the trolley?
   b) How many boxes can Joy get into each of these trolleys?

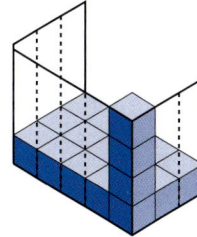

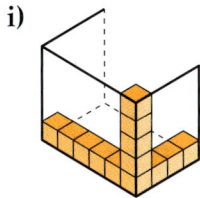

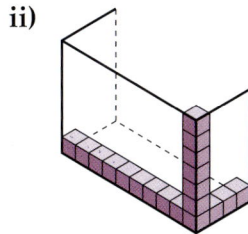

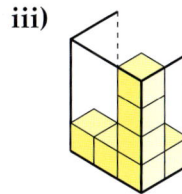

   i)   **ii)**   **iii)**

3 Work out the volume of each of these cuboids.

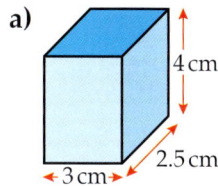

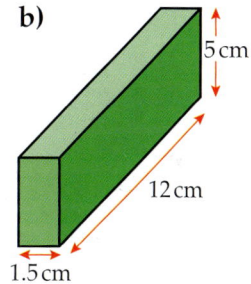

a) 4 cm, 2.5 cm, 3 cm

b) 5 cm, 12 cm, 1.5 cm

Remember the formula is: $V = w \times l \times h$.

4 Calculate the volume of these boxes.

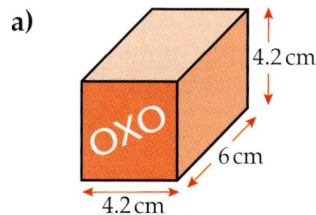

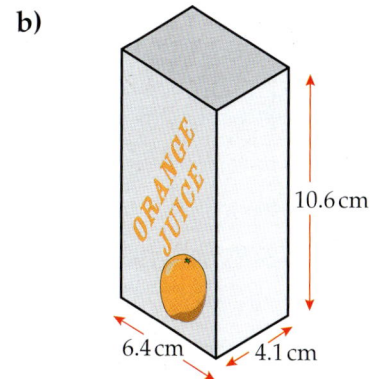

a) OXO — 4.2 cm, 6 cm, 4.2 cm

b) ORANGE JUICE — 10.6 cm, 6.4 cm, 4.1 cm

5 Mr Harding has built a rectangular pond for his garden.
The pond is 1 m deep. The length is 2 m and the width is 2.5 m.
What is the volume of Mr Harding's pond?

Volume 2

◈ Calculate the volume of shapes made from cuboids

The **formula** for the **volume** of a cuboid is: $w \times l \times h$

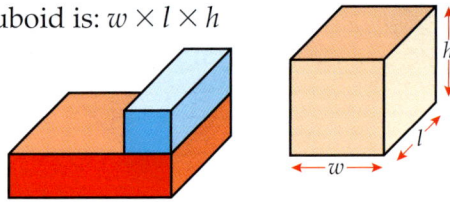

This shape is made from two cuboids.

The volume of the shape can be calculated by working out the volumes of the two separate cuboids and then adding.

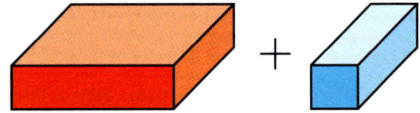

Total volume = volume of red cuboid + volume of blue cuboid

Example 1   Calculate the volume of this shape.

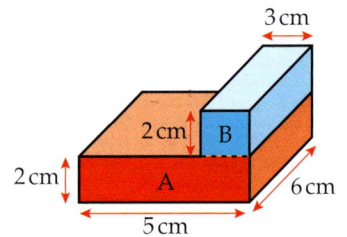

Volume of A = 5 cm × 6 cm × 2 cm = 60 cm³

Volume of B = 3 cm × 6 cm × 2 cm = 36 cm³

Volume of shape = 60 cm³ + 36 cm³ = 96 cm³

Example 2   Kathy is packing butter into boxes.
The butter is 9 cm by 6 cm by 5 cm.
The box is 27 cm by 24 cm by 10 cm.

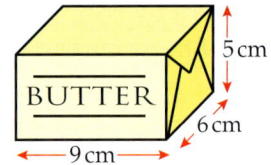

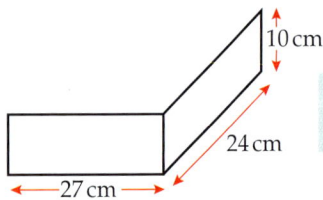

The butter in the box acts just like a 'cube' in a cuboid.

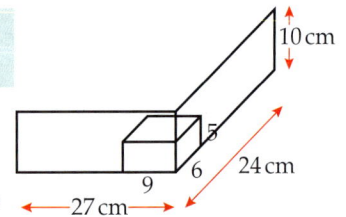

She puts the butter this way round in the box.
How many packs of butter fit into the box this way?

The box is 10 cm high.

The butter is 5 cm high.

So she will get 2 layers of butter in the box.

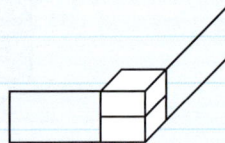

The box is 27 cm wide.

The butter is 9 cm wide.

So she will get 3 packs of across along the box.

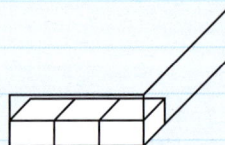

The box is 24 cm long. The butter is 6 cm long.

So she will get 4 packs along the box.

Total packs of butter = 2 × 3 × 4 = 24

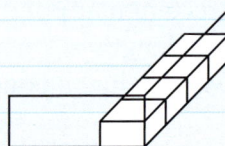

Exercise 6.6

1 Work out the volume of each of these shapes.

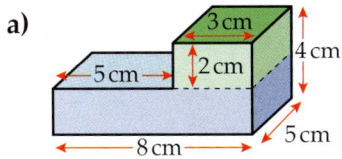

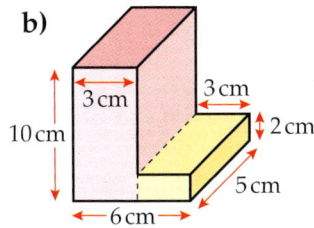

a)

b)

2 Eddie is packing instant soup into boxes.
The soup packs are 6 cm by 4 cm by 3 cm.

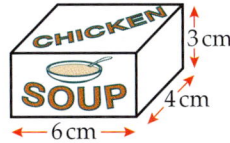

The box is 36 cm by 24 cm by 30 cm.

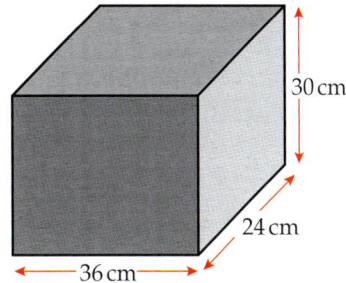

He puts the soup this way round in the box.
How many packs of soup fit into the box?

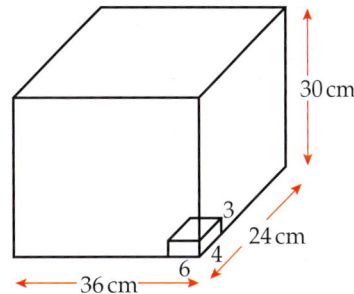

3 Calculate the volume of each of these shapes.

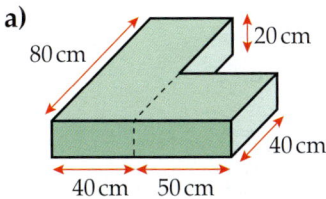

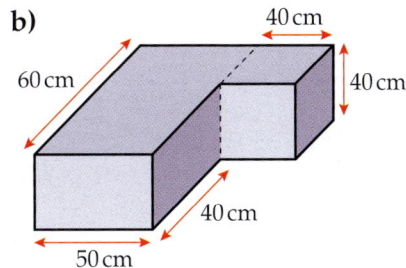

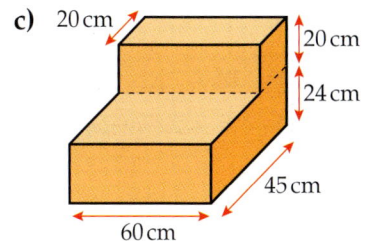

a)

b)

c)

Investigation

4 Using a plain sheet of A4 paper, design an
open box with the largest possible volume.

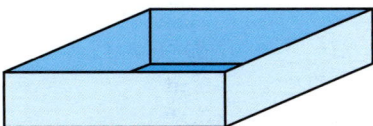

This is what a pattern
for your box might
look like. The width of
the box is *a*, the height
is *b* and the length is *c*.

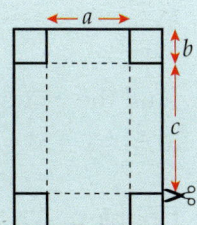

Mental calculations 1

◈ Using doubling and halving to simplify mental calculations

Mental **calculations** are calculations done 'in the head'.

For a multiplication of two numbers, if one number is **halved** whilst the other is **doubled**, the product remains the same.

For example:
$$12 \times 10 = 120$$
$$6 \times 20 = 120$$
$$3 \times 40 = 120$$

Doubling and halving can be used to make mental multiplications easier.

It works well when one number can be easily doubled and the other easily halved. Numbers whose last digit is 5 are ideal for doubling.

For example:
$$28 \times 5 = 14 \times 10 = 140$$
$$16 \times 4.5 = 8 \times 9 = 72$$
$$2.4 \times 3.5 = 1.2 \times 7 = 8.4$$
$$^-14 \times {}^-2.5 = {}^-7 \times {}^-5 = {}^+35$$

Each time, the changed multiplication is easier to calculate than the original multiplication.

Example

Work out
a) 6×3.5 b) 4.5×18 c) $^-12 \times {}^-5.5$ d) 4.8×2.5

a) $6 \times 3.5 = 3 \times 7 = 21$

b) $4.5 \times 18 = 9 \times 9 = 81$

c) $^-12 \times {}^-5.5 = {}^-6 \times {}^-11 = {}^+66$

d) $4.8 \times 2.5 = 2.4 \times 5 = 1.2 \times 10 = 12$

Numbers that end in 5 are easily doubled.

When multiplying integers, same signs $= {}^+$ve

You can double and halve twice to make it easier.

Exercise 7.1

1 Work out
a) 4×15 b) 55×6 c) 14×25 d) $^-35 \times {}^+12$

2 Find the value of
a) 14×3.5 b) 7.5×8 c) $^-4.5 \times {}^-16$ d) 6×12.5

3 Double and halve more than once to find the answer to the following:
a) 2.5×8.48 b) 16×2.25 c) 12×1.25 d) 2.5×12.4

4 Using mental methods, find the area of this picture.

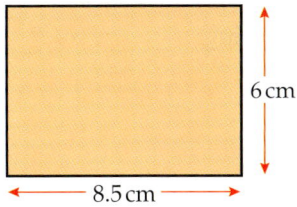

6 cm

8.5 cm

5 A bus holds 45 people. If there are 12 full buses, how many people are there altogether?

6 A coin is 0.25 cm thick. What would be the height of 24 coins?

7 Tickets cost £1.75 each. How much would 28 cost?

8 Use mental methods to answer the clues and complete the cross number puzzle.

Across	Down
1) 5×8.26	1) 86×5
3) 480×2.5	2) 2.5×140.8
5) $^-5 \times {}^-1.06$	3) 5×2.68
6) 2.5×36.8	4) 0.06×5
7) 8.6×5	6) 5×180.8
8) 6×15	7) 8.2×5
9) 5×6.82	11) 2.5×144
10) 86.2×5	12) 2.5×1.28
12) 5×6.6	14) 1.5×28
13) 120×5	15) 46×1.5
15) 8×7.5	16) 12.4×2.5
16) 5×64.8	17) 3.5×14
18) 22×5.5	

9 Find the total cost of 16 jumpers, each costing £3.50.

10 What is the area of a field that is 480 m long by 25 m wide?

Mental calculations 2

⊕ Multiply 'near tens' mentally by multiplying by 'tens' and then adjusting

Looking for 'near tens' is another method of making multiplications easier.

For a multiplication of two numbers, if one is a 'near ten', **partition** it (or split it up) to include a multiple of ten, for example:

For 43×21 the second number is 'near 20'
So, $43 \times 21 = (43 \times 20) + (43 \times 1)$ ————————— $21 = 20 + 1$ is a 'near ten'.

For 16×29 the second number is 'near 30'
So, $16 \times 29 = (16 \times 30) - (16 \times 1)$ ————————— $29 = 30 - 1$ is a 'near ten'.

The partitioning makes the multiplication easier to **calculate** mentally.

Example   Work out   **a)** 31×13 **b)** £2.34 $\times$ 9

a) $31 = 30 + 1$ ———————— 31 is near to 30.

     $31 \times 13 = (30 \times 13) + (1 \times 13)$

           $= 390 + 13$

           $= 403$

b) $9 = 10 - 1$ ———————— 9 is near 10.

     £2.34 $\times$ 9 = (£2.34 $\times$ 10) − (£2.34 $\times$ 1)

           = £23.40 − £2.34

           = £21.06

Exercise 7.2

1 To multiply a number by 51 we could use $(\times 50) + (\times 1)$. How would you multiply these values?

   a) 21   **b)** 39   **c)** 71

   d) 49   **e)** 22   **f)** 58

2 Work out the following

   a) 11×15 **b)** 21×15 **c)** 31×15 **d)** 51×15

3 Find the value of

   a) 7×9 **b)** 7×19 **c)** 7×29 **d)** 7×99

4 What is the cost of 19 stamps at 25p each?

5 How long would 21 pieces of wood each measuring 13 cm be?

6 If 1 cake has a mass of 43 g, what would be the mass of 39 cakes?

7 If a chocolate egg cost £2.45, what will 19 eggs cost?

8 A glass of lemonade holds 220 ml. What would be the volume of lemonade in 18 similar glasses?

9 Find the area of this rectangle.

6 cm

28 cm

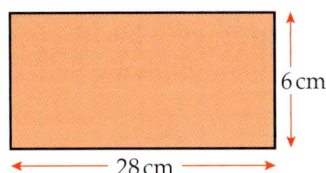

10 Find the coded message. Work out each multiplication. The letter goes above the answer in the message. (The answer can appear more than once.) The first one has been done for you.

											d	
462	58.3	73.8	434	836	756	462	58.3	434	51.7	667	702	627

462	836	28.8	58.3	552	434	58.3	836	627	357	

$39 \times 18 = d$ ($39 \times 18 = 702$ so $702 = d$)

$11 \times 5.3 = e$ $9 \times 3.2 = k$

$69 \times 8 = i$ $21 \times 36 = l$

$21 \times 22 = m$ $29 \times 23 = o$

$19 \times 44 = a$ $11 \times 4.7 = h$

$9 \times 8.2 = n$ $19 \times 33 = s$

$31 \times 14 = t$ $51 \times 7 = y$

Multiplying and dividing by 0.1 and 0.01

- ⊕ Multiply and divide whole numbers and decimal numbers by 0.1 and 0.01
- ⊕ Understand the effect of multiplying and dividing by a number less than 1

When multiplying by 10, 100 or 1000, the **digits** move 1, 2 or 3 places to the left.
When dividing by 10, 100 or 1000, the digits move 1, 2 or 3 places to the right.

Th	H	T	U•	t	h	th	
			3	2			3.2
		3	2				3.2 × 10
	3	2	0				3.2 × 100
3	2	0	0				3.2 × 1000
			0	3	2		3.2 ÷ 10
			0	0	3	2	3.2 ÷ 100

Multiplying by 0.1 ($\frac{1}{10}$), is equivalent to finding one **tenth**, or dividing by 10.
Multiplying by 0.01 ($\frac{1}{100}$), is equivalent to finding one **hundredth**, or dividing by 100.

Dividing by 0.1 ($\frac{1}{10}$), 'how many tenths in…?', is equivalent to multiplying by 10.
Dividing by 0.01 ($\frac{1}{100}$), 'how many hundredths in…?', is equivalent to multiplying by 100.

$$\times\, 0.1 \longleftrightarrow \div\, 10$$
$$\times\, 0.01 \longleftrightarrow \div\, 100$$
$$\div\, 0.1 \longleftrightarrow \times\, 10$$
$$\div\, 0.01 \longleftrightarrow \times\, 100$$

Dividing a number by 0.1 or 0.01 makes the number greater.
Multiplying a number by 0.1 or 0.01 makes the number smaller.

Example 1 Use **8.4** to perform the following calculations.

a) × 0.1   b) × 0.01   c) ÷ 0.1   d) ÷ 0.01

A place value grid will help

		H	T	U .	t	h	th
				8 . 4			

a) 8.4 × 0.1 (or ÷ 10)   0 . 8 4
b) 8.4 × 0.01 (or ÷ 100)   0 . 0 8 4
c) 8.4 ÷ 0.1 (or × 10)   8 4 .
d) 8.4 ÷ 0.01 (or × 100) 8 4 0 .

Example 2 A sheet of paper is 0.1 mm thick. What would be the thickness of 240 sheets?

240 × 0.1 mm = 240 ÷ 10 mm = 24 mm or 2.4 cm

Exercise 7.3

1 Copy and complete the following. You may use a place value grid to help.

a) 16×100 b) $70 \div 10$ c) 4.32×100 d) $16.42 \div 10$

e) 0.53×10 f) $172 \div 100$ g) $9 \div 10$ h) 5.7×100

2 Use **7.6** to perform the following calculations. A place value grid may help.

a) $\times 0.1$ b) $\times 0.01$ c) $\div 0.1$ d) $\div 0.01$

3 Copy and complete the following calculations. The first one has been done for you.

a) $6.4 \div 0.1 = 6.4 \times 10 = 64$ b) 12.4×0.1

c) 16.3×0.01 d) $14.6 \div 0.1$

e) $3.62 \div 0.01$ f) $7.2 \div 0.01$

4 A grain of sand has a mass of 0.01 g. What would be the mass of 6500 grains?

5 A chain of cells is 20 mm long. How many cells which are 0.1 mm long does it contain?

6 Copy and complete this table.

	$\times 100$	$\div 10$	$\times 0.1$	$\div 0.1$	$\times 0.01$	$\div 0.01$
23		2.3				
15.21						
17.4						
6.53				65.3		
21						
9.45						

7 A box contains silver leaves with a mass of 25 g. If each silver leaf has a mass of 0.1 g, how many silver leaves are in the box?

8 The number 6.4 has been multiplied or divided by 0.1 or 0.01 to make the following numbers. Write down the calculation that has been used.

```
      H   T   U . t   h   th
              6 . 4
a)        6   4                = 6.4 ÷ ____
b)            0 . 6   4        =
c)            0 . 0   6   4    =
d)  6     4   0                =
```

9 True or False?

a) Multiplying by a number greater than 1 gives an answer larger than the original number.   *Try multiplying by 2.*

b) Multiplying by 1 gives a larger answer than the original number.

c) Multiplying by a number smaller than 1 gives an answer smaller than the original number.   *Try multiplying by $\frac{1}{2}$ or 0.1.*

d) Dividing by a number greater than 1 gives an answer smaller than the original number.

e) Dividing by 1 gives a smaller answer than the original number.

f) Dividing by a number smaller than 1 gives an answer larger than the original number.

Rounding

Key words
nearest
  hundredth
round
nearest tenth
round up

- ⊕ Round whole numbers to any power of 10 (i.e. to nearest 10, 100, 1000, ...)
- ⊕ Round decimal numbers to the nearest whole number, or one or two decimal places

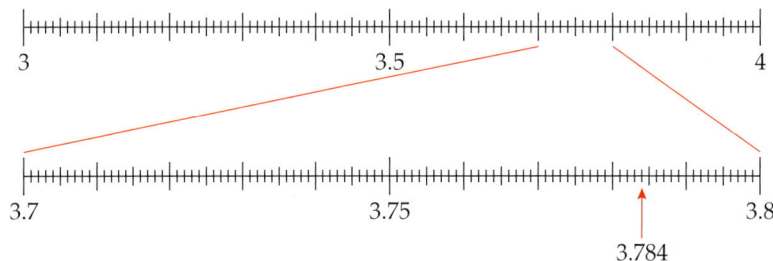

3.784 lies between the 'hundredths' 3.78 and 3.79 – the **nearest hundredth** is 3.78
'**Rounding** to the nearest hundredth' is called 'rounding to two decimal places'.

3.784 lies between the 'tenths' 3.7 and 3.8 – the **nearest tenth** is 3.8
'Rounding to the nearest tenth' is called 'rounding to one decimal place'.

'One decimal place' is shortened to 1 d.p.

We can also round this number to the nearest whole number.
3.784 lies between the whole numbers 3 and 4 – the nearest whole number is 4.

3.75 lies exactly halfway between the tenths 3.7 and 3.8.
When this happens, we always **round up**, so the nearest tenth is 3.8.

Example 1   283 657   Round this number to the nearest:

- **a)** hundred thousand
- **b)** ten thousand
- **c)** thousand
- **d)** hundred
- **e)** ten

a)	300 000	It lies between 200 000 and 300 000, more than halfway (250 000), so round up.
b)	280 000	It lies between 280 000 and 290 000, less than halfway (285 000), so round down.
c)	284 000	It lies between 283 000 and 284 000, more than halfway (283 500), so round up.
d)	283 700	It lies between 283 600 and 283 700, more than halfway (283 650), so round up.
e)	283 660	It lies between 283 650 and 283 660, more than halfway (283 655), so round up.

Example 2   3.573   Round this number to:

- **a)** 2 d.p.
- **b)** 1 d.p.
- **c)** nearest whole number

a)	3.57	It lies between 3.57 and 3.58, less than halfway (3.575), so round down.
b)	3.6	It lies between 3.5 and 3.6, more than halfway (3.55), so round up.
c)	4	It lies between 3 and 4, more than halfway (3.5), so round up.

Exercise 7.4

1 Round 3259 to the nearest: **a)** thousand **b)** hundred **c)** ten.

2 Round these numbers to the nearest whole number.
a) 4.3 **b)** 26.7 **c)** 15.28 **d)** 114.53

3 Round these to the nearest tenth (1 d.p.)
a) 6.49 **b)** 5.83 **c)** 15.25 **d)** 37.33

4 Round to the nearest hundredth (2 d.p.)
a) 5.364 **b)** 8.347 **c)** 25.748 **d)** 66.666

5 The population of Wales is 2 903 000. What is this to the nearest:
a) million **b)** hundred thousand.

6 The mass of a Christmas Turkey was 7.382 kg. What is this to the nearest:
a) 2 d.p. **b)** 1 d.p. **c)** kg (whole number)

7 Which of these numbers would round to 1 d.p. to 3.3?
3.23 3.24 3.25 3.26 3.27 3.28 3.29 **3.3** 3.31 3.32 3.33 3.34 3.35 3.36

8 Convert the following fractions into decimals using a calculator. Round your answers correct to two decimal places.
a) $\dfrac{3}{8}$ **b)** $\dfrac{4}{7}$ **c)** $\dfrac{1}{6}$ **d)** $\dfrac{13}{9}$

9 Which numbers in this cloud would round to 2 d.p. to 8.72?

8.714
8.719
8.696
8.725
8.715
8.722
8.731
8.723

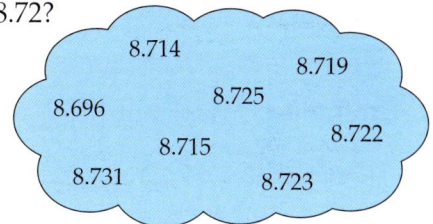

Investigation

10 You will need number cards 0–9 and a dice.
Shuffle the cards and place them in this order to make a 5 digit number.

$\square\,\square\,.\,\square\,\square\,\square$

Now throw your dice to find out how to round your number.

Repeat this several times.

Dice	Rounding
1	1 d.p.
2	2 d.p.
3	Whole number
4	Ten
5	Hundredths
6	Tenths

7.5

Key words
estimate
rounding
digit
carrying

Adding and subtracting decimals

⊕ Add whole numbers and decimal numbers using standard written methods
⊕ Subtract whole numbers and decimal numbers using standard written methods
⊕ Estimate answers by rounding

When adding or subtracting using column methods:
- Write an **estimate** of the answer by **rounding** each number.
- Write the numbers in columns underneath each other, making sure each **digit** is in its correct column.
- Compare the answer with the estimate as a check.

For example, 32.34 + 17.63:
- Estimate: 30 + 20 = 50
- Add: 32.34
             +17.63
            ‾‾‾‾‾‾‾
             49.97
            ‾‾‾‾‾‾‾
- Check estimate: 49.97 is close to 50 so it is a sensible answer.

When adding:
Start adding from the right, **carrying** into the next column on the left, if necessary.

When subtracting:
Start subtracting from the right, 'requesting' from the next column on the left when necessary.

Example 1   Work out 1.73 + 6.5 + 7 + 0.29.

Estimate 2 + 7 + 7 + 0 = 16

        1 . 7 3
        6 . 5
        7 .
    +   0 . 2 9
    ‾‾‾‾‾‾‾‾‾‾‾
      1 5 . 5 2
        1 1   1

Check estimate: 15.52 is close to 16 so it is a sensible answer.

Round to whole numbers.

7 is 7 units, so it goes to the left of the point.

Starting from the right 3 + 9 = 12, write 2 down and carry 1 tenth to the next column.

Example 2   Mahmet had £3.30. He spent £1.37 on a magazine. How much does he have left?

Estimate £3 − £1 = £2

      ² ¹² ¹
    £ 3̶ . 3̶ 0
  − £ 1 . 3 7
  ‾‾‾‾‾‾‾‾‾‾‾
    £ 1 . 9 3

Check estimate: £1.93 is close to £2, so it is a sensible answer.

Round to whole pounds.

Starting from the right 0 − 7, we need to request a number from the next column. We take a 1 from 3. This gives a 10 in the next column. We can now take 7 from the 10.

Exercise 7.5

1 By using a standard written method find the value of the following. Remember to make an estimate first and check it against your answer to see if it is sensible.
   a) £6.25 + £1.05 + £3 + £2.68
   b) 4.2 + 1.157 + 0.36 + 3.242
   c) 13.8 + 2.03 + 4 + 0.635
   d) 15.3 kg + 6.075 kg + 5.237 kg + 12 kg + 0.23 kg
   e) 12.3 m + 15.27 m + 4.595 m + 0.065 m + 0.009 m
   f) 16.53 + 6 + 12.826 + 0.9 + 0.587 + 23

2 Complete these subtractions. Remember to make an estimate first and then check it against your answer.

> Set out £16 as 16.00.

   a) 4.85 − 2.6   b) 3.23 − 1.15   c) 19.36 m − 7.82 m
   d) 5.24 g − 1.87 g   e) £16 − £3.38   f) 7.3 − 0.725

3 What is the total length of three pieces of ribbon measuring 4.3 m, 6.25 m and 5.575 m?

4 What is the difference between 6.73 litres and 4.29 litres?

5 Jimmy buys a pen costing £1.35, an eraser costing 87p and a note pad costing £2.99.
   a) How much did he spend altogether?
   b) How much change did he get from £10?

> Make sure the 87p is in the correct place. It can be written as £0.87.

6 Alice is 149.5 cm tall and Adam is 153 cm tall. How much taller is Adam than Alice?

7 Zoë gets some money for her birthday. She gets £10 from her Grandmother, £15 from her Uncle and £2.50 from her little sister. She wants to buy a CD costing £15.99, a bag costing £7.45 and some sweets costing £3.75.
   a) Does she have enough money to buy everything?
   b) How much does she have left over or how much does she need?

8 Find the sum and the difference of 15.08 and 8.73.

9 $a = 3.56$, $b = 2.07$, $c = 1.38$, $d = 4.6$
   Find a) $a + b + c$ b) $b - c$ c) $d - a$ d) $a + c - d$

10 Find the missing values in these calculations.
   a) $\quad 3.84$ b) $\quad 4.13$ c) $\quad 3.82$
       $- \underline{\quad\quad}$ $+ \underline{\quad\quad}$ $- \underline{\quad\quad}$
       $\quad 1.31$ $\quad 6.75$ $\quad 2.35$

Investigation

11 You will need a set of 0–9 cards and a coin.
   Shuffle the cards and make two 3 digit numbers.
   Place a decimal point in each number.
   Toss a coin – *heads* for addition and *tails* for subtraction.
   Now set out and complete the calculation.
   Do this several times.

Multiplying decimals

◈ Multiply whole numbers and decimal numbers by decimal numbers using the standard column method

◈ Understand where to position the decimal point

◈ Estimate the result of a calculation by rounding

◈ Check the result by comparing it with the estimate

Always start with an **estimate** .
- Estimate the answer by rounding, then multiplying the rounded numbers.
- Complete the **multiplication** .
- Compare the result with the estimate to check if it is sensible.

A **standard method** for 1.56×2.4:
- Estimate: $2 \times 2 = 4$
- Change the first decimal number by multiplying by 100, and the second decimal number by multiplying by 10. Altogether the calculation has been multiplied by 1000, so, $1.56 \times 2.4 = 156 \times 24 \div 1000$
- Calculate the whole number multiplication, i.e. $156 \times 24 = 3744$

$$
\begin{array}{r}
1\ 5\ 6 \\
\times \quad 2\ 4 \\
\hline
3\ 1\ 2\ 0 \quad 20 \times 156 \\
6\ 2\ 4 \quad 4 \times 156 \\
\hline
3\ 7\ 4\ 4 \\
\end{array}
$$

- Divide by 1000: $3744 \div 1000 = 3.744$
- Compare the answer with the estimate: 3.744 is close to 4, so it is a sensible answer.

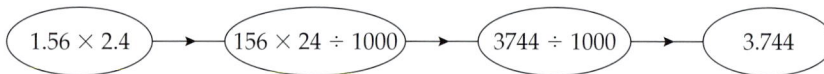

$$1.56 \times 2.4 \longrightarrow 156 \times 24 \div 1000 \longrightarrow 3744 \div 1000 \longrightarrow 3.744$$

Example   A picture is 1.25 m long and 0.85m wide. What is the area of the picture?

Estimate $1 \times 1 = 1\,m^2$

$1.25 \times 100 = 125$

$0.85 \times 100 = 85$

$$
\begin{array}{r}
1\ 2\ 5 \\
\times \quad 8\ 5 \\
\hline
6\ 2\ 5 \quad \times 5 \\
1\ 0\ 0\ 0\ 0 \quad \times 80 \\
\hline
1\ 0\ 6\ 2\ 5 \\
\end{array}
$$

The multiplication can be done by any method, i.e. a grid or as separate calculations.

$$
\begin{array}{r}
1\ 2\ 5 \\
\times \quad 5 \\
\hline
6\ 2\ 5 \\
\end{array}
+
\begin{array}{r}
1\ 2\ 5 \\
\times \quad 8\ 0 \\
\hline
1\ 0\ 0\ 0\ 0 \\
\end{array}
= 10625
$$

$10\,625 \div 100 \div 100 = 1.0625\ m^2$

Check: 1.0625 is close to estimate 1 and so the answer is sensible.

Exercise 7.6

1. Work out **a)** 52×73 **b)** 126×34

2. Which of the numbers, 10, 100 or 1000, do I need to multiply these decimals by to make whole numbers?
   a) 4.2 **b)** 6.37 **c)** 0.72 **d)** 2.253

3. Copy and continue these number sentences. The first one has been done for you.
   a) $5.15 \times 0.6 = 515 \times 6 \div 100 \div 10 = 515 \times 6 \div 1000$
   b) $6.2 \times 0.7 =$ **c)** $6.3 \times 7.5 =$ **d)** $8.63 \times 2.4 =$ **e)** $3.42 \times 3.6 =$

4. Now complete the multiplications in **Q3** using a standard written method. Remember to estimate the answer before you begin and check your answer against the estimate at the end.

5. What is the total length of 142 pieces of metal each 4.5 m long?

6. A cinema ticket costs £2.45. What would be the cost of 27 tickets?

7. Find the area of this rectangle which measures 8.3 cm by 9.4 cm.

   8.3 cm

   ← 9.4 cm →

8. Rope costs £3.24 per metre. How much would 3.6 m cost?
   Give your answer to the nearest penny.

9. I want to put a picture 11.3 cm long by 6.2 cm wide on my T-shirt.
   a) What is the area of the picture?
   The printers charge 7.5p for every full square centimetre of picture.
   b) How much will it cost?

10. Copy and complete this multiplication pyramid.
    Each brick is found by multiplying the two numbers below it.

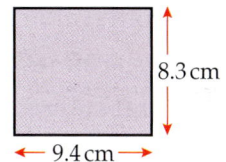

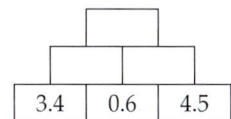

    | 3.4 | 0.6 | 4.5 |

Investigation

11. This question requires a set of 0–9 cards.
    Shuffle the cards and make a number with 3 digits like

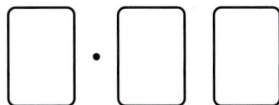

    ☐ . ☐ ☐

    Shuffle the remaining cards and make a 2 digit number like

    ☐ . ☐

    Now estimate the answer you will get from multiplying your numbers.
    Complete the calculation and check against your estimate.
    Now repeat.

Dividing decimals

- ⊕ Divide whole numbers and decimal numbers by decimal numbers using a standard written method
- ⊕ Estimate the result of a calculation by rounding
- ⊕ Check the result by comparing it with the estimate

Key words
division
divisor
decimal
estimate
tenths
hundredths

Division by a number is equivalent to repeated subtraction of that number. We call the number we are dividing by the **divisor**.

The answer to a division remains the same if both the number and the divisor are multiplied or divided by the same number.

For example, $240 \div 20$, $24 \div 2$, $2.4 \div 0.2$ all have the same answer, 12.

When dividing by a **decimal** number:

- Convert the division into an equivalent one which has a whole number divisor.
- Write an **estimate** of the answer.
- Start subtracting as many 100s of the divisor as you can, then as many 10s of the divisor as you can, then as many units of the divisor as you can, then as many **tenths** of the divisor, and so on.
- Round the remainder to the nearest whole number, nearest tenth or nearest **hundredth**, depending on the context of the calculation.
- Compare the answer with the estimate.

Example   Work out $19.2 \div 0.6$.

$0.6 \times 10 = 6$

$19.2 \times 10 = 192$

Estimate $180 \div 6 = 30$

$$
\begin{array}{r}
6\overline{)\,1\,9\,2} \\
-\ 6\,0 \quad 6 \times 10 \\
\hline
1\,3\,2 \\
-\ 6\,0 \quad 6 \times 10 \\
\hline
7\,2 \\
-\ 6\,0 \quad 6 \times 10 \\
\hline
1\,2 \\
-\ 1\,2 \quad 6 \times 2 \\
\hline
0 \quad + \\
\hline
3\,2
\end{array}
$$

$192 \div 6 = 32$ so $19.2 \div 0.6 = 32$

Check estimate: 32 is close to 30, so it is a sensible answer.

To make the divisor a whole number multiply by 10, so both numbers are multiplied by 10.

Choose a close, easy number to divide to find your estimate.

$6 \times 10 = 60$, subtract 60.

We could use $6 \times 10 = 60$ too small
$6 \times 20 = 120$ too small
$6 \times 30 = 180$
and subtract 180 in one go.

Exercise 7.7

1 What would you multiply both numbers by to make the divisor a whole number?
  - **a)** $17.2 \div 0.4$
  - **b)** $92.4 \div 0.7$
  - **c)** $3.81 \div 0.03$
  - **d)** $16.2 \div 0.05$
  - **e)** $4.23 \div 0.09$
  - **f)** $191.7 \div 0.9$

2 Copy and complete a number sentence for each part of **Q1** showing the result of multiplying both numbers. Then complete the calculation using a standard written method. The first one has been done for you.
  - **a)** $17.2 \div 0.4 = 172 \div 4 = 43$

3 How many pieces of rope 0.7 m long, can be cut from a piece 16.1 m in length?

4 How many paper clips with a mass of 0.08 g would be in a 14 g box?

5 A spoonful of honey has a volume of 0.005 litres. How many spoonfuls would I get from a 0.25 litre bottle?

6 To take off a wheel in a motor race takes 1.2 seconds. How many wheels could be taken off in 1 minute?

> Change the minute into seconds.

7 **a)** Without doing any calculations find the question which gives a different answer from the rest.
  - **i)** $3.24 \div 0.12$
  - **ii)** $32.4 \div 1.2$
  - **iii)** $0.324 \div 1.2$
  - **iv)** $324 \div 12$
  - **b)** What is the answer that 3 of these give?

8 Will these answers be larger or smaller than 32? You may not have to work them out.
  - **a)** 32×7
  - **b)** $32 \div 7$
  - **c)** 32×0.4
  - **d)** $32 \div 0.01$
  - **e)** $32 \div 0.4$
  - **f)** $32 \div 1.5$

Investigation

9 **a)** Copy and complete this spider diagram with divisions that give the answer 5. No dividing by 1, 10, 100 or 1000 is allowed.
  - **b)** Can you make another diagram where all the divisors are decimals?
  - **c)** Change the answer number and make another diagram for your partner to complete. Now check to see if they were right.

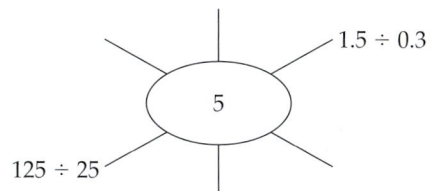

$1.5 \div 0.3$

5

$125 \div 25$

Square roots

Key words
square number
square root
positive
negative
factorisation
factor

⊕ Know that a positive integer has two square roots, one positive and one negative

⊕ Know how to use factorisation to find square roots

Square numbers are found by multiplying a whole number by itself.

36 is a square number because $6^2 = 6 \times 6 = 36$.   'Six squared is thirty-six.'

The inverse of 'square' is ' **square root** '. $\sqrt{36} = 6$.   'The square root of thirty-six is six.'

Since $^-6 \times {}^-6$ is also 36, then 36 has two square roots: $^+6$ and $^-6$.

All **positive** integers (whole numbers) have two square roots, one positive and one **negative** . It is convention to assume that $\sqrt{36}$ means the positive solution.

The square roots of some larger numbers can be found by **factorisation** , if the **factor** pair contains two well-known squares.
For example, $\sqrt{1600} = \sqrt{16} \times \sqrt{100} = 4 \times 10 = 40$.

Example 1   Find the square roots of the following:

a) 25   b) $^-81$ c) 900

a) $\sqrt{25} = 5$

So 25 has $^-5$ and $^+5$ as its square roots.

$^+5 \times {}^+5 = {}^+25$
$^-5 \times {}^-5 = {}^+25$, so 25 has 2 square roots.

b) $\sqrt{^-81}$ = not possible

c) $\sqrt{900} = \sqrt{9} \times \sqrt{100}$

You can only make $^-81$ with different numbers, $^-9$ and $^+9$, so you cannot find its square root.

$= 3 \times 10$

$= 30$

So 900 has $^-30$ and $^+30$ as its square roots.

We look for pairs of factors that make 900. e.g.
9×100, 18×50, 36×25, 2×450, 4×225
Choose a pair made up of square numbers.

Example 2   Between which 2 whole numbers does $\sqrt{43}$ lie?

Square numbers are 1, 4, 9, 16, 25, 36, 49, 64, 81, 100

$36 < 43 < 49$

So $\sqrt{36} < \sqrt{43} < \sqrt{49}$

$6 < \sqrt{43} < 7$

$\sqrt{43}$ lies between 6 and 7

43 lies between the square numbers 36 and 49.

Exercise 7.8

1. Find the positive and negative square roots of the following:

   a) 16   b) 25   c) 49   d) 9   e) 36

2. Which of the following have whole number square roots?

   a) $\sqrt{8}$ b) $\sqrt{4}$ c) $\sqrt{^-25}$ d) $\sqrt{24}$ e) $\sqrt{64}$

3. a) If $2.5 \times 2.5 = 6.25$, what are the square roots of 6.25?

   b) If $^-3.2 \times ^-3.2 = 10.24$, what are the square roots of 10.24?

   c) If $137 \times 137 = 18\,769$, what are the square roots of 18 769?

   > How many answers does each one have?

4. Copy and continue the sequence to find the first 20 square numbers.

Square	1×1	2×2	3×3	4×4	5×5 ....
Square number	1	4	9	16	

5. Find the following:

   a) $\sqrt{100}$ b) $\sqrt{81}$ c) $\sqrt{121}$ d) $\sqrt{64}$ e) $\sqrt{144}$

6. Using the square numbers you know, find two whole numbers which these square roots lie between.

   > Look at Example 2.

   a) $\sqrt{70}$ b) $\sqrt{120}$ c) $\sqrt{340}$ d) $\sqrt{159}$ e) $\sqrt{88}$

7. Copy and complete these number sentences. The first one has been done for you.

   a) $400 = 4 \times 100 : \sqrt{400} = \sqrt{4} \times \sqrt{100} = 2 \times 10 = 20$

   b) $1600 = 16 \times 100 : \sqrt{1600} =$

   c) $144 = 9 \times 16 : \sqrt{144} =$

   d) $196 = 4 \times 49 : \sqrt{196} =$

   e) $256 = 4 \times 64 : \sqrt{256} =$

8. $\sqrt{9} \times \sqrt{4}$ can be used to find $\sqrt{36}$.
   What square root would these help us find?

   a) $\sqrt{25} \times \sqrt{4}$ b) $\sqrt{100} \times \sqrt{25}$ c) $\sqrt{4} \times \sqrt{36}$

9. $324 = 9 \times 36$ $1296 = 16 \times 81$ $225 = 25 \times 9$

   $1936 = 121 \times 16$ $3969 = 81 \times 49$ $576 = 144 \times 4$

   Use these facts to find the following:

   a) $\sqrt{324}$ b) $\sqrt{3969}$ c) $\sqrt{225}$

   d) $\sqrt{1296}$ e) $\sqrt{576}$ f) $\sqrt{1936}$

10. Find the following square roots by first finding 2 square number factors.

    a) $\sqrt{2500}$ b) $\sqrt{6400}$ c) $\sqrt{625}$ d) $\sqrt{484}$

Cubes and cube roots

- ⊕ Use index notation to write squares and cubes
- ⊕ Use a calculator to find squares and cubes
- ⊕ Know the cubes of 1, 2, 3, 4, 5 and 10 and the corresponding cube roots

Key words
square number
square root
cube number
powers
cube root
index

Some examples of **square numbers** are:

$$1^2 = 1 \times 1 = 1$$
$$2^2 = 2 \times 2 = 4$$
$$3^2 = 3 \times 3 = 9$$
$$4^2 = 4 \times 4 = 16$$
....
$$10^2 = 10 \times 10 = 100$$

25 is a square number.
$5^2 = 25$

'Five squared is twenty-five' or 'five to the power of two is twenty-five'.

The inverse is $\sqrt{25} = 5$.

'The **square root** of twenty-five is five'.

Remember that the other square root of twenty-five is negative five.

Some examples of **cube numbers** are:

$$1^3 = 1 \times 1 \times 1 = 1$$
$$2^3 = 2 \times 2 \times 2 = 8$$
$$3^3 = 3 \times 3 \times 3 = 27$$
$$4^3 = 4 \times 4 \times 4 = 64$$
....
$$10^3 = 10 \times 10 \times 10 = 1000$$

8 is a cube number.
$2^3 = 8$

'Two cubed is eight' or 'two to the **power** of three is eight'.

The inverse is $\sqrt[3]{8} = 2$.

'The **cube root** of eight is two'.

In the statement $2^3 = 8$, 3 is called the **index** or power.

Example   Find the value of the following:

- **a)** 10^3
- **b)** 6 to the power 2
- **c)** 5 squared
- **d)** 3 cubed
- **e)** cube root of 8
- **f)** $\sqrt[3]{-64}$

a) 10^3 means $10 \times 10 \times 10 = 1000$

b) 6 to the power 2 means 6^2 or $6 \times 6 = 36$

c) 5 squared means 5^2 or $5 \times 5 = 25$

d) 3 cubed means 3^3 or $3 \times 3 \times 3 = 27$

e) cube root of $8 = \sqrt[3]{8} = 2$ (because $2 \times 2 \times 2 = 8$)

f) $\sqrt[3]{-64} = {}^-4$ (because ${}^-4 \times {}^-4 \times {}^-4 = ({}^+16) \times {}^-4 = {}^-64$)

Exercise 8.1

1 Copy and complete this table of squares and cubes.

	1	2	3	4	5	6	7	8	9	10
Squared	1	4	9	16						
Cubed	1	8	27							

2 Find, where possible, the following squares and square roots.

    a) 4^2 **b)** $\sqrt{25}$ **c)** 8^2

    d) $\sqrt{-36}$ **e)** $\sqrt{121}$ **f)** 10^2

3 Calculate the following cubes and cube roots.

    a) 4^3 **b)** $\sqrt[3]{8}$ **c)** 10^3

    d) $\sqrt[3]{125}$ **e)** 6^3 **f)** $\sqrt[3]{27}$

4 Copy and complete the following sentences.

    a) 3 squared equals ____.   **b)** ____ is the square root of 100.

    c) 7 cubed equals ____.   **d)** ____ is the cube root of 8.

    e) ____ is the cube root of ⁻8.   **f)** ____ to the power 2 equals 81.

    g) 4 to the power 3 equals ____.   **h)** 27 is the cube of ____.

    i) ____ is the cube root of 125.   **j)** $3 \times 3 \times 3$ is the same as 3____.

5 Find the following, giving your answers correct to 1 d.p. where appropriate.

    a) $\sqrt{144}$ **b)** $\sqrt[3]{3375}$ **c)** $\sqrt{85}$ **d)** $\sqrt[3]{120}$ **e)** $\sqrt[3]{385}$

6 Find the length of 1 edge of a cube with a volume of 512 cm³.

7 A cube has an edge length of 9 cm. What is its volume?   Volume = length³

8 A cube has a volume of 250 cm³. What is the length of 1 edge correct to 1 d.p.?

9 Use your table in **Q1** to find between which two numbers these cube roots lie. The first one has been done for you.

    a) $\sqrt[3]{750}$ $729 < 750 < 1000$

                       $\sqrt[3]{729} < \sqrt[3]{750} < \sqrt[3]{1000}$

                       $9 < \sqrt[3]{750} < 10$ $\sqrt[3]{750}$ lies between 9 and 10.

    b) $\sqrt[3]{-40}$ **c)** $\sqrt[3]{283}$ **d)** $\sqrt[3]{635}$ **e)** $\sqrt[3]{149}$

Investigation

10 You will need a set of 0–9 cards and a dice.

Shuffle the cards and make a 3-digit number. Roll the dice – an even number means find the square root and an odd number means find the cube root.

    a) Use your calculator to find the answer correct to 1 d.p. Repeat this several times.

    b) Now throw the dice. If it lands on 1 or 5 make a 1-digit number. If it lands on 2 or 4 make a 2-digit number and if it lands on 3 or 6 make a 3-digit number.

    Make your number. Now turn over the next card. If it is odd find the cube of your number, if it is even find the square of your number. Repeat several times.

Powers of 10

⊕ Know the meaning of powers of 10

Key words
powers of 10
million
billion
place value

10^2 is read as 'ten squared' and 'ten to the power of two'.
10^3 is read as 'ten cubed' and 'ten to the power of three'.

These are examples of different ' **powers of 10** '.

The powers of 10 are:

10^1	$= 10$	ten
10^2	$= 10 \times 10$	hundred
10^3	$= 10 \times 10 \times 10$	thousand
10^4	$= 10 \times 10 \times 10 \times 10$	ten thousand
10^5	$= 10 \times 10 \times 10 \times 10 \times 10$	hundred thousand
10^6	$= 10 \times 10 \times 10 \times 10 \times 10 \times 10$	thousand thousand (**million**)

Also 10^9 $= 1000 \times 1000 \times 1000$ thousand million (**billion**)

The column headings on a **place value** grid can be written as powers of 10:

$$10^6 \ \ 10^5 \ \ 10^4 \ \ 10^3 \ \ 10^2 \ \ 10 \ \ \ 1$$

			Th	H	T	U $\bullet$	t	h

Large numbers can be written as a multiple of a power of 10.
For example, $47\,000 = 47 \times 10^3$, $15\,600\,000 = 15.6 \times 10^6$

Example 1   **a)**   Find the value of 10^8.
b)   Write one thousand as a power of 10.

a) $10^8 = 10 \times 10 \times 10 \times 10 \times 10 \times 10 \times 10 \times 10 = 100\,000\,000$

b)   One thousand $= 1000 = 10^3$ ———————————— $10 \times 10 \times 10 = 1000$

Example 2   Find the value of   **a)** 8×10^3 **b)** 6.4×10^5

a) $8 \times 10^3 = 8 \times (10 \times 10 \times 10) = 8 \times 1000 = 8000$

b) $6.4 \times 10^5 = 6.4 \times (10 \times 10 \times 10 \times 10 \times 10) = 6.4 \times 100\,000 = 640\,000$

$6.4 \times 10 = 64$, $64 \times 10 = 640$
$640 \times 10 = 6400$, $6400 \times 10 = 64\,000$
$64\,000 \times 10 = 640\,000$

Exercise 8.2

1 Find the value of the following:

    a) 10^3 **b)** 10^7 **c)** 10^6 **d)** 10^1 **e)** 10^9

2 Write these numbers as a power of 10:

    a) one hundred   **b)** ten thousand   **c)** one million   **d)** one billion

3 Copy and complete these sentences.

    a) 10^6 is worth one _____

    b) A thousand can be written as 10 to the power ___

    c) 10 to the power 5 is worth _____ thousand

    d) 10 000 can be written as _____

    e) ____ is worth one billion.

4 Copy and complete, writing in the power of ten the number could be multiplied by.

10^6	10^5	10^4	10^3	10^2	10^1	tenths	can be written as
5	6	0	0	0	0 .	0	$5.6 \times 10^{[\ ]}$
	5	6	0	0	0 .	0	$5.6 \times 10^{[\ ]}$
		5	6	0	0 .	0	$5.6 \times 10^{[\ ]}$
			5	6	0 .	0	$5.6 \times 10^{[\ ]}$
				5	6 .	0	5.6×10^1
					5 .	6	5.6×1

5 Using a place value chart to help, write down as many 'multiplication by a power of 10' calculations as you can for the following numbers.

    a) 70 000   **b)** 2300   **c)** 4 200 000

6 Find the value of the following.

> Look back at Example 2.

    a) 3×10^3 **b)** 7×10^6 **c)** 11×10^4

    d) 2×10^9 **e)** 4.5×10^2 **f)** 5.3×10^1

7 A space ship reported the distance between two moons as 3.4×10^7 miles. How far is this in ordinary numbers?

8 A scientist was estimating the number of fish on a reef.
He said there were three thousand million. How would he write this as 3 times a power of 10?

9 Which number is larger?

> Change into ordinary numbers to compare them.

    a) 3×10^5 and 3×10^6 **b)** 3×10^3 and 5×10^2

    c) 4×10^8 and 7×10^6 **d)** 6×10^4 and 9×10^7

Investigation

10 Look for a book in the Library, or search the Internet to find out the distances between the planets in our solar system.

Are the distances given as a multiplication with a power of 10? If not put them into this type of number.

If the distances are given as multiplications with a power of 10 put them into ordinary numbers.

Prime factors

- Recognise prime numbers
- Write a number as a product of its prime factors

Key words
product
factor
factorisation
factor pair
prime number
prime factor
index notation

We can write a number as a **product** of its **factors**, for example:

$36 = 4 \times 9$, this is called a **factorisation** of 36

4 and 9 are a **factor pair**.

$500 = 5 \times 100$, this is called a factorisation of 500

5 and 100 are a factor pair.

Prime numbers are numbers that have exactly 2 factors.
There are 25 prime numbers less than 100.
They are:

2, 3, 5, 7, 11, 13, 17, 19, 23, 29, 31, 37, 41, 43, 47, 53, 59, 61, 67, 71, 73, 79, 83, 89, 97

1 is not a prime number – it only has 1 factor.

Every non-prime number can be written as a product of **prime factors**.

For example: $36 = 2 \times 2 \times 3 \times 3$, this is called the prime factorisation of 36.
For example: $500 = 2 \times 2 \times 5 \times 5 \times 5$, this is called the prime factorisation of 500.

We usually write the prime factors of a number using **index** (power) **notation**
For example: $36 = 2^2 \times 3^2$ $500 = 2^2 \times 5^3$

Example 1   How many factors does 12 have?

$1 \times 12, 2 \times 6, 3 \times 4$

Factors of 12 are 1, 2, 3, 4, 6, 12

12 has 6 factors.

Divide by 1, 2, 3, … where possible. Stop when a number is repeated.

Example 2   Find the **prime factorisation** of 60.

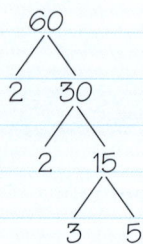

60
2   30
2   15
3   5

Divide by the smallest prime number you can. Stop when you only have prime numbers.

Prime factorisation of 60 is: $2 \times 2 \times 3 \times 5 = 2^2 \times 3 \times 5$

Check to make sure it multiplies to give 60.

Exercise 8.3

1 Find all the factor pairs of:

   a) 20   **b)** 50   **c)** 35   **d)** 42   **e)** 49

2 Which of the following are prime numbers?

   a) 4   **b)** 7   **c)** 9   **d)** 17   **e)** 31

   f) 81   **g)** 43   **h)** 73   **i)** 92   **j)** 23

3 Copy and complete the factor tree to find the prime factorisation of 48.

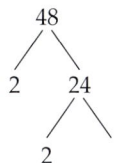

```
      48
     /  \
    2    24
        /  \
       2
```

4 How many factors do the following numbers have?   First find all the factor pairs.

   a) 16   **b)** 22   **c)** 14   **d)** 27   **e)** 100

5 What numbers have these prime factorisations?

   a) 3×5 **b)** $2 \times 3 \times 7$ **c)** $2^2 \times 3$ **d)** $2^3 \times 5^2$

6 Sally has written her prime factorisation answers like this:

   a) $2 \times 2 \times 2 \times 3 \times 3$ **b)** $2 \times 3 \times 3 \times 5 \times 5$

   Re-write her answers using index notation.

7 Use factor trees to find the prime factorisations of the following.
Give your answers using index notation.

   a) 16   **b)** 45   **c)** 100   **d)** 24   **e)** 80

8 **a)** How many factors do each of the following numbers have?

       2, 3, 5, 7, 11

   b) What can you say about prime numbers and the number of factors?

9 Ali says that 1 is a prime number and Sanji says that it is not.
Who is right? Give a reason for your answer.

10 **a)** List the factors of 16.

   b) List the factors of 20.

   c) Look in both lists to find any numbers the same (common factors).
Write them in order.

   d) What number is the highest common factor?

11 Repeat **Q10** for the following pairs of numbers.

   a) 10 and 35   **b)** 40 and 60.

Index notation

⊕ Simplify algebraic expressions using index notation

Key words
index
power
index notation
square
cube

We can write $3 \times 3 \times 3 \times 3$ as 3^4.

The raised 4 is the ' index ' or power – it tells us how many times to multiply 3 by itself. We read 3^4 as '3 to the power of four'.

You can use a calculator to find the value of 3^4 by pressing:

$$3 \quad x^y \quad 4 \quad =$$

This gives us: $\quad 3^4 = 81$

We can use index notation for unknown values too.

For example, $\quad b \times b = b^2.$ $\qquad$ We call this 'b squared ' or 'b to the power of two'.

$\qquad\qquad\qquad b \times b \times b = b^3.$ $\qquad$ We call this 'b cubed ' or 'b to the power of three'.

Example 1 Write the following using index notation. Use the x^y key on your calculators to find its value.

$$4 \times 4 \times 4 \times 4 \times 4 \times 4$$

$4 \times 4 \times 4 \times 4 \times 4 \times 4 = 4^6$

$4^6 = 4096$

4 is multiplied by itself 6 times, so we write 4 to the power 6.

Press $\quad 4 \quad x^y \quad 6$

Example 2 Simplify the following algebraic expressions using index notation:

$\qquad$ **a)** $c \times c \times c \times c \times c$ $\qquad$ **b)** $3 \times r \times r \times r \times r \times r \times r$

a) $c \times c \times c \times c \times c = c^5$

b) $3 \times r \times r \times r \times r \times r \times r = 3r^6$

The c is multiplied by itself 5 times, so we write c to the power 5.

The r is multiplied by itself 6 times, so we write r to the power six (r^6). The r is also multiplied by 3. We usually write the numbers before the letters.

Exercise 8.4

1 Copy and complete the following tables.

a)

$2^?$	2	2
2^2	2×2	?
2^3	?	8
?	$2 \times 2 \times 2 \times 2$	?
2^5	?	32

b)

c^5	?
r^5	?
$q^?$	$q \times q \times q \times q \times q$

2 Use **Q1** to help you find the value of   **a)** 2^6 **b)** 3×2^3

3 Write the following using index notation.
Use the x^y key on your calculator to find the value of each.

a) $5 \times 5 \times 5$ **b)** $9 \times 9 \times 9 \times 9 \times 9$ **c)** $1 \times 1 \times 1 \times 1 \times 1 \times 1 \times 1$

d) $12 \times 12 \times 12$ **e)** $2 \times 2 \times 2 \times 2$ **f)** $10 \times 10 \times 10 \times 10 \times 10 \times 10$

4 Write the following algebraic expressions using index notation:

a) $t \times t \times t \times t \times t \times t$ **b)** $r \times r \times r \times r$ **c)** $w \times w \times w \times w \times w \times w \times w$

d) $h \times h \times h \times h$ **e)** $j \times j \times j \times j \times j$ **f)** $p \times p$

5 Simplify the following algebraic expressions using index notation:

a) $3 \times t \times t \times t \times t$ **b)** $6 \times w \times w$

c) $5 \times p \times p \times p \times p \times p \times p$ **d)** $q \times q \times 3 \times q$

e) $x \times x \times 2$ **f)** $y \times y \times y \times 3 \times y \times y \times y \times y \times y$

6 In the following diagram the expression in each cell is found by multiplying the values in the two cells below it:

The value in this cell is $p \times p \times p$. ——————

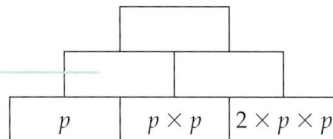

| p | $p \times p$ | $2 \times p \times p$ |

Copy and complete the diagram, writing each expression using index notation.

7 Mr Wong is making an outdoor chess board from paving slabs.
He charges 2 pence for the 1st square on the chess board.
2×2 pence for the 2nd square on the chess board.
$2 \times 2 \times 2$ pence for the 3rd square on the chess board, and so on.

a) How much does he charge for the 10th square on the chess board?
Write your answer in index notation.

b) How much is this in pence?

c) How much is this in pounds?

d) Work out how much he charges for the   **i)** 20th square   **ii)** 25th square

e) Do you think these charges are fair?

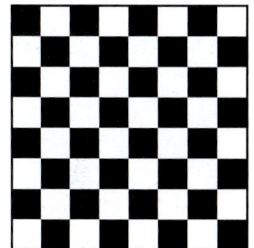

Investigation

8 **a)** When $n = 2$ find the value of: **i)** $2n$ **ii)** n^2

b) What do you notice about your two answers in part **a)**?

c) When $n = 3$ find the value of: **i)** $2n$ **ii)** n^2

d) Does your answer follow the same pattern as in part **b)**?

e) Investigate the values of $2n$ and n^2 for other values of n.

Substitution and powers

⊕ Substitute values into expressions involving indices

In the order of operations, **indices** come before multiplication, division, addition or subtraction.

For example $5 \times 3^2 + 12 = 5 \times 9 + 12$ ──── We calculate the value of 3^2 before we do anything else.

$$= 45 + 12$$
$$= 57$$

We **substitute** values into algebraic **expressions** involving indices by replacing the letters with numbers.

For example, if $x = 5$ we can find the value of $3x^2 + 10$ like this:

$$3x^2 + 10 \quad = \quad 3 \times 5^2 + 10$$ ──── Replace the x with 5, and then follow the order of operations.
$$= \quad 3 \times 25 + 10$$
$$= \quad 75 + 10$$
$$= \quad 85$$

Example   Find the value of the following expressions when $r = 3$:

a) $4r^2 - 5$ b) $\dfrac{r^3}{9} + 1$

Remember $4r^2$ means $4 \times r^2$.

a) $4r^2 - 5 \quad = \quad 4 \times 3^2 - 5$ b) $\dfrac{r^3}{9} + 1 \quad = \quad \dfrac{3^3}{9} + 1$
$\qquad\qquad = \quad 4 \times 9 - 5$ $\qquad\qquad\qquad\qquad = \quad \dfrac{27}{9} + 1$
$\qquad\qquad = \quad 36 - 5$ $\qquad\qquad\qquad\qquad = \quad 3 + 1$
$\qquad\qquad = \quad 31$ $\qquad\qquad\qquad\qquad = \quad 4$

Substitute $r = 3$ into the expression.

Follow the order of operations: indices, then division, then addition.

Exercise 8.5

1 When $x = 4$, find the value of:
   a) x^2 b) $2x^2$ c) $x^2 + 2$ d) $\dfrac{x^2}{2}$

2 Find the value of each of the following expressions when $x = 5$.
   a) x^4 b) $3x^4$ c) $x^4 - 5$ You can use a calculator to work out 5^4.
   d) $x^4 + 12$ e) $\dfrac{x^4}{5}$

3 Calculate the value of $r^3 - 6$ when:
   a) $r = 3$ b) $r = 7$ c) $r = 2$ d) $r = 10$

4 Work out the value of each of the following expressions when $q = 6$.

a) q^5 **b)** $6q^4$ **c)** $q^4 + 6$ **d)** $7q^4 - 6$

5 What is the value of each of the following expressions when $m = 11$?

a) m^2 **b)** m^3 **c)** $m^2 + m^3$ **d)** $5m^2 - m^3$

6 Find the value of each of the following expressions when $x = 7$:

a) $3x^2$ **b)** $\dfrac{x^2}{7}$ **c)** $2x^3 - 24$ **d)** $150 - x^4$ **e)** $13 + 4x^5$

7 **a)** A factory manufactures square picture frames.
They use a square piece of wood like this:
Write down an algebraic expression for
the area of wood used.

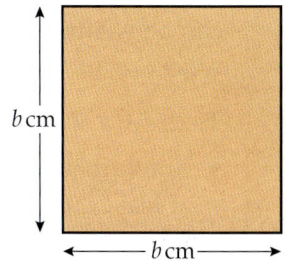

b cm

b cm

b) To make the frame they cut a square of
wood out of the middle, like this:
Write an expression for the area of
wood in the frame.

What is the area of
the piece cut out?

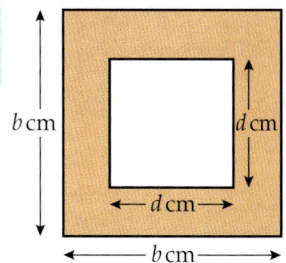

b cm

d cm

d cm

b cm

c) For one set of frames they use a 12 cm square.
Find the area of wood in the picture frame when the square cut out has sides:

i) 3 cm **ii)** 10 cm **iii)** 9 cm.

8 A cardboard box has the following dimensions:

a) Write down and simplify an algebraic
expression for the volume of the box.

Remember $3p$
means $3 \times p$.

b) Find the volume of the box when:

i) $p = 1$ cm **ii)** $p = 5$ cm **iii)** $p = 2$ cm.

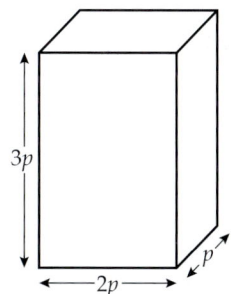

$3p$

p

$2p$

Investigation

9 To raise a negative number to a power using a calculator you need to put brackets
round the number.

For example, to calculate $(^-3)^2$ press: (— 3) x^y 2 =

a) Find the value of n^2 when:

i) $n = {}^-1$ **ii)** $n = {}^-2$ **iii)** $n = {}^-3$ Remember the brackets!

iv) $n = {}^-4$ **v)** $n = {}^-5$

b) Are your answers to part **a)** positive or negative?

c) Find the value of n^3 when:

i) $n = {}^-1$ **ii)** $n = {}^-2$ **iii)** $n = {}^-3$

iv) $n = {}^-4$ **v)** $n = {}^-5$

d) Are your answers to part **c)** positive or negative?

e) Investigate for other powers of n. Describe any patterns you notice.

Drawing graphs

Key words
graph
axes
quadrant
equation

⊕ Draw graphs by plotting points in all four quadrants

⊕ Decide whether a point lies on a graph

We draw a **graph** on a pair of **axes** :

All **equations** of straight-line graphs can be written in the form $y = mx + c$, where m and c are numbers.

Each of the four sections are called **quadrants**.

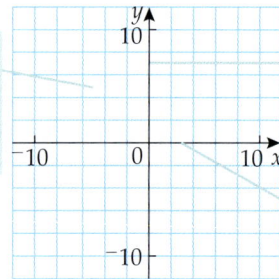

This is the y-axis.

This is the x-axis.

To draw a straight-line graph we:

• draw up a table of values and calculate at least three points

• plot these points

• join them with a straight line.

We can find out whether a point lies on the line by substituting the x-coordinate into the equation for the line and finding the corresponding y-coordinate.

Example 1 a) Complete the table of values for the graph $y = 2x + 1$.

b) Plot the points from the table and draw the graph of $y = 2x + 1$.

x	⁻4	0	4
y			

a)

x	⁻4	0	4
y	⁻7	1	9

b)

$y = 2x + 1$

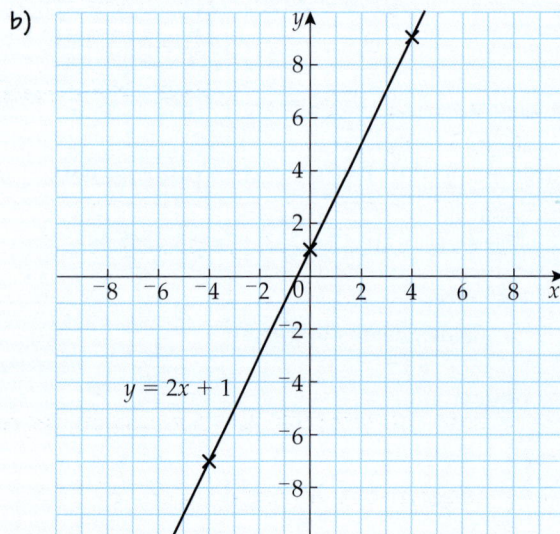

To find the values of y we substitute the value of x into the equation:
$y = 2x + 1$
So when $x = {}^-4$:
$$y = 2 \times {}^-4 + 1$$
$$= {}^-8 + 1$$
$$= {}^-7$$

To draw the graph, first draw a pair of axes.

Plot the points from the table and join them with a straight line.

Extend the line to the edges of the grid.

Example 2   Without drawing the graph, decide whether the following points lie on the graph of $y = 2x - 20$:

a) $(10, 0)$ b) $(1, {}^-22)$

a) When $x = 10$

    $y = 2x - 20 = 2 \times 10 - 20 = 20 - 20 = 0$

    Yes the point $(10, 0)$ lies on the graph.

b) When $x = 1$

    $y = 2x - 20 = 2 \times 1 - 20 = {}^-18$

    No the point $(1, {}^-22)$ does not lie on the graph.

> Substitute the *x*-coordinate into the equation of the graph to calculate the corresponding *y*-coordinate.

> From the equation, when $x = 10, y = 0$, so the point $(10, 0)$ lies on the graph.

> When $x = 1, y = {}^-18$ so the point $(1, {}^-22)$ cannot lie on the graph.

Exercise 8.6

1 Copy and complete the table of values for each of the following graphs. Plot all the graphs on the same pair of axes.

> Label both axes from $^-10$ to 10.

a) $y = 5x + 1$

x	$^-1$	0	1
y			

b) $y = -3x$

x	$^-2$	1	3
y			

c) $y = -2x - 1$

x	$^-5$	0	3
y			

2 a) Draw the graph of $y = 3x - 1$, on a pair of axes labelled from $^-10$ to 10.

> Draw up a table of values first.

    b) Use your graph to find the *y*-coordinate when the *x*-coordinate is:

        i) 1.5   **ii)** $^-0.5$ **iii)** 2.5

    c) Use your graph to find the *x*-coordinate when the *y*-coordinate is:

        i) 8   **ii)** $^-1$ **iii)** $^-4$

3 Draw all the following graphs on the same pair of axes.

> Label each graph clearly with its equation.

a) $y = x$ b) $y = -2x + 1$ c) $y = 5x - 4$

4 Which of the following points lie on the graph: $y = -5x - 7$?

> Do not draw the graph!

A $(3, 8)$ B $(^-2, 3)$ C $(0.5, {}^-9.5)$ D $(^-3, {}^-8)$

5 a) Copy and complete the following table for the graph of $y = -x$.

x	$^-8$	$^-5$	0	2	7
y					

    b) Without doing any calculations, write down the coordinates of five more points on the graph.

6 Brian uses a graph whose equation is $y = 2x + 30$ to convert from temperature in degrees Celsius to degrees Fahrenheit.

y = temperature in degrees Fahrenheit and x = temperature in degrees Celsius.

Do these points lie on Brian's graph?

a) $(2, 34)$ b) $(10, 40)$ c) $(0, 2)$

d) $(^-5, 25)$ e) $(^-10, 10)$ f) $(15, 0)$

8.7 The gradient

⊕ Investigate straight line graphs of the form $y = mx + c$

The **gradient** of a **graph** is a measure of how steep the graph is.

The equation of a straight line graph can be written in the form $y = mx + c$.
m is the gradient of the line and c is the **y-intercept**.

Look at the graphs of $y = 3x + 1$ and $y = 2x + 1$:

These graphs have positive gradient.
The graph of $y = 3x + 1$ has a steeper gradient than the graph of $y = 2x + 1$.

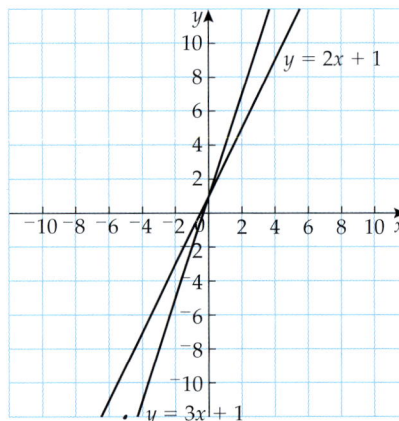

Look at the graphs of $y = -2x$ and $y = -3x - 2$:

These graphs have negative gradient.
The graph of $y = -3x - 2$ has a steeper gradient than the graph of $y = -2x$.

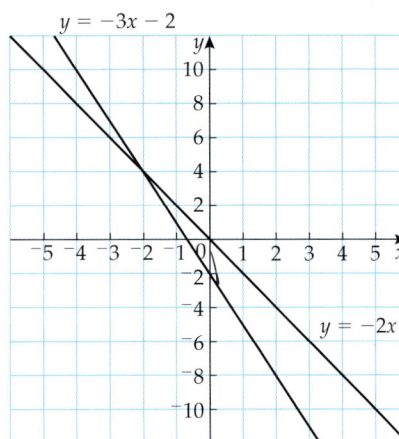

Two graphs are parallel when their equations have the same value of m (the same gradient).

Example   Draw the graph of $y = 4x - 2$.
   a) Where does the graph cross the y-axis?   b) What is the gradient?

x	-3	0	3
y	-14	-2	10

a) $(0, -2)$ b) 4

You can see this on the graph, and in the equation where $c = -2$.

In the equation of the graph, $m = 4$.

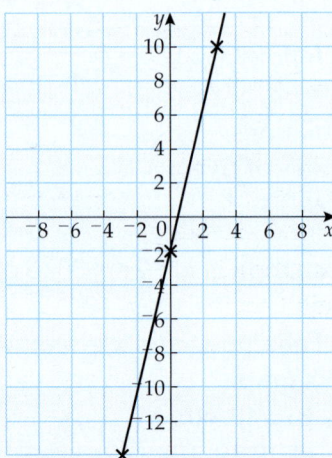

Exercise 8.7

1 Draw up a table of values for each of the following equations.

  a) Plot these graphs on the same pair of axes, labelled from $^-10$ to $^+10$ on both axes.

  i) $y = x$ **ii)** $y = 2x$ **iii)** $y = 4x$

  b) Describe what happens to the graphs as the number in front of the x increases.

2 a) Plot these graphs on the same pair of axes, labelled from $^-10$ to $^+10$ on both axes.

  i) $y = x + 2$ **ii)** $y = 2x + 2$ **iii)** $y = 4x + 2$

  Compare your graphs with those in **Q1**.

  b) How does the value for 'c' affect the graph?
  How does the value for 'm' affect the graph?

3 a) Plot these graphs on the same pair of axes, labelled from $^-10$ to $^+10$ on both axes.

  i) $y = -x$ **ii)** $y = -2x$ **iii)** $y = -4x$

  b) Describe what happens to the gradient of the graphs as
  the number in front of the x gets lower.

  > -4 is lower than -2

4 a) Find the y-intercept of each of
  these graphs.
  The graph drawn in blue has
  equation $y = -2x + 1$.

  b) Use this fact to write down the
  equations of the other graphs in
  the diagram.

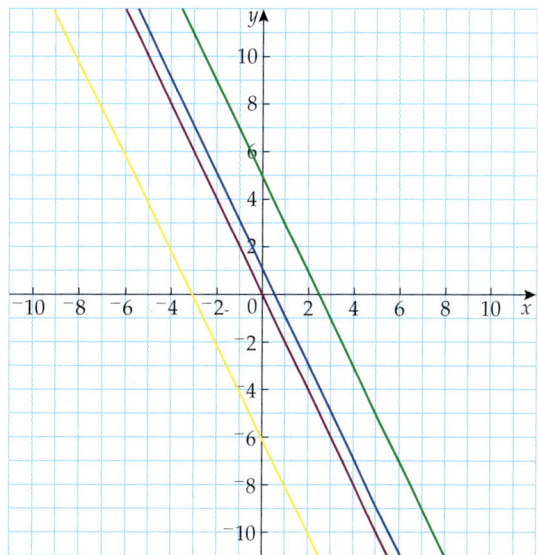

5 a) Copy and complete this table of
  values for the graph $y = 2x$.

  b) When the x-value increases by 1
  what happens to the y-value?

x	0	1	2	3	4
y					

  c) Repeat parts **a)** and **b)** for the following graphs:

  i) $y = 3x$ **ii)** $y = 2x + 1$ **iii)** $y = -2x$

  d) How is what happens to the y-values related to the equation of the graph?

6 a) Where does the black straight line
  graph cross the y-axis?

  b) The gradient of a horizontal line is
  zero. Use this fact and your answer
  to part **a)** to write down and simplify
  the equation of the black graph.

  c) Write down the equation of the
  red graph.

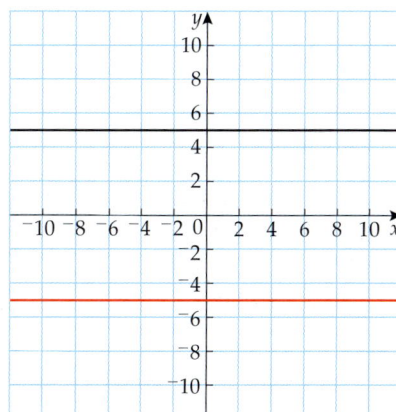

Plotting real-life graphs

⊕ Plot graphs from real-life data, that are not straight lines

So far we have drawn graphs involving straight lines.

In real life graphs are often **curved** or straight-line sections joined together.

Remember, when **plotting** graphs:

1. Always use a sharp pencil
2. Use a ruler for any straight lines
3. Always label the **axes**
4. Ensure the scales are kept regular

Example In a science experiment, frozen peas were added to a pan of boiling water. The temperature of the pan of peas and water was measured every 10 seconds. The results were:

Time (seconds)	0	10	20	30	40	50	60
Temperature of water (°C)	100	94	88	86	88	94	100

Plot a graph to show how the temperature changes in the pan over time.

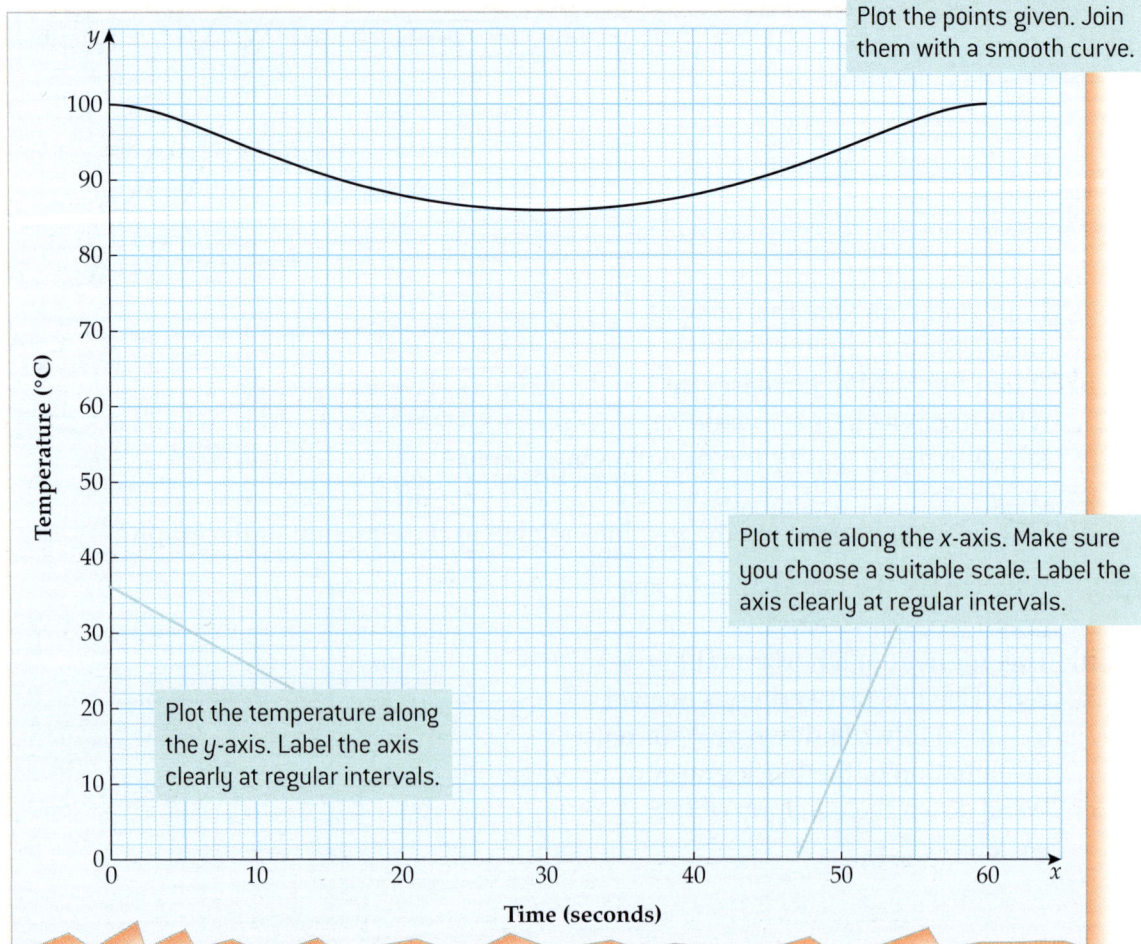

Plot the points given. Join them with a smooth curve.

Plot time along the x-axis. Make sure you choose a suitable scale. Label the axis clearly at regular intervals.

Plot the temperature along the y-axis. Label the axis clearly at regular intervals.

Exercise 8.8

You will need graph paper for this exercise.

1 A farmer breeds prize rams. He started with 6 prize rams in his flock of sheep.
Each year he keeps the best rams from all the lambs born in the flock.
The table shows the number of prize rams he keeps over 6 years:

> Year 0 means the 365 days from when he started the breeding program. Year 1 started one year later.

Year	0	1	2	3	4	5	6
Number of prize rams	6	8	11	14	19	24	29

Follow the steps below to plot a graph to show the number of prize rams over this period.
a) Draw an x-axis from 0 to 6, allowing 2 cm to represent 1 year. Label the axis 'Year'.
b) Draw a y-axis from 0 to 30, allowing 2 cm to represent 5 prize rams. Label the axis 'Number of prize rams'.
c) Plot the points given in the table.

> The first point to plot is (0, 6).

d) Join the points with straight lines.

2 When you wash up, the water level in the washing up bowl varies.
A scientist records the following data while doing the washing up one evening:

> Some water is lost when you take a clean plate out of the bowl. When you put a large pan in the bowl, the water level rises.

Time (mins)	0	2	4	6	8	10	12	14	16	18	20
Water level (cm)	0	70	90	75	100	60	70	80	40	10	0

Plot a graph to show the water level in the bowl over time, following the steps below:
a) Draw an x-axis from 0 to 20, allowing 2 cm to represent 4 minutes. Label the axis 'Time (minutes)'.
b) Draw a y-axis from 0 to 120, allowing 2 cm to represent 10 and label it 'Water level (cm)'.
c) Plot the points given in the table.
d) Join each pair of consecutive points with a straight line.

3 In the womb a baby grows at an incredible rate.
Look at the table below:

Age of baby (in weeks)	0	6	10	14	18	22	26	30	34	40
Length of baby (cm)	0	0.4	2.5	9	13.5	18.5	25	28	32	36

Plot a graph to show the length of a baby during its time in the womb by following the steps below:
a) Draw an x-axis from 0 to 40, allowing 2 cm to represent 5 weeks. Label the axis 'Age (weeks)'.
b) Draw a y-axis from 0 to 36, allowing 2 cm to represent 10 cm. Label the axis 'Length of baby (cm)'.
c) Plot the points given in the table.
d) Join the points with a smooth curve.

4 The table shows the total annual rainfall (in cm) over the last 10 years for Bilanbong.

Year	0	2	4	6	8	10
Total rainfall (cm)	95	84	75	70	64	60

Choose suitable scales for the axes, plot the data given and join the points with straight lines.

Interpreting real-life graphs

⊕ Interpret graphs from real-life

We can show a relationship between two **variables** by **plotting** a graph.

Graphs are not only used in mathematics.
You will often see graphs in Science, Geography and History.

Graphs do not have to be just straight lines.
They can be curves or a series of different straight lines.

For example, this graph shows the temperature of a
cup of tea that has been left to cool.

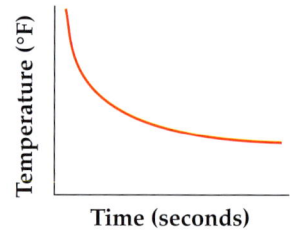

Example   The graph shows the population of fruit bats in Borongboro over a five-year period:

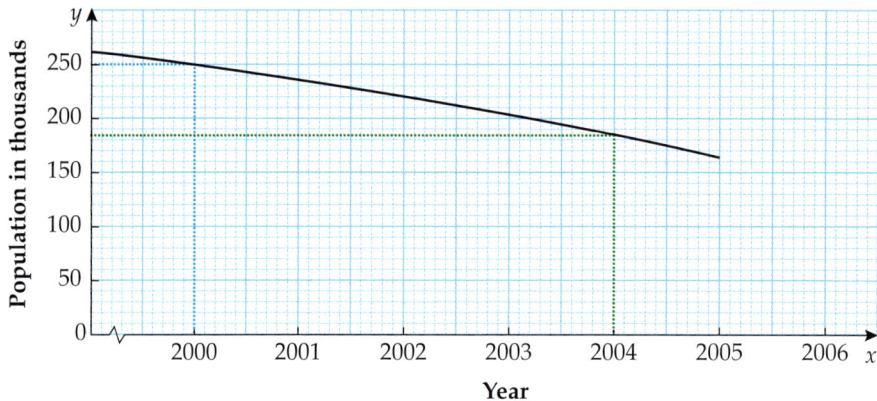

a)   What was the population of fruit bats in 2000?

b)   What was the population of fruit bats in 2004?

c)   Describe in words what is happening to the population.

d)   How does the shape of the graph show this?

e)   What do you think the population will be in 2006?
     Give your reasons.

a)   The population of fruit bats in 2000 was 250 000

b)   The population of fruit bats in 2004 was 184 000

c)   The population of fruit bats is decreasing.

d)   The graph is sloping downwards:

     it has negative gradient.

e)   139 000. If the graph is extended to 2006, we can estimate

     what the population will be by reading off the new graph.

See the blue dotted line.
Note: the population of bats is
given in thousands.

See the green dotted line.

As the value of x (the number of
years) increases, the value of y
(the population) decreases.

Exercise 8.9

1 The graph shows the number of rabbits in a field over a period of 30 months:

a) What happens to the number of rabbits in the field as time passes?

> What does the shape of the graph show?

b) How many rabbits are there in the field after 10 months?

c) How many rabbits are there in the field after 30 months?

d) How many rabbits do you think there will be in the field after 60 months?
Give your reasons.

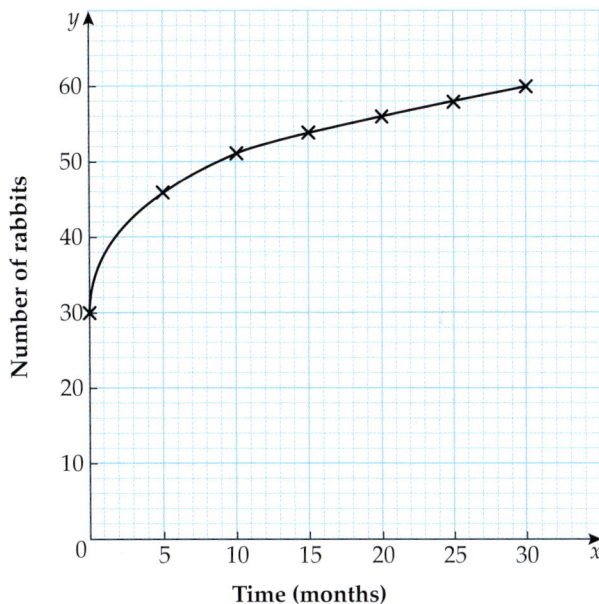

2 The following shows a graph of the amount of water in a bath over a period of 30 minutes.

a) How much water is in the bath after 4 minutes?

b) How much water is in the bath after 8 minutes?

c) What is do you think is happening between 0 and 8 minutes?

d) What do you think is happening between 8 and 24 minutes?

> Explain what you think is happening to the bath in real life.

e) How much water is in the bath after 24 minutes?

f) How much water is in the bath after 30 minutes?

g) What do you think is happening between 24 and 30 minutes?

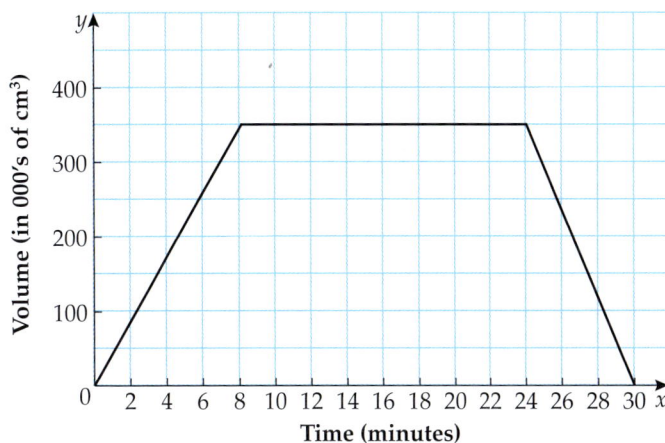

3 Match the following sketch graphs with their titles:

a) Graph to show the amount of ice cream in a cone over a period of time

b) Graph to show the numbers of cars on the road since 1900

c) Graph to show the number of pages in this textbook over the next 10 years

d) Graph to show the volume of petrol in a car on a journey, where it stops to fill the tank once

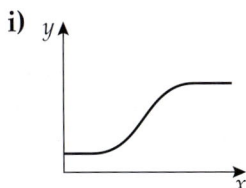

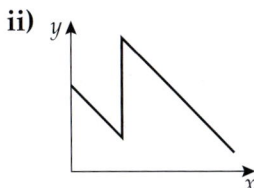

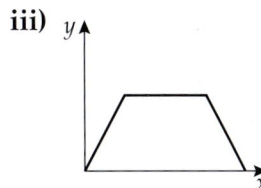

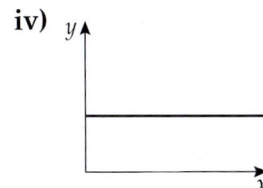

Probability

⊕ Know that if the probability of an event is p, then the probability of it not happening is $1 - p$

A probability is a measure of the chance of an **event** happening.

It should only be written as a fraction, decimal or percentage.

Theoretical probability of an **outcome** $= \dfrac{\text{number of ways the outcome can happen}}{\text{the total number of outcomes}}$

If the probability of an event is p, then the probability of it not happening is $1 - p$.

If the probability of an outcome happening $= \frac{3}{11}$, the probability of the outcome **not** happening is $1 - \frac{3}{11} = \frac{11}{11} - \frac{3}{11} = \frac{8}{11}$.

Example 1 Ten digit cards numbered from 0 to 9 are shuffled. The top card is turned over. What is the probability that this card is

    a) odd   **b)** not odd   **c)** less than 4   **d)** not less than 4?

a) $\frac{5}{10} = \frac{1}{2}$ **b)** $1 - \frac{1}{2} = \frac{1}{2}$

c) $\frac{4}{10} = \frac{2}{5}$ or 0.4 **d)** $1 - 0.4 = 0.6$

Example 2 Ben buys a lollipop from a machine. The probability of the lollipop being his favourite flavour is 20%. What is the probability that it will not be his favourite flavour?

$100\% - 20\% = 80\%$

Exercise 9.1

1 A dart is thrown at random at the board. It always hits the board. What is the probability that the dart lands on

    a) a 6?   **b)** not a 6?

    c) an even number?   **d)** not an even number?

    e) a number greater than 6?   **f)** a number not greater than 6?

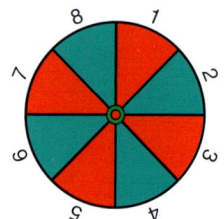

2 Copy and complete the table to show the probabilities of each outcome when this spinner is spun.

Outcome	Probability of outcome happening	Probability of outcome not happening
1		
5		
Odd		
Less than 6		
4		

3 In a biscuit tin there are nine chocolate, six jam and five plain biscuits. A biscuit is chosen at random. What is the probability that the biscuit is
a) jam?
b) not jam?
c) chocolate or jam?
d) not chocolate or jam?
Write your answers as both decimals and percentages.

4 A bag contains 28 dominoes, seven of which are 'doubles'. A domino is removed at random. What is the probability that the domino is not a 'double'?

5 The probability that Kim will win a swimming race is 55%. What is the probability that she will not win?

6 This two-way table shows the writing hand of a class of students.

	Boys	Girls
Left-handed	2	1
Right-handed	10	12

A student is chosen at random. What is the probability that the student is
a) a right-handed girl?
b) not a right-handed girl?
c) a boy?
d) right-handed?

How many students are in the class?

7 A shop sells scratch cards. Each card is divided into squares. Some of the squares have spots hidden on them. Just one square is scratched and a prize is won if a spot appears. Which cards have
a) the greatest chance of winning a prize?
b) the least chance?

i)

ii)

Calculate the probabilities for each card as percentages or decimals.

iii)

iv)

Possible outcomes 1

◈ Find and record all possible outcomes in a systematic way, using diagrams and tables

A table can often be drawn to find all possible outcomes of two events.

If a table cannot be used, then a **systematic** or ordered method should be used so no outcomes are overlooked.

Example

A café gives a choice of potato and vegetables with its meals.

Show all possible outcomes by
a) drawing a table
b) using another systematic method.

Menu

Potato	Vegetable
Chips	Peas
Mashed	Carrots
Boiled	

a)

	Peas	Carrots
Chips	Chips & Peas	Chips & Carrots
Mashed	Mashed & Peas	Mashed & Carrots
Boiled	Boiled & Peas	Boiled & Carrots

b) Chips & Peas   Mashed & Peas   Boiled & Peas

Chips & Carrots   Mashed & Carrots   Boiled & Carrots

Exercise 9.2

1 Sharon has digit cards 1, 2, 3. Mike has digit cards 0, 2, 4.
Complete the table showing all possible outcomes when Sharon and Mike each choose a card at random from their pile and
a) add the two numbers together

+	0	2	4
1			
2			
3			

b) multiply the two numbers together.

×	0	2	4
1			
2			
3			

c) For each table what is the probability that the answer will be
   i) even?   ii) not even?   iii) greater than 0?

2 A menu offers different choices of meals.

Starter	Main course	Dessert
Soup	Pasta	Ice cream
Melon	Pie	Cake
	Salad	

    a) Juan chooses a main course and dessert. What are the possible combinations he could have?

    b) Liam chooses a starter, main course and dessert. What possible combinations could he have?

3 **a)** Complete the sample space diagram to show all of the outcomes when these two dice are thrown and their values added together.

+	⁻3	⁻2	⁻1	1	2	3
⁻2						
⁻2						
⁻1						
1						
3						
3						

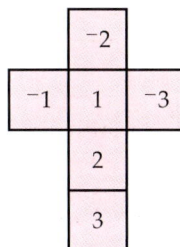

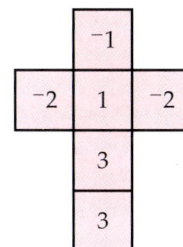

(First die net: ⁻2 on top, ⁻1, 1, ⁻3 across, 2, 3 below)
(Second die net: ⁻1 on top, ⁻2, 1, ⁻2 across, 3, 3 below)

    b) Which total is most likely?
    c) Which total is least likely?

4 Leanne is making 2-digit numbers from these digit cards.

> 75 is a 2-digit number that she could make.

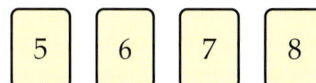

| 5 | 6 | 7 | 8 |

    a) What numbers can she make?

    b) What is the probability that the 2-digit number will be
      i) even?   **ii)** not even?   **iii)** divisible by 5?   **iv)** greater than 70?

    c) What 3-digit numbers can she make?

5 Throw four *heads* and win a prize!

    a) Complete the table to find all possible combinations of *heads* and *tails* when four coins are thrown.

Total number of *heads*	0	1	2	3	4
Outcome	tttt	httt thtt …			

> If 16 people played this game, how many would win?

    b) What is the probability of throwing four *heads*?

    c) If 80 people play this game, how many would you expect to win?

Investigation

6 In the game 'scissors, paper, stone' scissors beats paper, paper beats stone and stone beats scissors.

Copy and complete the table to show the winner each time or write 'draw' if they are the same.

	Scissors	Paper	Stone
Scissors	Draw	Scissors	
Paper			
Stone			

Use your table to explain why this is a fair game.

Estimating probabilities

◈ Estimate probabilities from experimental data

Key words
estimate
theoretical probability
experimental probability

The data from an experiment can be used to find an **estimate** of the **theoretical probability** . For some investigations this may be the only type of probability that can be calculated for an experiment.

The **experimental probability** (or estimated probability) is calculated in the same way as the theoretical probability.

$$\text{experimental probability} = \frac{\text{number of times an outcome happens}}{\text{number of times the experiment was carried out}}$$

Example   Simi is performing an experiment to explore the hypothesis 'toast always lands butter side down'. She uses a piece of card with 'butter' written on one side for her experiment.

a)   Estimate the probabilities of the two outcomes from her data.

Direction of toast	Butter facing up	Butter facing down
Frequency	53	47

b)   Simi carries out the experiment another 30 times. Use your answer from part a) to estimate how many times it will land 'butter facing down'.

a)

Direction of toast	Butter facing up	Butter facing down
Frequency	53	47
Estimated probability	$\frac{53}{100} = 0.53$	$\frac{47}{100} = 0.47$

b) $30 \times 0.47 = 14.1$. The toast will land on the butter side about 14 times.

Exercise 9.3

1   Some pupils throw three coins, recording the number of *heads* showing each time.

Pupil	Number of throws	0 *heads*	1 *head*	2 *heads*	3 *heads*
A	30	4	13	10	3
B	120	13	48	44	15
C	50	5	19	20	6

a)   Which pupil's results should be the most accurate and why?
b)   Use all of the above results to find the total frequency of the four outcomes for the experiment being carried out 200 times. Record these in the table below.

Number of *heads*	0	1	2	3
Total frequency				
Experimental probability				

c) Find the estimated probabilities for each of the number of *heads* being thrown.

d) Find the sum of the experimental probabilities.

> What is the total when you add all your experimental probabilities?

2 Requires three dice.

a) Throw the three dice. The numbers showing will be one of the outcomes below.

Outcome	3 numbers the same	2 numbers the same	3 consecutive numbers	Other outcome
Tally				
Frequency				
Experimental probability				

b) Use the table to record the outcomes of 40 throws.

c) Calculate the estimated probabilities from your table for each outcome.

d) Find the sum of the experimental probabilities.

3 Meg counts the number of drawing pins in 46 boxes. 27 boxes have less than 50 drawing pins in. What is the probability that the next box Meg counts will have

a) less than 50 drawing pins in it?

b) 50 or more drawing pins?

> Use the information given to estimate the probability.

4 Terry records the colour of a traffic light he passes on his way to school for 80 journeys.

Colour of light	Red	Amber	Green
Frequency	28	12	40
Estimated probability			

a) Copy and complete the table showing the estimated probabilities.

b) In 12 journeys approximately how many times should the light be showing red?

Investigation

5 Requires digit cards

a) Use cards 0 and 1. Shuffle the cards and deal face up. Are they in numerical order? Record the result in a copy of the table below.

	In order	Not in order
Tally		
Frequency		
Experimental probability		

Repeat the experiment 40 times. Use your data to calculate the probability of the two cards being dealt in order by copying and completing the table.

b) Repeat the above experiment using digit cards 0, 1 and 2. Each time calculate the experimental probability of the cards being dealt in order.

> The data collection sheet will be the same for each of these experiments.

c) Repeat using digit cards 0, 1, 2 and 3?

Comparing probabilities

- Compare experimental and theoretical probabilities in a range of contexts
- Understand the difference between mathematical explanation and experimental evidence

Key words
random
event
experimental
probability
theoretical
probability

When a dice is thrown it is a **random event**, so we do not know beforehand what number the dice will show. We can throw the dice a number of times and use the results to calculate the **experimental probability** of throwing a 6. We can also work out the **theoretical probability** of throwing a 6. We do not expect these two values to always be equal but it can be interesting to compare them.

Example A coin is thrown different numbers of times and the number of *tails* counted. This is used to calculate the probability of throwing one *tail*.

Number of throws	20	40	60	80	100	120	140	160	180	200
Estimated probability	0.45	0.4	0.483	0.525	0.52	0.492	0.507	0.4875	0.494	0.505

a) What is happening to the estimated probability as the number of throws increases?

b) The experimental probability after 1000 throws is equal to 0.487. Explain why this does not mean that the coin is biased.

> Biased means unfair.

a) The theoretical probability is 0.5. As the number of throws increases, the experimental probability becomes closer to this value.

b) We do not expect the experimental probability to have exactly the same value as the theoretical probability. As 0.487 is close to 0.5, the coin is probably not biased.

Exercise 9.4

1 Two tetrahedral dice, numbered 1 to 4, are thrown. The numbers on the three uppermost faces are added up. This is done again and the two totals are summed together and recorded.

a) What are the four possible totals for throwing one dice and adding the uppermost faces?

> What are the possible faces that the dice could land on?
>
> If the dice shows 1, 2 and 3 the sum equals 6.

b) Sam carries out this experiment, recording his results in a frequency table. Calculate the experimental probabilities for his table.

Total	12	13	14	15	16	17	18
Frequency	4	12	17	19	14	9	5
Experimental probability							

c) Complete this sample space diagram for this experiment.

+	6	7	8	9
6				
7				
8				
9				

A **sample space diagram** records all the possible outcomes of an experiment.

d) Copy and complete this frequency table for the table in part **c)**.

Total	12	13	14	15	16	17	18
Frequency							
Theoretical probability							

How many times does each score appear in the sample space diagram?

e) Use the table to compare the experimental and theoretical probabilities.

f) How could the experimental probabilities be made more accurate?

What is the total number of scores shown in the sample space diagram?

2 a) Conduct an experiment using a dice to calculate the experimental probability of throwing the number 5. Record your results in a table.

	Throwing a 5	Not throwing a 5
Tally		
Frequency		
Experimental probability		

Throw the dice at least 20 times.

b) Calculate the experimental probability of throwing a 5 on a dice.

c) What is the theoretical probability of throwing a 5 on one dice?

d) Compare the two probabilities. Were they close?

Convert both probabilities to decimals to compare them.

Investigation

3 This question requires ten counters, some blue and some white, and a table like the one shown below. Work with a partner.

a) Put your counters in a bag. Do not let your partner know how many of each colour there are. Ask your partner to choose a counter from the bag, record its colour then replace it. Repeat this ten times.

b) Ask your partner to guess how many counters of each colour are in the bag. Record this in the table.

	Blue	White
Frequency after 10 trials		
Estimated number of each colour		
Frequency after 20 trials		
Estimated number of each colour		

c) Repeat the experiment another ten times.

d) Ask your partner to make a new guess of the number of each colour in the bag.

e) Repeat the experiment for 20 trials, then 30 trials, up to 100 trials in groups of ten. Each time ask your partner to estimate the number of each coloured counter.

f) At the end of the experiment empty the bag. Did your partner get better at estimating the number of each counter, as the number of trials increased?

Combining transformations

Key words
reflection
rotation
translation
object
image
equivalent point

⊕ Transform 2-D shapes using combinations of reflections, rotations and translations on paper and using ICT

Reflection , **rotation** and **translation** are types of transformation.

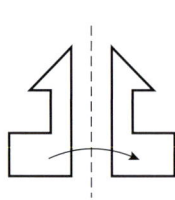

Reflection

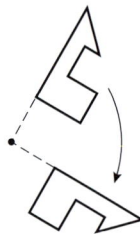

Rotation

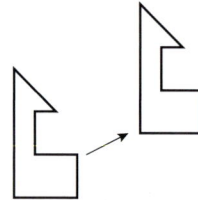

Translation

A transformation moves a shape to a new position, from the **object** to the **image** .
Each point on the object has an **equivalent point** on the image.
We can also transform shapes by combining transformations.
The shape and size of the object will stay the same no matter how many times we reflect, rotate or translate it.

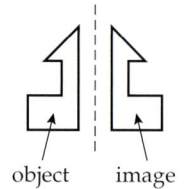

object   image

Example   Translate the object A 1 right and 3 up and call the image B.
Rotate B clockwise 90° around the point O.
Call the image C.

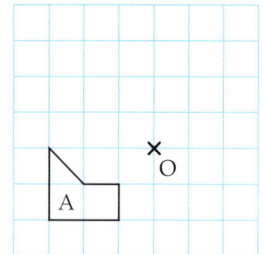

Label the vertices.

Translate one vertex 1 right and 3 up and mark P'. Repeat for the

other vertices and join up the points. Label the image B.

Trace B onto some tracing paper. Put a pencil point on the cross

and rotate the shape B by 90° around O. Label the image C.

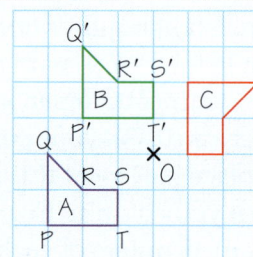

Exercise 10.1

❶ Copy the diagram. Reflect the object P in the mirror line M_1.
Call the image Q. Reflect Q in the mirror line M_2. Call the image R.
Reflect R in the mirror line M_3.
Call the image S.

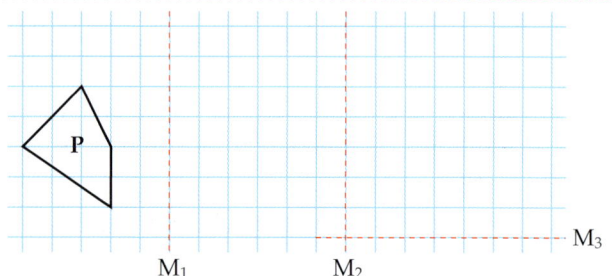

2 Copy this diagram.
Translate the triangle using the three different translations shown below:
a) 3 right, 1 up followed by 1 left, 2 up
b) 4 left, 3 down followed by 1 right, 2 up
c) 2 right, 1 up followed by 5 left, 2 up

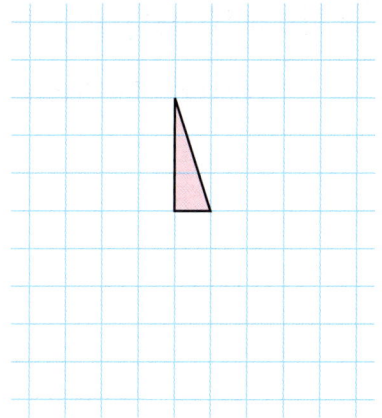

3 Copy this diagram:
Draw the image of A after a rotation of 90° clockwise about (0, 0). Label the image B.
Draw the image of A after a rotation of 90° anticlockwise about (0, 0). Label the image C.
What single transformation maps B on to C?

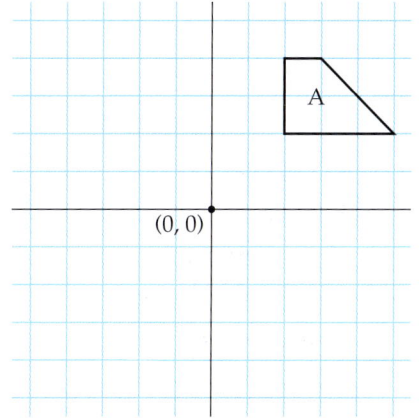

4 Look at this diagram:
What single transformation will map:
i) A onto B
ii) A onto C
iii) C onto D?

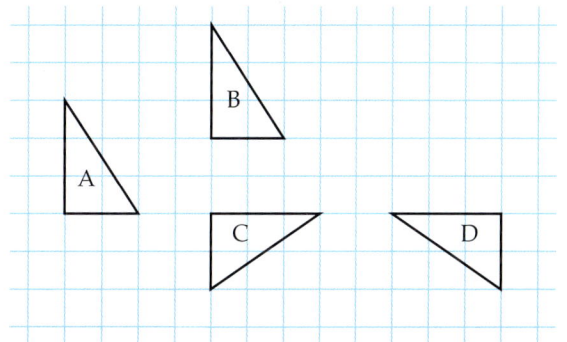

Investigation

5 Look at this diagram:

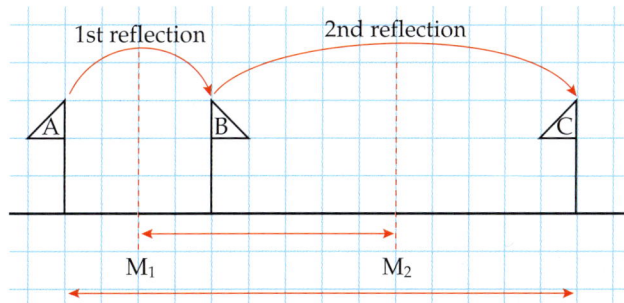

a) Measure the distance between the object A and the image C.
b) Measure the distance between the two mirror lines, M_1 and M_2. What do you notice?
c) What can you say about the distance between the two mirror lines compared to the distance between the same points on the object and its image?

⊕ Identify all the symmetries of 2-D shapes

Key words
line of symmetry
symmetrical
reflection symmetry
order of rotation
  symmetry

A **line of symmetry** exists where one half of a shape reflects on to the other.

Shapes which are **symmetrical** about a line have **reflection symmetry** .

The **order of rotation symmetry** is the number of ways a shape can fit onto itself in a complete 360° turn about its centre.

A rectangle has two lines of symmetry and rotation symmetry order 2

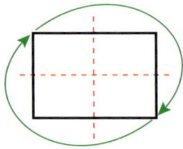

A square has four lines of symmetry and rotation symmetry order 4

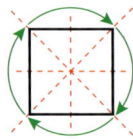

A kite has one line of symmetry and rotation symmetry order 1

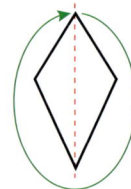

Example   Describe all the symmetries of these shapes:
   a) Isosceles triangle
   b) Parallelogram
   c) Rhombus.

a) **Isosceles triangle**

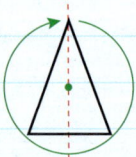

1 line of symmetry, which is the perpendicular bisector of the base.

Rotation symmetry of order 1.

b) **Parallelogram**

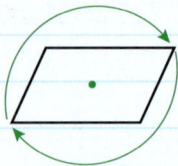

No lines of symmetry.

Rotation symmetry of order 2.

The centre of rotation is the intersection of the diagonals.

c) **Rhombus**

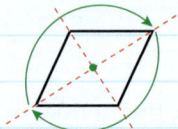

The diagonals are the lines of symmetry.

Rotation symmetry of order 2.

The centre of rotation is the intersection of the diagonals.

Exercise 10.2

1 Describe all the symmetries of these shapes:

a)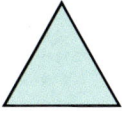

Equilateral triangle

b)

Isosceles trapezium

c)

Arrowhead or Delta

2 Identify which quadrilateral each pair of diagonals belongs to and give reasons for your answers. In which quadrilaterals are the pair of diagonals also lines of symmetry?

a) 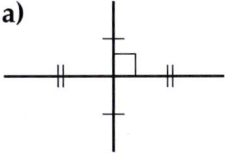   b) 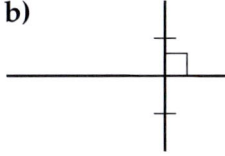   c) 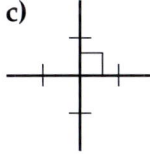   d)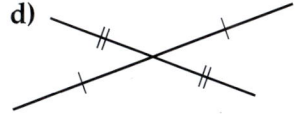

3 On square dotted paper draw the right-angled triangle shown in this diagram.

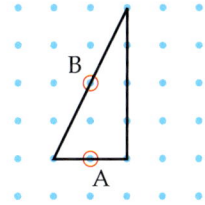

a) Rotate the triangle through 180° about the point A.
b) Name the shape that is formed.
c) Draw any lines of symmetry of the shape.
d) Write the order of rotation symmetry.

4 Draw another copy of the triangle from **Q3**.

a) Rotate the triangle about the point B.
b) Name the shape that is formed.
c) Draw any lines of symmetry of the shape.
d) Write the order of rotation symmetry.

5 Draw the triangle in the diagram on 1 cm square paper.

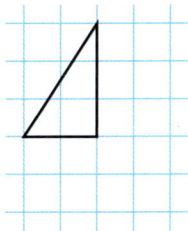

Here is an example of a tessellation using another triangle. A tessellation is a tiling pattern with no gaps.

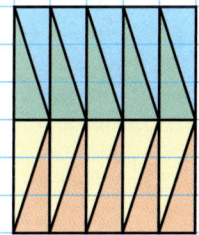

Cut out the triangle and on another sheet of squared paper draw a tessellating pattern by drawing around your shape after reflecting, rotating and translating it.

Investigation

6 Using ICT or square dotted paper, design a tessellation using a quadrilateral of your choice. You can either repeatedly reflect or rotate it, or use a combination of reflections, rotations and translations.

- Know and understand the meaning of congruence
- Know that if 2-D shapes are congruent then corresponding sides and angles are equal
- Be able to recognise congruent shapes

Congruent shapes are exactly the same shape and the same size.
All corresponding lengths are equal.
All corresponding angles are equal.
If you cut out congruent shapes they will fit exactly over each other. Sometimes the shapes need to be turned over to check for congruence.
In this diagram, triangle A is congruent to triangle B and quadrilateral C is congruent to quadrilateral D.

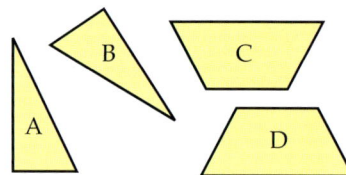

Example 1   Write down the letters of the congruent shapes in this diagram:

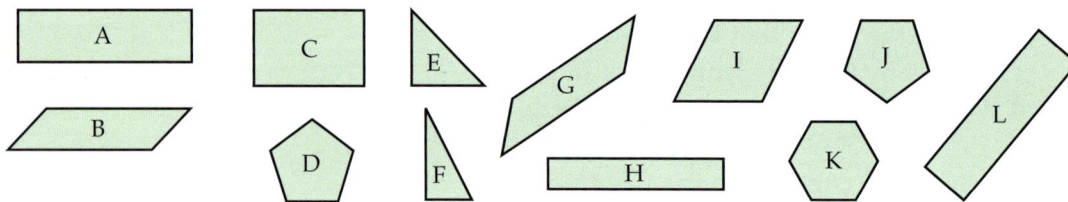

A and L are congruent. B and G are congruent.

D and J are congruent.

Example 2   a)   Write down the letters of the shapes that are congruent to A.
b)   What type of transformation maps A onto each congruent shape?

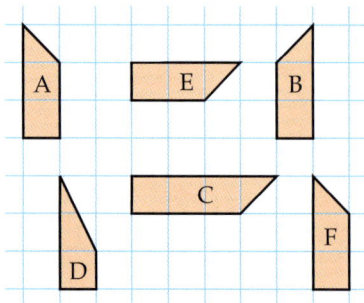

a)   B, E and F
b)   B – reflection, E – rotation, F – translation

Exercise 10.3

1 Write down the letters of the congruent group of shapes in this diagram:

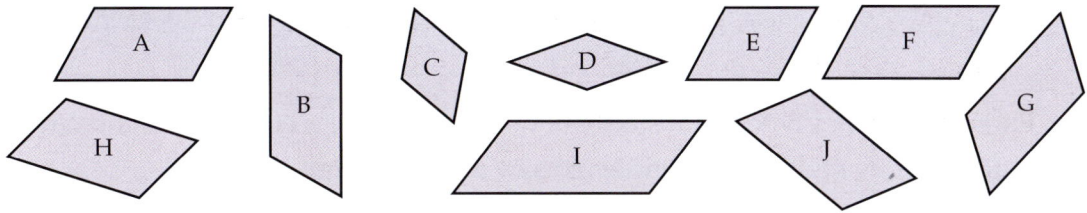

A B C D E F G H I J

2 Write down the letters of three congruent pairs of shapes in this diagram.

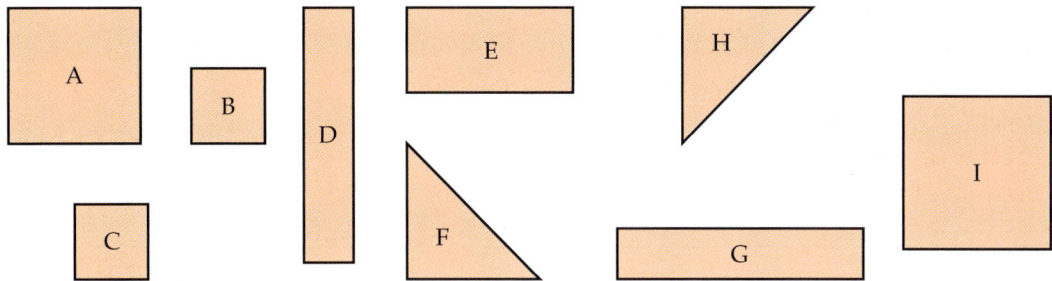

A B C D E F G H I

3 Make a quadrilateral of your choice, using a 5 by 5 pinboard.
Find all the congruent quadrilaterals you can make on the pinboard by reflecting, rotating or translating the original shape. Record the position of each congruent quadrilateral that you find, and write down which transformation you used.

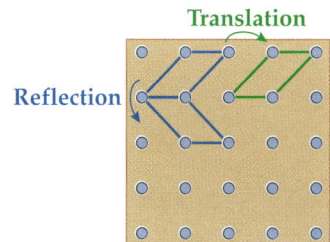

Translation

Reflection

4 **a)** Write down the letters of the shapes that are congruent to A.

b) Describe the transformation that maps A on to each congruent shape.

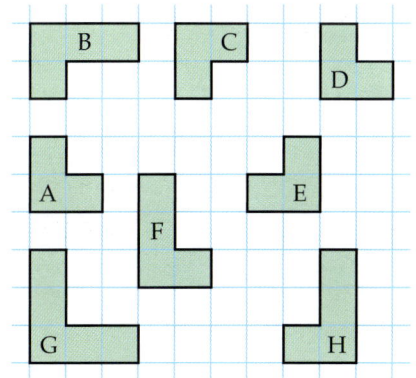

B C D A F E G H

Investigation

5 How many different ways can you divide a 4 by 4 pinboard into two congruent halves (see the diagram)?
How many ways can you divide it into four congruent quarters?
Investigate how many ways you can divide up pinboards of other sizes. For example, try a 5 by 5 pinboard. What sort of shapes are the congruent halves or quarters?

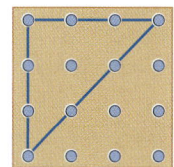

Enlargement

◈ Enlarge shapes given a centre of enlargement

Enlargement is a type of transformation. When a shape is enlarged, all the sides are made bigger by multiplying their lengths by a **scale factor**.

Every enlargement has a **centre of enlargement**.

Lines joining equivalent points on the object and image meet at the centre of enlargement.

Here the triangle ABC has been enlarged by a scale factor of 3.

The enlargement is labelled A′B′C′

The image is three times the distance from the centre O as the object.

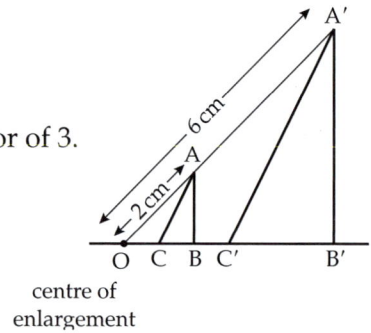

centre of enlargement

Example Enlarge the kite ABCD by a scale factor of 2, using the point S as the centre of enlargement.

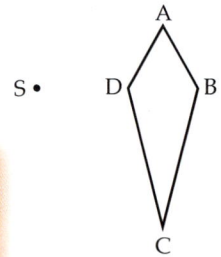

Draw the kite ABCD. Draw lines connecting the point S to the vertices A, B, C and D and extend them. Measure the lengths SA, SB, SC and SD. Multiply each measurement by two and then measure the new distances **from the point S**. Mark the points A′B′C′D′ and join them.

Exercise 10.4

1 Trace each shape and enlarge it, from centre O, by the given scale factor.

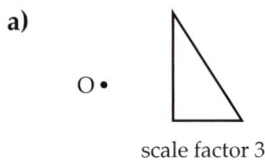

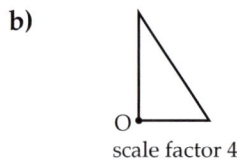

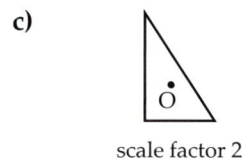

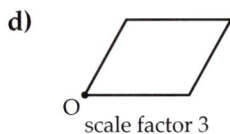

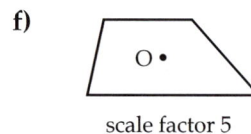

a)

O•

scale factor 3

b)

O•

scale factor 4

c)

O•

scale factor 2

d)

O•

scale factor 3

e)

O

scale factor 2

f)

O•

scale factor 5

② Look at shape A.
Which of the other shapes
are enlargements of A?

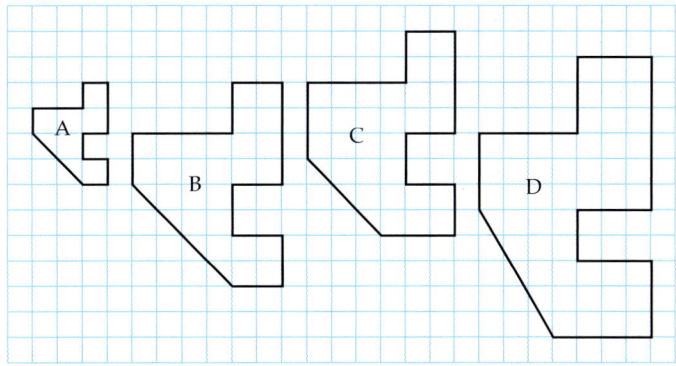

③ In these diagrams, A has been enlarged to give B. Trace the diagrams and find the centre of enlargement for each.

a)

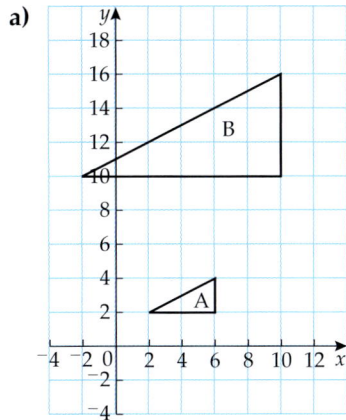

b)

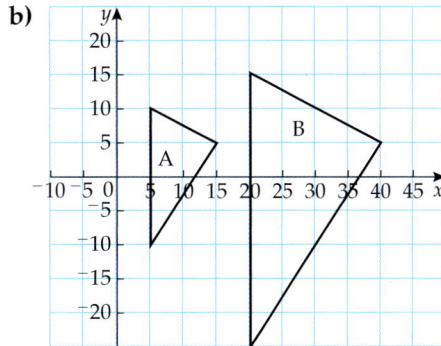

Investigation

④ Make a copy of the triangle on axes as shown in the diagram. Using the centre of enlargement (0, 0), enlarge the shape by scale factors of your choice (for example scale factor 2, scale factor 3 and scale factor 5). Investigate what happens to the coordinates of the vertices of the shape when enlarged.

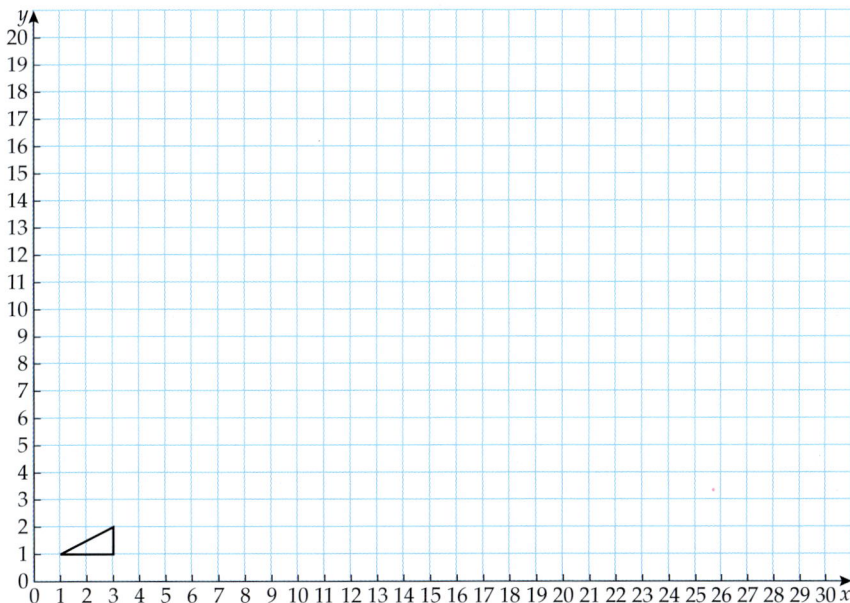

Scale factors and ratio

⊕ Understand ratio as related to an enlargement

⊕ Understand and use the scale factor of an enlargement

The triangle T is an enlargement of triangle S.

Each side of T is 2 times the length of the **corresponding** side on S:

AB = 4 cm and A′B′ = 8 cm, $4 \times 2 = 8$
AC = 2 cm and A′C′ = 4 cm, $2 \times 2 = 4$
BC = 5 cm and B′C′ = 10 cm, $5 \times 2 = 10$

The **scale factor** of the enlargement is 2.

The **ratio** of the sides of S to T is 1 : 2.

For any enlargement, if the scale factor is n then the ratio of the corresponding sides is 1 : n.

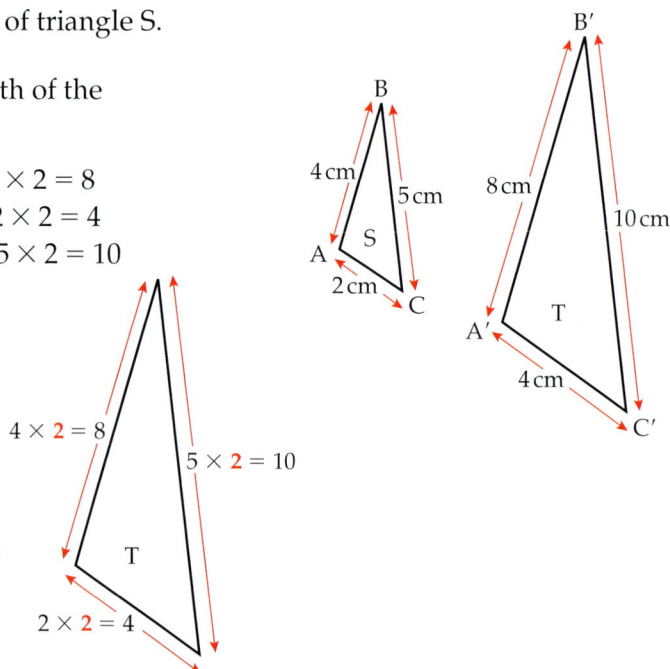

Example Shape Y is an enlargement of shape X, write the scale factor and ratio for the enlargement.

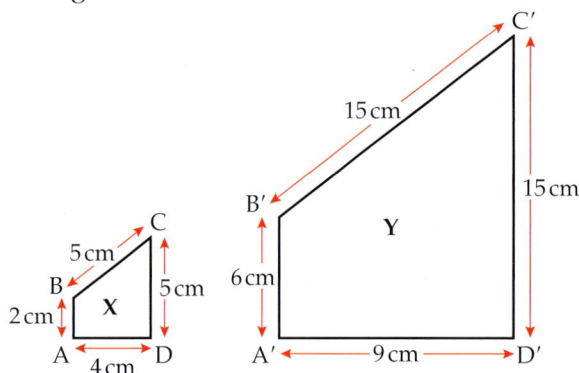

AB = 2 and A′B′ = 6, $2 \times 3 = 6$

AD = 4 and A′D′ = 12, $4 \times 3 = 12$

By calculating the scale factor for these two sides it is clear that the scale factor of the enlargement is 3.

Just checking the other sides: $5 \times 3 = 15$ (for both).

As the scale factor is 3 the ratio of X : Y is 1 : 3.

Exercise 10.5

1 Measure the following diagrams and calculate the scale factor for each enlargement.

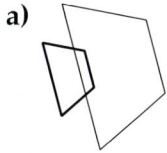

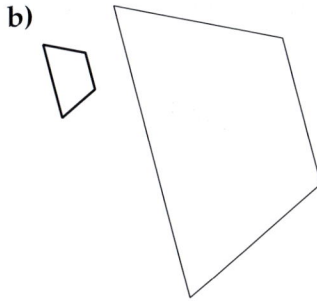

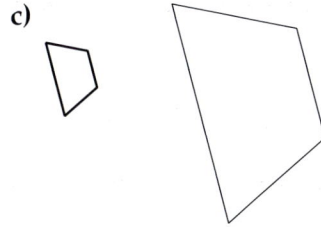

a)

b)

c)

2 Work out the scale factor and ratio of enlargement for each pair of diagrams.

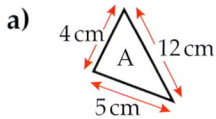

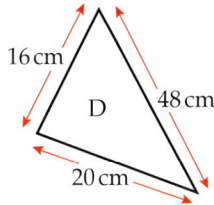

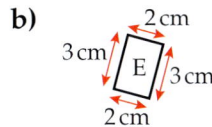

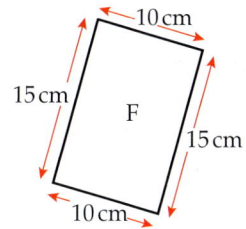

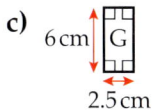

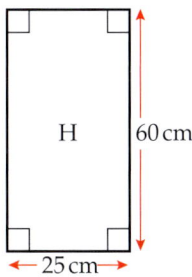

a) 4 cm, A, 12 cm, 5 cm — 16 cm, D, 48 cm, 20 cm

b) 2 cm, 3 cm, E, 3 cm, 2 cm — 10 cm, 15 cm, F, 15 cm, 10 cm

c) 6 cm, G, 2.5 cm — H, 60 cm, 25 cm

3 Find the scale factor and the ratio of the enlargement for each pair of diagrams.

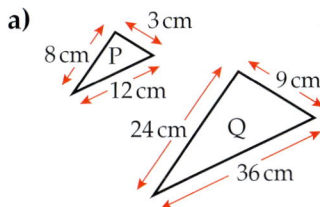

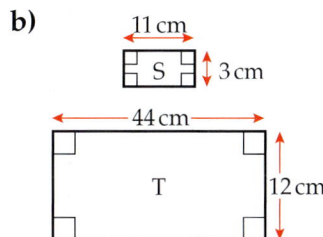

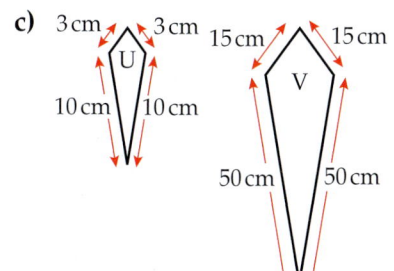

a) 3 cm, 8 cm, P, 12 cm — 9 cm, 24 cm, Q, 36 cm

b) 11 cm, S, 3 cm — 44 cm, T, 12 cm

c) 3 cm, 3 cm, U, 10 cm, 10 cm — 15 cm, 15 cm, V, 50 cm, 50 cm

4 Trace the triangle ABC. Using the centre of enlargement O, enlarge the triangle by scale factor 4. Label your enlarged triangle A'B'C'. Measure the lengths OA and OA'.
Write the ratio OA : OA'.
Draw some shapes of your own and enlarge them by scale factor 4. For each write the ratio OA : OA'.
Write down anything you notice.

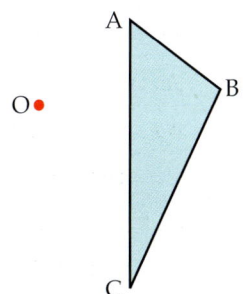

10.6 Scale drawings

⊕ Make simple scale drawings

A **scale drawing** is a drawing that represents a real object.

This scale drawing shows a plan of a room.

The actual room is 8 m long and 4 m wide.

On the plan, the room is 4 cm long and 2 cm wide.

The plan and the room are in proportion – 1 cm on the plan represents 2 m in real life.

To write this as a **ratio**, the 2 metres is converted to centimetres.

1 cm represents 200 cm so the ratio of the **scale** is 1 : 200.

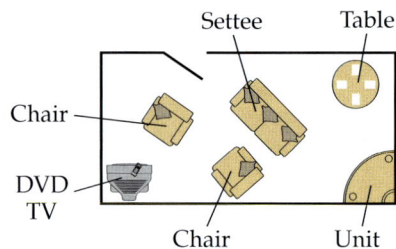

Settee   Table

Chair

DVD
TV

Chair   Unit

Example 1   A rectangular classroom is 8 m by 5.6 m. Make a scale drawing of the room. Use the following scale: 1 cm represents 2 m.

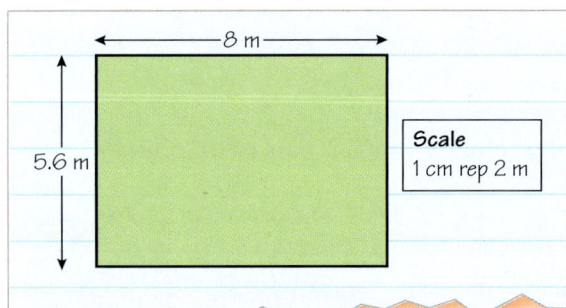

8 m

5.6 m

Scale
1 cm rep 2 m

1 cm on the scale drawing represents 2 m in real life. So 4 cm represents 8 m and 2.8 cm represents 5.6 m. Remember to write the scale next to the scale drawing.

Example 2   What is the scale of a plan of a room where 5 cm represents 1 m?

Plan	Real life
5 cm	100 cm
1 cm	20 cm

Convert to the same units.

Now simplify.

Scale is 1 : 20.

Exercise 10.6

1 A rectangular room is 10 m by 6 m.

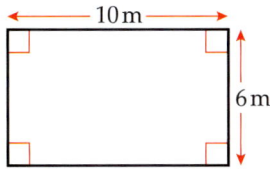

Make a scale drawing of the room. Use the following scale: 1 cm represents 2 m.

2 The diagram shows an outline sketch of a school sports field.

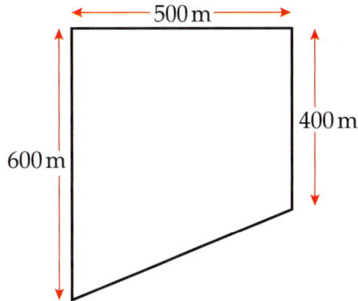

Make a scale drawing of the field. Use the following scale: 1 cm represents 100 m.

3 Find the scales of the following drawings.
   a) A map of a field where 2 cm represents 1 m.
   b) A plan of a garden where 10 cm represents 5 m.
   c) A drawing of a bedroom where 5 mm represents 50 cm.

4 The diagram shows a sketch for a plan of a garden.

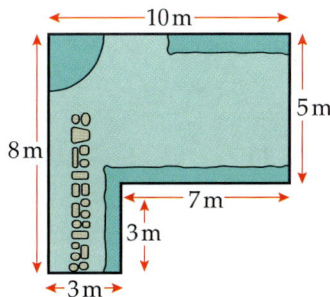

The plan is to be drawn to a scale of 2 cm to 1 m. What are the lengths on the plan?

5 Draw a sketch of your ideal study room showing clearly the actual measurements. Make a scale drawing of your study room stating clearly your scale. Work out some approximate measurements for some pieces of furniture and draw them on your plan to the same scale.

6 Design a year 9 common room using cut outs for large fittings. Clearly state your scale.

This is a set of revision questions covering Units 6–10. If you have a problem with a question, look back at the lesson shown in the box to refresh your memory.

Questions 1–20 are non-calculator questions.

1 Using mental methods, work out

Lesson 7.1
Lesson 7.2

a) 5×28　　b) 4.5×18　　c) 11×24　　d) 19×8

2 Find the mid-points of the following pairs of coordinates by plotting points and drawing the lines.

Lesson 6.1

a) (5, 2) and (5, 6)　　b) (3, 2) and (9, 2)　　c) (1, ⁻2) and (5, 4)

3 Simplify the following algebraic expressions using index notation.

Lesson 8.4

a) $a \times a \times a \times a \times a$　　b) $5 \times b \times b \times b$　　c) $3 \times c \times c \times c \times c \times c$

4 A bag of sweets contains 6 red, 4 green and 2 black sweets. A sweet is chosen at random. What is the probability that the sweet is:

Lesson 9.1

a) red?　　b) not red?　　c) green?

d) not green?　　e) not black?　　f) red or green?

How many sweets are in the bag?

Give your answers as fractions.

5 Describe all the symmetries of the following shapes.

Lesson 10.2

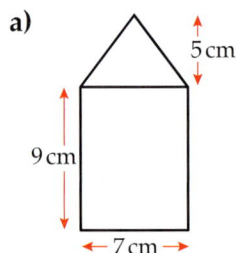

square　　　　rectangle　　　　parallelogram

6 a) A small 'Post-it' note has a mass of 0.01 g. What would be the mass of 5000 small 'Post-it' notes?

Lesson 7.3

b) A book is 12 mm thick. If each page is 0.1 mm thick, how many pages are there?

7 Find the areas of the following shapes.

Lesson 6.3
Lesson 6.4

a) 5 cm, 9 cm, 7 cm

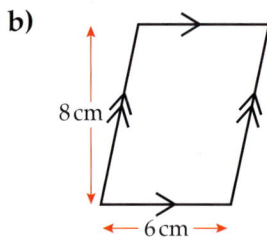

b) 8 cm, 6 cm

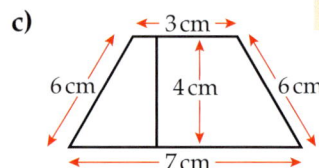

c) 3 cm, 6 cm, 4 cm, 6 cm, 7 cm

8 **a)** Find the value of 10^6.

Lesson 8.2

    b) Write ten thousand as a power of 10.

    c) Find the value of 4×10^3.

9 Li has a choice of packed lunch from the following:

Lesson 9.2

Sandwich	Drink
Savoury cheese	Water
Ham Salad	Milk
Chicken	Orange juice

List all the possible outcomes if she chooses a sandwich and a drink.
(Use the initial letter only for your list i.e. *S* to stand for Savoury cheese).

10 A farmer has 3 pieces of fencing measuring 8.72 m, 15 m and 4.532 m.

Lesson 7.4
Lesson 7.5

    a) What is the total length of fencing?

    b) He uses 13.97 m. How much does he have left?

    c) Round your answer to **a)** correct to 1 decimal place.

    d) Round your answer to **b)** correct to 2 decimal places.

11 Draw a set of axes from ⁻10 to 10. Plot the points (2, 1), (5, 1) and (5, 3). Join the points to make a triangle and label it A

Lesson 10.1

    a) Translate A 1 right and 3 up. Label the image B.

    b) Translate B 2 left and 2 down. Label the image C.

    c) State a single transformation that will move triangle A to triangle C.

    d) Reflect C in the *y*-axis. Label the image D.

    e) Reflect D in the *x*-axis. Label the image E.

    f) What single rotation would move triangle C onto triangle E?

12 Find all the square roots of the following, where possible.

Lesson 7.8

    a) $\sqrt{36}$ **b)** $\sqrt{-100}$ **c)** $\sqrt{400}$

13 State which of the following shapes are congruent.

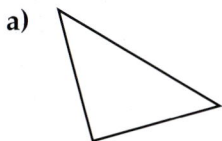

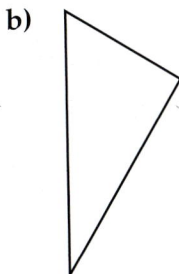

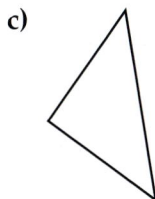

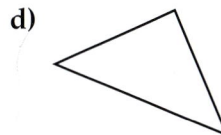

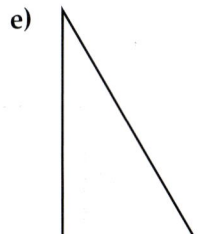

Lesson 10.3

a)   **b)**   **c)**   **d)**   **e)**

14 a) Copy and complete the table of values for the graph $y = 2x - 1$.

Lesson 8.6

x	0	2	4
y			

b) Draw a set of axes from ⁻10 to 10. Plot the points and draw the graph of $y = 2x - 1$.

15 Find the volume of this shape.

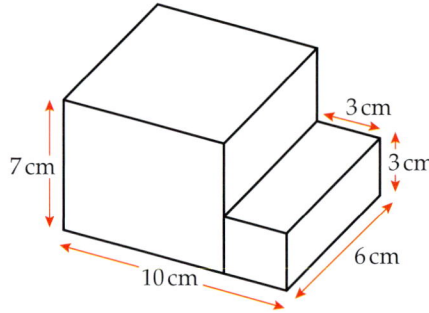

Lesson 6.6

3 cm
7 cm
3 cm
10 cm
6 cm

16 How many pieces of pipe that are 0.4 m long can be cut from a piece 13.2 m long?

Lesson 7.7

17 A straight line graph has the equation $y = 5x + 3$.

Lesson 8.7

a) Without drawing the graph state:
  i) the gradient of the line
  ii) where it cuts through the y-axis (the intercept)

b) Will the line $y = 5x - 1$ be parallel to the line $y = 5x + 3$?

18 Trace each shape and enlarge it from centre O, by the scale factor shown.

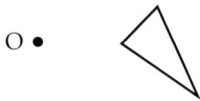

Lesson 10.4

O •

scale factor 2

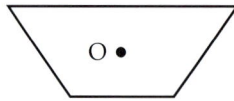

O •

scale factor 3

19 Use a factor tree to find the prime factorisation of 96.

Lesson 8.3

20 In an experiment the number of live bacteria was measured after being placed in different temperatures for 24 hours. The results were:

Lesson 8.8
Lesson 8.9

Temp (°C)	10	15	20	25	30	35	40	45	50
No. of bacteria	5	9	19	42	50	51	37	20	0

a) Draw axes with temperature along the x-axis, using 1 cm for 5 °C and Number of bacteria up the y-axis using 1 cm for 5 bacteria.

b) Plot the points in the table and join with straight lines.

c) Using your graph, what statement can you make about the effect of temperature on live bacteria?

21 a) Convert the following metric units into approximate imperial equivalents.

Lesson 6.2

  i) 3 kg   **ii)** 6 m   **iii)** 48 km

b) Convert the following imperial units into their approximate metric equivalents.
  i) 25 miles   **ii)** 44 pounds   **iii)** 10 pints.

22

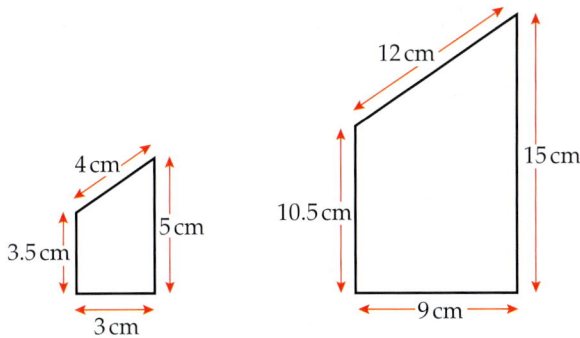

a) Work out the scale factor of the enlargement

b) What is the ratio of the enlargement?

23 Find the value of each of the following expressions when $t = 8$.

a) t^3 b) $3t^2 + 2$ c) $\dfrac{t^2}{4}$ d) $2t^4 - 3t^3$

24 Find the volume of a box 32.5 cm long, 12.5 cm wide and 8.5 cm high.

25 Find the value of the following:

a) 7^3 b) 12 cubed   c) cube root of 27   d) $\sqrt[3]{125}$

26 A 4-sided spinner, numbered 1 to 4 is spun 60 times. The results are:

Number	1	2	3	4
Frequency	18	12	14	16

a) Work out the experimental probability for each outcome. Round your answers to 2 decimal places where necessary.

b) If I spun the spinner 180 times, how many times would I expect it to land on 1?

c) If this is a fair spinner, what is the theoretical probability for each outcome?

d) Compare the experimental probability and the theoretical probability and comment on whether you think the spinner is biased.

e) How could you make the experimental probability more accurate?

27 This is a sketch of the floor plan of a flat.

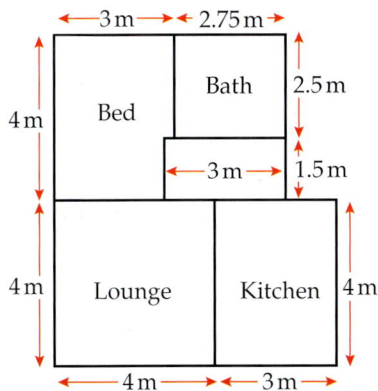

a) Make a scale drawing of the plan using 2 cm to represent 1 m.

b) Without a calculator work out the area of the bathroom.

⊕ Multiply an unknown value over a bracket

⊕ Simplify algebraic expressions

To **simplify** expressions it is sometimes necessary to **expand** the brackets. We can use a multiplication grid:

$$b(b-3) \rightarrow b \begin{array}{|c|c|} \hline b^2 & 3b \\ \hline \end{array}$$

Remember $b \times b$ is written b^2.

$$b(b-3) = b^2 - 3b$$

When an algebraic expression has brackets and other terms, we expand the brackets first. Then we collect like terms.

For example, to simplify the expression $b(b-3) + 5b$:

$$b(b-3) + 5b = b^2 - 3b + 5b$$
$$= b^2 + 2b$$

First expand the brackets, then collect like terms.

Example 1 Expand the brackets in each of the following expressions.

a) $3(t-5)$

b) $x(x+10)$

a) $3(t-5) \rightarrow 3 \begin{array}{|c|c|} \hline 3t & 15 \\ \hline \end{array}$

$$3(t-5) = 3t - 15$$

The operation in the bracket is subtract.

b) $x(x+10) \rightarrow x \begin{array}{|c|c|} \hline x^2 & 10x \\ \hline \end{array}$

$$x(x+10) = x^2 + 10x$$

Example 2 Simplify the following expression: $x(x+5) - 12 + 3x$

$x(x+5) \rightarrow x \begin{array}{|c|c|} \hline x^2 & 5x \\ \hline \end{array}$

First expand the bracket.

$$x(x+5) = x^2 + 5x$$
$$x(x+5) - 12 + 3x = x^2 + 5x - 12 + 3x$$
$$= x^2 + 8x - 12$$

Next collect together like terms.

Exercise 11.1

1 Expand the brackets in each of the following expressions:

a) $4(x + 5)$ **b)** $6(x - 3)$

c) $5(x + 2)$ **d)** $2(a + 4)$

e) $9(b - 2)$ **f)** $11(r - 5)$

g) $12(10 + g)$ **h)** $7(2 - r)$

i) $3(5 - b)$ **j)** $8(6 + x)$

> See Example 1 part **a)**.

2 Expand the brackets in each of the following expressions.

a) $a(a + 5)$ **b)** $b(b - 4)$ **c)** $c(c + 10)$

d) $d(d - 12)$ **e)** $e(5 + e)$ **f)** $f(10 - f)$

3 Simplify the following algebraic expressions.

a) $3(x + 4) - 2x$ **b)** $5(x - 2) + 12$ **c)** $x(x + 5) + 4x$

d) $5x + 6(x - 3)$ **e)** $2x + x(x + 1)$ **f)** $x(x - 3) - 7x$

> Expand the brackets first.

4 a) For each rectangle:

Write an algebraic expression for the area, using brackets.

Expand the brackets in your expression.

i)   **ii)**   **iii)**

b) Write down and simplify an expression for the area of the following shape.

> The shape is made from the rectangles in part **a)**.

5 Decide which of the following expressions are identical.

a) $4(3x - 5)$ **b)** $10x + 2(x - 3)$

c) $5(2x - 2) - 2x - 10$ **d)** $8x + 2(2x + 3) - 12$

6 In the diagram, you make each expression by adding the two cells below it.

Copy and complete the diagram.

Write the missing expressions as simply as possible.

Investigation

7 a) Find the value of $2(x + 5) - 2x + 10$ when

     i) $x = 1$ **ii)** $x = 2$ **iii)** $x = {}^-6$ **iv)** $x = 0$

b) Describe what you notice.

c) Explain why this is.

d) Write another algebraic expression that will give you similar answers to **b)** and **c)**.

⊕ Simplifying expressions involving powers of x

We can **simplify** algebraic expressions by collecting like terms.
Like terms have exactly the same letters and **powers** .

For example,
$$3x^2 + 4x^3 + 2x^2$$
Look at the terms involving x^2: $3x^2 + 2x^2 = 5x^2$
Look at the terms involving x^3: $4x^3$

So the expression simplifies to: $4x^3 + 5x^2$

Example   Simplify the following algebraic expressions:

   a) $2b^3 + 5b^3 - 2b^3$ **b)** $5a^2 + 7a^5 - 3a^2 + 4a^5$

a) $2b^3 + 5b^3 - 2b^3$	$= 7b^3 - 2b^3$
	$= 5b^3$
b) $5a^2 + 7a^5 - 3a^2 + 4a^5$	$= 5a^2 - 3a^2 + 7a^5 + 4a^5$
	$= 2a^2 + 11a^5$

Each term has exactly the same letters and powers, so we add together the values in front of the b^3's.

First group together all the terms with exactly the same letters and powers.

Now add (or subtract) like terms.

Exercise 11.2

1 The picture shows a bathroom tile.

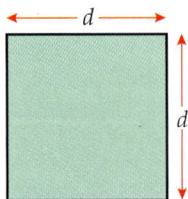

d across the top, *d* down the side

   a) Write down an expression for the area of this tile.
   b) If 125 tiles are used in a bathroom, write an expression for the total area they cover.
   c) Each tile has sides of 10 cm. What area do 125 tiles cover, in cm²?

2 Find the perimeter of each of the following shapes.
   Make sure you simplify your answer as much as possible.

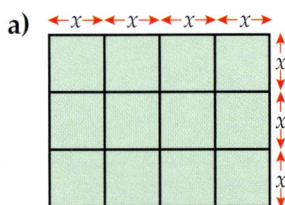

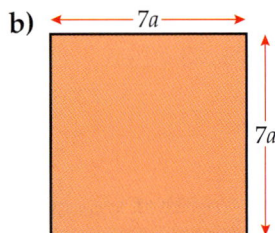

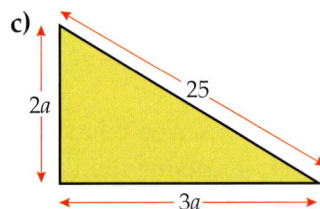

   a) x x x x along top, x x x down side

   b) $7a$ across top, $7a$ down side

   c) $2a$ on left side, 25 on hypotenuse, $3a$ along bottom

3 On a farm there are 12 fields.

Ten of the fields are square and each covers an area of b^2.

The remaining two fields cover an area three times greater than each of the ten square fields.

   a) Write down an expression for the area of one of the larger fields.

   b) Write down and simplify an expression for the total area covered by all 12 fields.

   c) If the length of one of the smaller fields is 0.5 km, what is the area of land that the farm covers?

4 The length of one side of cube is $3t$ cm.

Draw a net of the cube

Work out the total distance round the outside of the net.

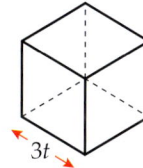

5 Simplify the following algebraic expressions:

   a) $b^2 + b^2 + b^2$ **b)** $m^7 + m^7 + m^7 + m^7 + m^7 + m^7 + m^7$

   c) $t^5 + t^5 + t^5 + t^5 + t^5$ **d)** $p^3 - p^3 + p^3 - p^3 + p^3$

6 Simplify the following as much as possible:

   a) $z^6 + z^6 + z^5 + z^5 + z^6$ **b)** $b^2 + b^3 + b^2 + b^3 + b^2$

   c) $m^4 + m^4 + m^5 + m^6 + m^6 + m^5 + m^6$ **d)** $t^2 + t^5 + t^2$

7 Simplify the following algebraic expressions.

   a) $a^2 + 3a^2$ **b)** $b^3 + 5b^3$ **c)** $3r^4 + 7r^4$

   d) $8m^2 - 5m^2$ **e)** $6w^3 - 5w^3$ **f)** $2q^2 - 3q^2$

8 Simplify the following algebraic expressions as much as possible:

   a) $4f^2 + 3f^3 + 2f^3$ **b)** $4x^7 - 3x^7 + 3x$

   c) $12q^3 - 5q^2 + 2q^2$ **d)** $3x^{11} - 5x^{12} - 3x^{11}$

   e) $5a + 6t^2 - 3a^2 - 4t^2$ **f)** $5y^3 - 3r^3 - 6r^3 - 5y^6$

> When you group like terms, remember to keep each term with its sign.

9 In a magic square the sums of the expressions in each row, column and diagonal are the same.

Show that this square is a magic square:

$a^5 + 6a^3$	$a^5 - 6a^3 - 2a^5$	$a^5 + 2a^5$
$a^5 - 6a^3 + 2a^5$	a^5	$a^5 + 6a^3 - 2a^5$
$a^5 - 2a^5$	$a^5 + 6a^3 + 2a^5$	$a^5 - 6a^3$

⊕ Substitute values into a formula

A **formula** is a rule that links two or more **variables** :

$$s = \frac{d}{t}$$ is a formula where s = speed, d = distance and t = time.

s, d and t are called variables, because they can stand for a range of different values.

We can substitute values into a formula to find an unknown value.

Example The formula for calculating the area of a triangle is:

$A = \frac{1}{2}bh$

where A = area, b = base, h = height

Calculate the area of this triangle:

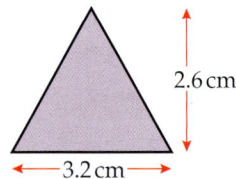

2.6 cm

3.2 cm

Area $= \frac{1}{2} \times 3.2 \times 2.6$ ———— Substitute the values b = 3.2 and h = 2.6 into the formula.

$= 4.16 \text{ cm}^2$ ———— The base and height are in cm, so the area is in cm^2.

Exercise 11.3

① To calculate the number of ice creams sold a shop owner uses the formula:

$I = 5C + 10$

where I = number of ice creams and C = temperature in degrees Celsius.

a) Copy and complete the table to show the number of ice creams sold in the first week in July:

Day	Monday	Tuesday	Wednesday	Thursday	Friday	Saturday
Temperature (in degrees Celsius)	20	18	16	19	22	17
Number of ice creams sold	5 × ... + 10 =					

b) One day in January the temperature falls to ⁻5°C. How many ice creams would the shopkeeper sell at this temperature?

c) What is the problem with your answer to part **b)**?

2 In electrical circuits we use the following formula to calculate voltage:

$V = IR$ where V = voltage, I = current and R = resistance

Find the value of V when:

a) $I = 20, R = 1$ b) $I = 2, R = 5$ c) $I = 12, R = 7$

3 The following formula is used to calculate the approximate area of a circle:

$A = 3r^2$ where A = area, r = radius

> The radius is the distance from the centre to the edge of a circle.

Calculate the approximate areas of the following circles:

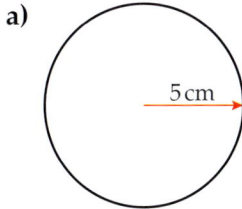

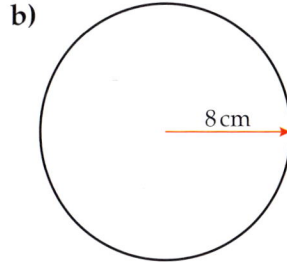

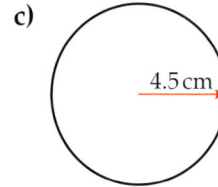

a)

5 cm

b)

8 cm

c)

4.5 cm

4 The formula for the nth term of a sequence is $T(n) = 5n^2$. Find:

a) $T(5)$ b) $T(12)$ c) $T(8)$ d) $T(15)$ e) $T(20)$

5 To calculate how fast something has travelled, the following formula is used:

$$s = \frac{d}{t}$$ where s = speed, d = distance and t = time

Find out how fast a car has travelled when:

a) $d = 20$ miles, $t = 1$ hour

b) $d = 100$ miles, $t = 2$ hours
> Give your answers in miles per hour.

c) $d = 600$ miles, $t = 10$ hours

Investigation

6 The area of a rectangle is calculated by using the formula:

$A = l \times w$

Where A = area, l = length and w = width

This is one rectangle with area 100 cm²:

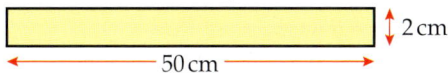

2 cm

50 cm

$A = l \times w = 50$ cm $\times$ 2 cm $= 100$ cm²

a) Sketch some other rectangles with the same area. Write the measurements for length and width on your sketch.

> Use whole numbers for length and width.

b) Which of your rectangles has the greatest perimeter?

c) Can you find one with a larger perimeter?

d) Repeat parts a)–c) for different areas. What do you notice?

Constructing formulae

⊕ Construct formulae
⊕ Check formula by substituting in values

A **formula** is a general rule that expresses a relationship between two or more variables.
We use formulae in Science and Geography as well as in Mathematics.

Einstein constructed a famous formula in his Theory of Relativity: $E = mc^2$.

If we have lots of similar problems to solve, we can **construct** a formula and substitute different values into it.

Example   A decorator charges £15 per hour plus the cost of the paint.

a)   Sam's room takes 12.5 hours and the paint costs £67.
How much does the decorator charge?

b)   Construct a formula the decorator can use to calculate the cost for different rooms. Use T = time in hours and P = cost of paint.

a)   Cost = £15 × 12.5 + £67

= £187.50 + £67

= £254.50

b)   Cost = $15T + P$

To work out the cost, multiply the number of hours by 15 and add on the cost of the paint.

Multiply the number of hours (T) by 15 and add on the cost of the paint (P).

Exercise 11.4

1   A shop increases all its prices by 10%.
a)   Copy and complete the table of prices below:

Product	Old Price	10% of old Price	New Price
McFlew CD	£12	£12 ÷ 10 = ……	…
Z Men Video	£11	………………	………………
The Tower DVD	£17	………………	………………

To find 10% of a value we divide by 10.

b)   Copy and complete the following formula for finding N (new price) when you know P (old price)

$$N = \frac{P}{10} + \dots$$

c)   Use your answer to b) to calculate the new price of the following items.

Round your answer to the nearest penny.

Wonderful North CD – £11.99
'West is West' DVD – £15.99
Box set of 'Tuffy' Videos – £45.98

2 In electrical circuits we use the following formula to calculate voltage:

$V = IR$ where V = voltage, I = current and R = resistance

Find the value of V when:

a) $I = 20, R = 1$ **b)** $I = 2, R = 5$ **c)** $I = 12, R = 7$

3 The following formula is used to calculate the approximate area of a circle:

$A = 3r^2$ where A = area, r = radius

> The radius is the distance from the centre to the edge of a circle.

Calculate the approximate areas of the following circles:

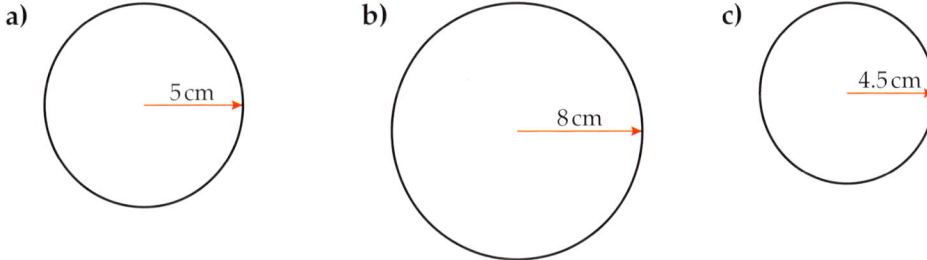

a)

5 cm

b)

8 cm

c)

4.5 cm

4 The formula for the nth term of a sequence is $T(n) = 5n^2$. Find:

a) $T(5)$ **b)** $T(12)$ **c)** $T(8)$ **d)** $T(15)$ **e)** $T(20)$

5 To calculate how fast something has travelled, the following formula is used:

$$s = \frac{d}{t}$$ where s = speed, d = distance and t = time

Find out how fast a car has travelled when:

a) $d = 20$ miles, $t = 1$ hour

b) $d = 100$ miles, $t = 2$ hours   > Give your answers in miles per hour.

c) $d = 600$ miles, $t = 10$ hours

Investigation

6 The area of a rectangle is calculated by using the formula:

$A = l \times w$

Where A = area, l = length and w = width

This is one rectangle with area 100 cm²:

2 cm

50 cm

$A = l \times w = 50$ cm $\times 2$ cm $= 100$ cm²

a) Sketch some other rectangles with the same area. Write the measurements for length and width on your sketch.

> Use whole numbers for length and width.

b) Which of your rectangles has the greatest perimeter?

c) Can you find one with a larger perimeter?

d) Repeat parts **a)**–**c)** for different areas. What do you notice?

Constructing formulae

- Construct formulae
- Check formula by substituting in values

A **formula** is a general rule that expresses a relationship between two or more variables.

We use formulae in Science and Geography as well as in Mathematics.

Einstein constructed a famous formula in his Theory of Relativity: $E = mc^2$.

If we have lots of similar problems to solve, we can **construct** a formula and substitute different values into it.

Example   A decorator charges £15 per hour plus the cost of the paint.

a) Sam's room takes 12.5 hours and the paint costs £67. How much does the decorator charge?

b) Construct a formula the decorator can use to calculate the cost for different rooms. Use T = time in hours and P = cost of paint.

a) $Cost = £15 \times 12.5 + £67$

To work out the cost, multiply the number of hours by 15 and add on the cost of the paint.

$= £187.50 + £67$

$= £254.50$

b) $Cost = 15T + P$

Multiply the number of hours (T) by 15 and add on the cost of the paint (P).

Exercise 11.4

1   A shop increases all its prices by 10%.

a) Copy and complete the table of prices below:

Product	Old Price	10% of old Price	New Price
McFlew CD	£12	£12 ÷ 10 = ……	…
Z Men Video	£11	………………	………………
The Tower DVD	£17	………………	………………

To find 10% of a value we divide by 10.

b) Copy and complete the following formula for finding N (new price) when you know P (old price)

$$N = \frac{P}{10} + \dots$$

c) Use your answer to **b)** to calculate the new price of the following items.

Round your answer to the nearest penny.

Wonderful North CD – £11.99

'West is West' DVD – £15.99

Box set of 'Tuffy' Videos – £45.98

2 A taxi driver charges £0.50 per mile.
Let n represent the distance in miles and P represent the cost of the journey.
   a) Write down a formula connecting P and n.
   b) Use your formula to calculate the cost of a journey of:
      i) 12 miles   **ii)** 250 miles   **iii)** 177 miles   **iv)** 23 miles.

3 A company logo is made of a square and a triangle.
The company uses several different sizes of logo.
For size 1 the square has sides of length 6 cm and
the height of the triangle is 3 cm.
   a) Calculate the area of the square.
   b) Calculate the area of the triangle.
   c) Calculate the total area of the logo.

What is the length of the base of the triangle?

For size 2 the square has sides of length 'a' and the height of the triangle is 'b'.
   d) Write down an algebraic expression for the area of the square.
   e) Write down an algebraic expression for the area of the triangle.
   f) Write down a formula for finding the total area of the logo (L)
   e) Use your formula to find the area of the following logos:

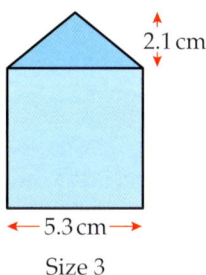

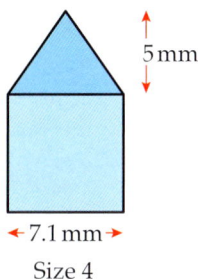

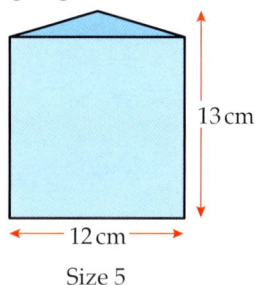

2.1 cm   5 mm   13 cm

5.3 cm   7.1 mm   12 cm

Size 3   Size 4   Size 5

4 A French restaurant serves bread with every meal. The chef allows $\frac{1}{2}$ a loaf of bread per customer.
   a) Write down an expression for the number of loaves (L) needed for N customers.
   b) The chef always orders an extra five loaves.
   Write down a formula to calculate the number of loaves he orders (L) for N customers.
   c) Use your answer to **b)** to work out how many loaves of bread the chef needs to order for these numbers of customers:
      i) 28   **ii)** 136   **iii)** 97

Investigation

5 An orange juice carton has the following dimensions:
   a) What is the volume of the carton?
   b) How many ml of juice will the carton hold? $1\ cm^3 = 1\ ml$
   c) How many litres is this?
   d) Write down a formula for calculating the capacity (in litres) of any carton.   Choose letters for the dimensions of the carton.
   e) Measure real juice cartons and use your formula to calculate the capacity.
   Compare your calculated capacity value with the volume of juice written on the side of the carton. Does your formula work?

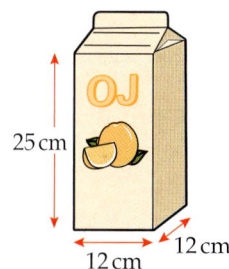

OJ   25 cm   12 cm   12 cm

11.5 Drawing distance–time graphs

⊕ Draw distance–time graphs

A **distance–time** graph shows a journey.

We always plot time on the *x*-axis and distance on the *y*-axis.

Always label the axes.

Use suitable scales on the axes.

Use a sharp pencil and a ruler.

Example   Alex goes for a ride on his motorbike. He leaves home and rides 40 km in 45 minutes. He stops at a petrol station for 5 minutes. Then he continues, travelling 35 km in 30 minutes.

Draw a distance–time graph to show his journey.
Use a scale of 1 cm = 10 minutes on the *x*-axis and 1 cm = 20 km on the *y*-axis.

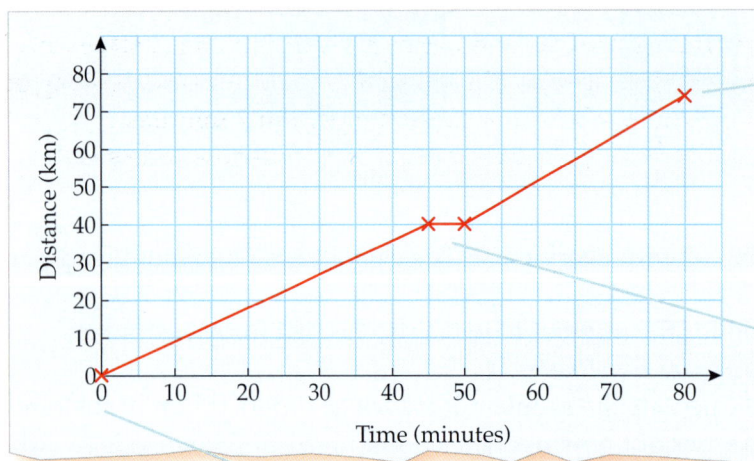

Plot the point half an hour from the previous point along and 35 km up from the previous point.

The graph is horizontal when he stops (distance staying the same).

Graphs starts at (0, 0) – the journey starts at time zero and the distance travelled is zero.

Exercise 11.5

You will need graph paper for this exercise.

❶ Emily goes for a bicycle ride every Saturday morning. She leaves home and cycles 10 km to the nearest town in 20 minutes. She then stops in town for a coffee for 30 minutes. Then she continues her journey, cycling another 20 km in 40 minutes.
   a) How far does she cycle in total?
   b) How long does the whole trip take her?
   c) Draw a distance–time graph to illustrate her journey.

Use a scale of 1 cm = 10 minutes on the *x*-axis and 1 cm = 5 km on the *y*-axis.

2 A train travels from Merryfield to Burybridge. The journey is 40 miles and the train travels at a constant speed of 80 miles per hour. It stops at a station exactly halfway for 5 minutes.

   a) How far does the train travel before it stops for 5 minutes?

   b) How long does the train take to travel the first 20 miles?

   c) How long does it take to travel the next 20 miles?

   d) How long does the whole journey take?

   e) Draw a distance–time graph to show the train's journey.

> A speed of 80 miles per hour means the train travels 80 miles in 1 hour. How long does it take to travel 20 miles?

> Remember to include the halfway stop.

> Use a scale of 2 cm = 10 mins on the x-axis and 2 cm = 10 miles on the y-axis.

3 A helicopter takes off from the flight deck of a ship. It takes 15 minutes to fly 20 km to another ship. It lands on the ship and waits for 40 minutes.
Then it flies to the first ship again, at a speed of 60 km per hour.

   a) How long does the helicopter take to fly the 20 km back to the first ship?

   b) How long does the whole journey take?

   c) Draw a distance–time graph showing this journey.

> Include the time when it is stationary.

> Use a scale of 2 cm = 10 minutes on the x-axis and 2 cm = 10 km on the y-axis.

4 Jude walks to school in the mornings. He leaves home at 8.00 am and walks 500 m in 4 minutes at a constant speed. He then spends 10 minutes in the corner shop looking at magazines. He walks the last 200 m to school at a constant speed in 2 minutes.
Copy the axes shown below and draw a distance–time graph to illustrate Jude's walk.

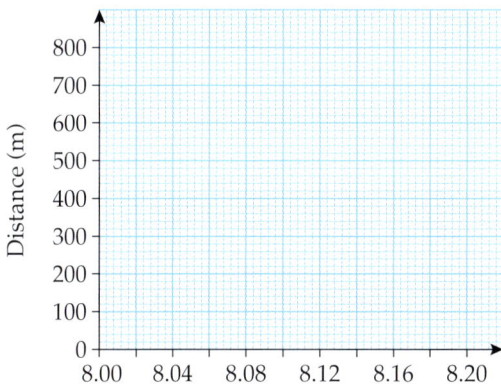

5 Denis rollerblades every morning. One morning he rollerblades a distance of 9 km in $\frac{1}{2}$ hour. Then he spends 10 minutes fixing a broken lace. After that he rollerblades another 4 km in 15 minutes.
Draw a distance–time graph to illustrate Denis's journey.

6 Draw a distance–time graph to show your journey to school this morning.

Interpreting distance–time graphs

◈ Read information from a distance–time graph

Key words
gradient
horizontal
speed

Distance–time graphs give us a lot of information about a journey.

For example, the following distance–time graph shows the distance travelled by a helicopter.

The **gradient** of a distance–time graph tells us about the **speed**. The greater the gradient, the faster the speed.

The graph showing the helicopter's journey has steepest gradient between 1 hr and 1 hr 15 minutes. This is when the helicopter's speed is greatest.

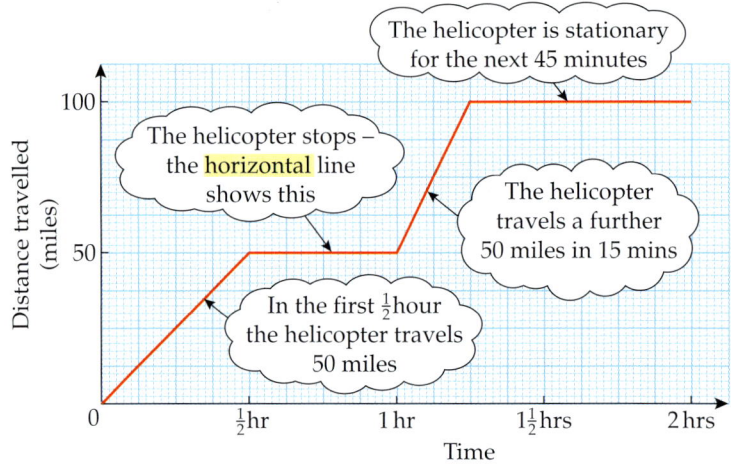

The helicopter is stationary for the next 45 minutes

The helicopter stops – the horizontal line shows this

The helicopter travels a further 50 miles in 15 mins

In the first ½ hour the helicopter travels 50 miles

Example Look at this distance–time graph showing Deborah's morning swim:
a) How far does Deborah swim in total?
b) How long does it take her to swim the first 400 m?
c) How long does it take her to swim the last 400 m?
d) What does she do 10 minutes into her swim? How is this shown on the graph?
e) When is Deborah's speed greatest?

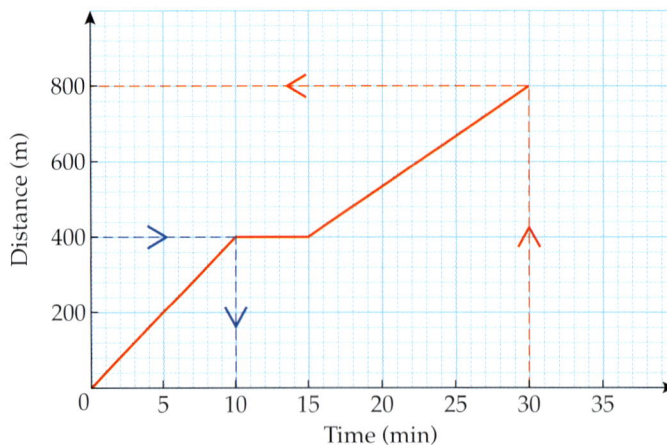

a) Total distance swum = 800 m — See the red dotted line.
b) First 400 m takes 10 minutes — See the blue dotted line.
c) Last 400 m takes 30 − 15 = 15 minutes — Time at 800 m − time at 400 m.
d) She has a rest, the graph is horizontal.
e) Greatest speed is between 0 and 10 minutes — The graph is steepest between these times.

Exercise 11.6

1 The following graph shows Mrs Garner's morning jog.
  a) How far does Mrs Garner jog in the first $\frac{1}{2}$ hour?
  b) When does she stop for a break? How long for?
  c) How long does her morning jog take?
  d) How far does Mrs Garner jog in the last $\frac{1}{2}$ hour?
  e) When is Mrs Garner's speed the greatest?

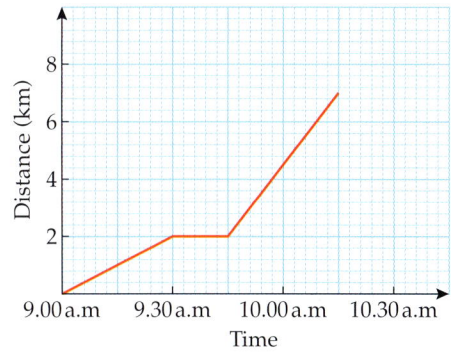

2 The following graph shows a train journey between Petershore and London.
  a) At what time does the train arrive in:
    i) Bunwich
    ii) Haseleby
    iii) London
  b) How many minutes does the train take to travel between:
    i) Petershore and Bunwich
    ii) Bunwich and Haseleby
    iii) Petershore and London?
  c) How long does the train stop for at: **i)** Bunwich   **ii)** Haseleby

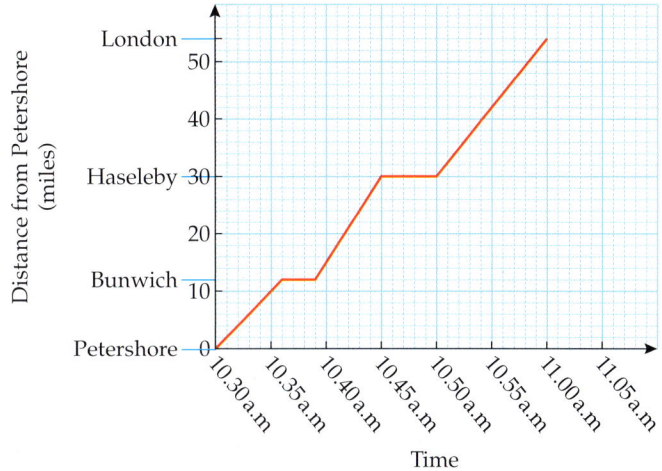

3 The following distance–time graph shows Oxford's Boat Race Team's normal training session.
  a) When are they travelling fastest?
  b) How do you know this?
  c) How far do they row in total?
  d) How long does their training session take?
  e) When do they take a break? How long for? How is this shown on the graph?

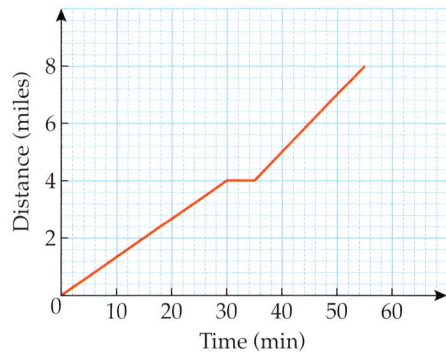

4 The following distance–time graph shows Wasim's Marathon run.
  a) Between which two times does he run fastest?
  b) Between which two times does he run slowest?
  c) Between which two times does he take a break?
  d) How long is the Marathon?
  e) How long does Wasim take to complete the Marathon?

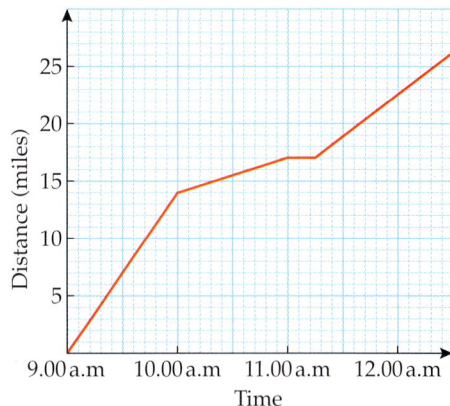

Solving ratio, proportion and percentage problems

- Identify the necessary information to solve a problem
- Use the unitary method to solve simple word problems involving ratio and direct proportion
- Use the equivalence of fractions, decimals and percentages to compare proportions, calculate percentages and find the outcome of a given percentage increase or decrease
- Use proportional reasoning to solve a problem, choosing the correct numbers to take as 100% or a whole

This chapter focuses on problem-solving. In this lesson you will look at the particular **strategies** that help to solve problems involving **ratio** , **proportion** and **percentages** . The questions are challenging, so that you have to focus on problem-solving strategies. You will find it helpful to work in a pair or small group.

Here are some of the strategies you will find useful for solving this type of problem:
1. Highlight the key information.
2. Put this information into a table.
3. Draw diagrams to help illustrate which value represents 100%.
4. If you are stuck, try replacing the numbers with easier ones, and see if you can solve it informally. Then use the same strategy on the real numbers.

Example   The local newspaper reports that accidents have decreased this year by 25%, since traffic-calming measures were introduced. The article states that there were 310 accidents this year. How many accidents were there last year?

100%
Last year

75%
or
310
This year

Now put the information in a table:

This year	Last year
310	?
75%	100%

÷ 75 × 100

$310 ÷ 75 × 100 = 413.33$

There were 413 accidents last year.

First, identify which number represents 100%. It helps to draw a diagram.

Do an estimate: 300 is $\frac{3}{4}$ of 400, so the answer must be just over 400.

Now put the information in a table.

There must have been a whole number of accidents, so round your answer.

Check your answer against your estimate, and by working backwards.

1 A bag of toffees is advertised as being 10% bigger. The new bag has 22 toffees. How many toffees were in the original bag?

2 A computer is advertised at £750.
The price includes a loyalty card discount of 25%.
Kerry does not have a loyalty card.
How much will the computer cost her?

Only £750
(with your 25% loyalty card discount)

3 Here is a recipe for tomato soup:

   500 ml stock
   600 g tomatoes
   2 onions
   100 ml double cream
   Salt and pepper

The recipe serves four people.
List the ingredients you would need to serve nine people.

4

| **Pay $\frac{3}{4}$ of original price** | **20% off** | **0.78 × original price** |

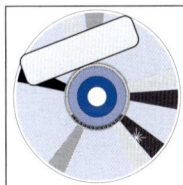

Make up a price for the CD.

   a) How much would you pay with each offer?
   b) What percentage of the original price do you pay with each offer?

€ 1.52 = £ 1
€ 1.00 = £ ?
÷ 1.52

5 Elina and Alexandra are going on holiday to Finland.
   a) They are comparing the cost of flights to Helsinki on the Internet.
   With Jet Air, the return flight costs £135 each. With Finn flights, the return flight costs €215. With the exchange rate £1 is worth €1.52. Which company should they fly with?
   b) They hire a car in Ivalo and drive to Nordkapp, a distance of 350 km. The hire car travels 14 km for every litre of petrol. How much petrol will they need to get there and back?
   c) Petrol costs €1.25 per litre. How much will the trip cost in Euros?

Solving geometrical problems

Key words
adjacent
vertically opposite
corresponding
parallel
alternate

- ⊕ Identify the necessary information to solve a problem
- ⊕ Solve geometrical problems using side and angle properties of equilateral, isosceles and right-angled triangles and special quadrilaterals
- ⊕ Explain and justify your solution clearly and logically

This lesson focuses on proving results about angles. You will need to remember and use the following key facts:

- The angle sum at a point is 360°.
- **Adjacent** angles on a straight line add up to 180°.
- The angle sum of a triangle is 180°.
- **Vertically opposite** angles are equal.

The later problems also use the following facts:

- **Corresponding** angles on **parallel** lines are equal.
- **Alternate** angles on parallel lines are equal.

Strategies that you will find useful include:

1. making a copy of the diagram and marking on what you know.
2. writing in any other angles you can work out, recording the order in which you found them.
3. using your record as a starting point for a proof.

Remember to write down the angle fact that you use to work out each angle.

Remember that the work in this chapter is deliberately challenging so that you focus on the problem-solving strategies. You will find it helps to work in a pair or small group.

Example

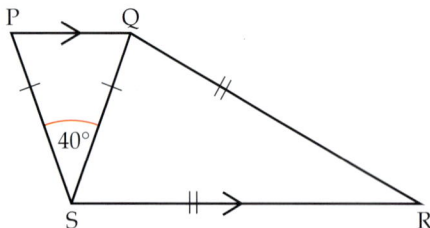

Length SR is equal to length QR.
Length PS is equal to length QS.
Find the size of angle QRS.

$\angle SPQ = \angle SQP$	(triangle SPQ is isosceles)
$\angle SQP = \frac{1}{2}(180° - 40°) = 70°$	(angles in a triangle add up to 180°)
$\angle QSR = 70°$	($\angle QSR$ is alternate to $\angle SQP$)
$\angle SQR = 70°$	(triangle SQR is isosceles)
$\angle QRS = 180° - 70° - 70° = 40°$	(angles in a triangle add up to 180°)

Exercise 12.2

1 Find the size of the angle marked ?.

Diagram not to scale

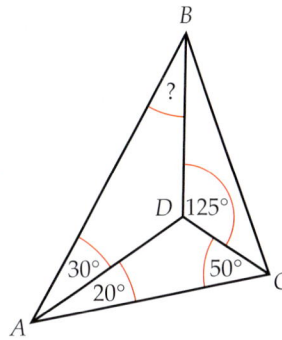

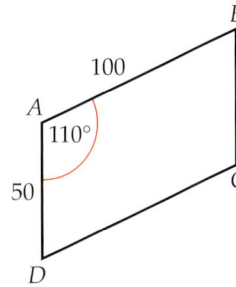

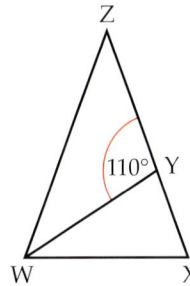

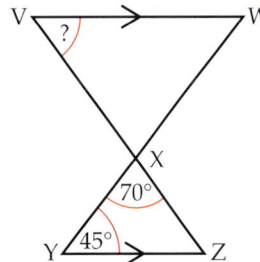

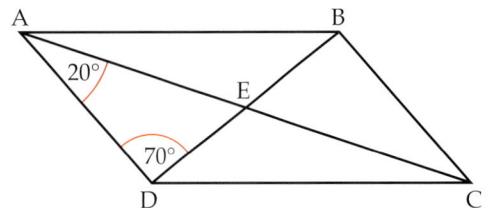

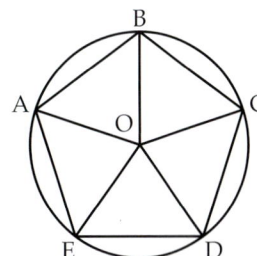

Start by making a sketch of the diagram.

2 Write LOGO instructions to draw this parallelogram.
Begin like this:
Forward 50
Right …
Explain how you worked out the angles.
Check that your instructions work!

Diagram not to scale

You will need to work out the other angles first. What can you remember about the angles in a parallelogram?

3 Length ZW is equal to length ZX.
Length WY is equal to length WX.
Find the size of angle WZX.

Diagram not to scale

4 Find the size of the angle marked ?.

Diagram not to scale

5 Quadrilateral ABCD is a parallelogram.
Find the size of angle ABE.

Diagram not to scale

6 ABCDE is a regular pentagon.
O is the centre of the circle.
Calculate the interior angle ABC.

Diagram not to scale

- Identify the necessary information to solve a problem
- Solve harder problems and evaluate solutions
- Represent problems and information in algebraic, geometric or graphical form
- Explain solutions clearly and logically, using symbols, graphs and text

In this lesson you will have a mixture of problems to solve. You may want to use some or all of the following **strategies** to help:

1. Highlight the important words and figures.
2. List what you know and what you need to know.
3. Draw a diagram.
4. Draw a graph.

The problems are quite demanding, so you will want to work as a pair or small group. Keep a record of the strategies that you use, and explain your solution clearly.

Example   Martin is landscaping his garden. He wants to cut down a tall tree. He needs to know if there is space in the garden to fell the tree, so he needs to know its height. He uses shadows to help. The shadow of the tree is 1.3 m long. The shadow of a cane 0.8 m high is 20 cm. Work out the height of the tree.

Drawing a diagram helps you to understand the situation.

Convert all the lengths to the same units.

	Height of object	Length of shadow
Cane:	0.8	0.2
Tree:	?	1.3

multiplier = 4

Height of tree = 1.3 × 4 = 5.2 m

Calculate the multiplier: 0.8 ÷ 0.2

Exercise 12.3

1 Kevin can earn £20 an hour overtime in his office job.

Cutting his hedge at home would take him 3 hours.

He could employ a gardener to do this for him.

The gardener charges £25 an hour, but would take only 2 hours to cut the hedge. Should Kevin cut the hedge himself, or work overtime and pay a gardener to do it?

2 Martin is working in his garden.
He has the following area which he wants to turf:

The diagram is drawn to a scale of 2 cm to 1 m.
Take any measurements you need to in order to calculate, to a sensible degree of accuracy, how much turf he needs. Draw a sketch to illustrate your calculations.

Turf costs £3.25 per square metre. How much will it cost him to buy the turf?

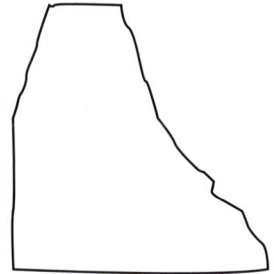

You could use tracing paper to copy the diagram.

3 Carla is designing paving patterns.
Here are the first three in the sequence:

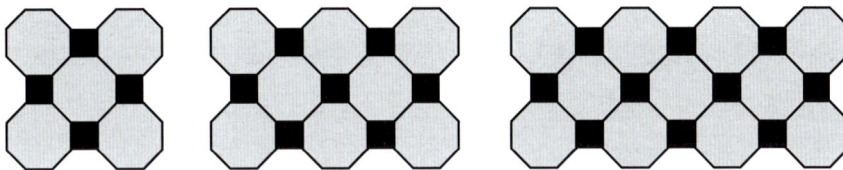

a) i) How many grey slabs will she need for the 10th pattern?

ii) How many black slabs will she need for the 10th pattern?

b) How many of each colour slab will she need for the 100th pattern?

c) Explain how to work out how many slabs she will need. Use algebra if you can.

4 Peter works in a shop selling mobile phones. He needs to advise customers about which phone to buy. For example, Mrs Round uses her mobile only for emergencies, but Miss Lim uses hers all the time to chat to her friends.

Organise the information about tariffs below so that Peter can advise customers quickly and easily.

Purple: No monthly charge; 40p per minute

P_3:   £15 per month; 15p per minute

Two to Two: £25 per month including 20 free minutes; 10p per minute

Multistep problems

- Identify the necessary information to solve a problem
- Solve harder problems and evaluate solutions
- Solve substantial problems by breaking them down into simpler tasks
- Represent problems and information in algebraic, geometric or graphical form
- Explain solutions clearly and logically, using symbols, graphs and text

The problems in this section are longer and more complex, but the mathematics that you need is no harder. Extra strategies that you will find helpful are:

1. Break the problem down into small tasks.
2. Work **systematically** .

You will have to do some rough working. Keep this, and record on it the problem-solving strategies that you used. Then write up a clear solution with enough explanation and working to show that it is correct.

Example

a) The cross-section of a ramp has an area of 2.85 m². Work out the horizontal length of the ramp needed to lift a wheelchair 1 metre.

b) How much concrete will be needed to make the ramp? You will need to make some assumptions to answer this question. State them clearly, with reasons.

a) First, we need to draw a diagram to show what we already know:

$$\text{Area of a triangle} = \frac{1}{2} \times \text{base} \times \text{height}$$
$$2.85 = \frac{1}{2} \times x \times 1$$

Use x to represent the unknown length.

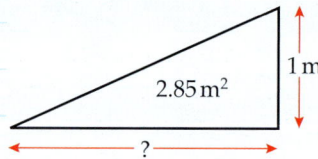

$$= \frac{1}{2}x$$
$$5.7\,\text{m} = x$$

b) Again, drawing a diagram will help to visualise the problem:

$$\text{Volume} = \text{area of cross-section} \times \text{width}$$

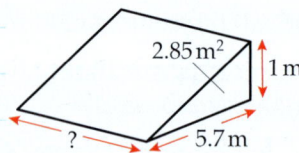

To work out the width of the ramp:

First consider how wide a wheelchair is. If you don't have a wheelchair around you can estimate by measuring the width of a chair, and adding on an extra piece for the wheels. A standard chair might be approximately 50 cm across. Allowing 15 cm on either side for the wheels gives a good safety margin.

Next, estimate how much room is needed on either side of the wheelchair to be
sure there is no danger of anyone falling off the ramp. 20 cm is a good estimate.
So the total width needed is:

$$50\,cm + 2 \times 15\,cm + 2 \times 20\,cm = 120\,cm$$

Convert this into metres as we have the area of the cross-section in metres:

$$120\,cm = 1.2\,m$$

Volume = area of cross-section × width

$$= 5.7\,m^2 \times 1.2\,m$$

$$= 6.84\,m^3$$

$6.84\,m^3$ of concrete is needed.

Exercise 12.4

1 Aaron is saving to buy a new car. He saves £200 per month. The interest rate is 0.4% per
month. If he keeps the interest in the account, how much will he have saved by the end of
the year?

2 Kerry is decorating her bedroom. The room is 3.8 metres by
2.9 metres. There is one door, and a window 1.2 metres square.
1 tin of the paint she has chosen covers 3 square metres.
How many tins of paint does she need?

> You will need to make some
> assumptions to answer this
> question: state them clearly.

3 Martin needs to make an accurate plan of his garden
so that he can work on a new design. He has drawn
a sketch and marked on the measurements.
Draw an accurate diagram, using compasses where
necessary. You will need to choose and state an
appropriate scale.

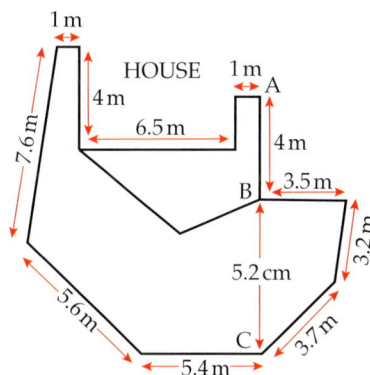

4 Carl runs a greengrocer's stall in the market. He buys 50 kg of bananas at £2.57 a kg, and
40 kg of tomatoes at £2.05 a kg.
He sells the bananas at a very small profit, at only £2.60 a kg, to attract people to his stall.
He needs to make £30 profit altogether.
How much does he need to charge for the tomatoes?

5 Zoë is making a birthday
cake using this recipe:
The recipe is for an 8 inch
square tin, but she wants
to make it in a tin
12 inches by 9 inches.
Work out the list of ingredients that she needs.

225g plain white flour	225g sultanas
10 ml mixed spice	1 medium egg, beaten
5 ml bicarbonate of soda	about 300 ml milk
175g butter or block margarine	10 sugar cubes (optional)
225g soft brown sugar	

12.5 Extended problems

◈ Solve substantial problems by breaking them down into simpler tasks

◈ Use trial and improvement to solve problems

◈ Represent problems and information in algebraic, geometric or graphical form

◈ Explain solutions clearly and logically, using symbols, graphs and text

◈ Suggest extensions to problems, conjecture and generalise

This section should take you two (or more) lessons. You will have the chance to spend longer on a problem and to ask and answer your own related questions. You are not expected to try all the questions. If you think you can predict the answer to a question, this is called a **conjecture** . You will then need to show that your conjecture is in fact correct. When you are working on extended problems, you will be assessed on the problem-solving strategies that you try, not just on the final solution. You should write up everything you try out, even if it doesn't work, so that your teacher can see how you tackled the problem.

Example   Take three consecutive numbers. Add them together.
Repeat for other sets of three consecutive numbers.
Look at your numbers. What do you notice?

Solving the problem

Start by collecting some results.

1 + 2 + 3 = 6

2 + 3 + 4 = 9

3 + 4 + 5 = 12

Already we can see that the numbers are going up in threes. In fact, they are all multiples of 3.

Be **systematic** about collecting your results.

Conjecture:

The sum of 3 consecutive numbers is a multiple of 3.

Check:

We will check our conjecture with a few more sums:

4 + 5 + 6 = 15

5 + 6 + 7 = 18

The conjecture seems to be correct, so we need to find out why.

Explanation

There is a balance in our sums. If we take one off the last number and add it to the first, we get three numbers the same. Adding three numbers the same is equivalent to multiplying one of the numbers by three, so we will get a multiple of 3.

Using algebra
To use algebra, we need to give the numbers names.
Lets call the middle number n.
The number before it is one less than n, so it is $n - 1$.
The number after it is one more than n, so it is $n + 1$.
The sum is $(n - 1) + n + (n + 1) = 3n - 1 + 1 = 3n$.
$3n$ is a multiple of 3.
Further ideas
What would have happened if we had called the first number n?
What would happen if we added four consecutive numbers together, or five consecutive numbers?

Exercise 12.5

1 In Exercise 12.1 you worked out ingredients for a recipe for nine people.
Prepare a spreadsheet that will calculate the ingredients for the recipe for any number of people.
Try to make your spreadsheet as easy to use as possible.

2 A game at a fair involves throwing two dice. You pay 10p to throw the dice. You win 50p if you get a double. Is the game worth playing? Design your own game, explaining clearly how much profit you expect to make.

3 Cardboard boxes are made from a single sheet of thick cardboard and fixed with tape. The cardboard measures 40 cm by 28 cm. It is cut and folded as shown:

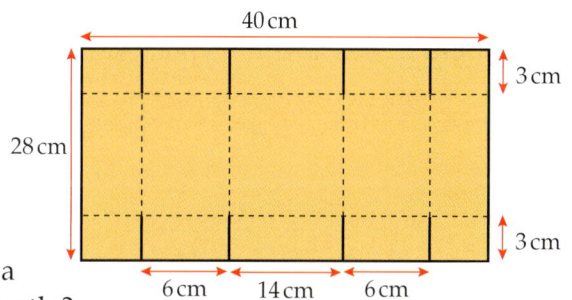

What is the volume of the box?

Using the same piece of card, can you make a box with a larger volume by folding it differently?

4 Ryan's company makes wire grids in different sizes. The small squares are always 10 cm by 10 cm. How much wire does he need to make a grid

   a) 3 squares by 3 squares

   b) 5 squares by 5 squares

   c) 9 squares by 9 squares.

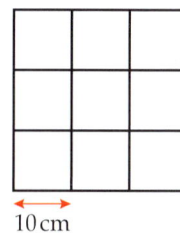

Work out a rule that Ryan can use to work out how much wire he needs for different sized grids. Use algebra if you can.

5 Investigate the 'Further ideas' in the Example.

Planning an investigation 2

⊕ Design a survey or experiment

⊕ Design, trial and refine data collection sheets

Key words
primary source
secondary source
sample size
continuous data

Evaluate results → **Specify the problem and plan** → **Collect data from a variety of sources** → **Process and represent data** → **Interpret and discuss data** → Evaluate results

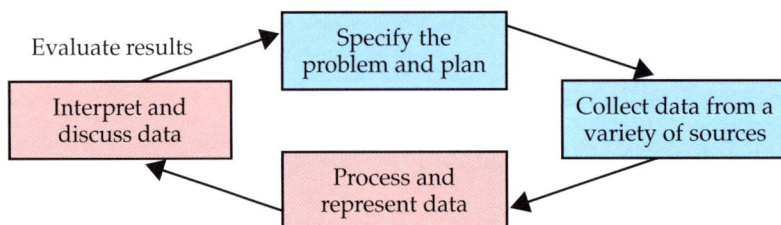

When you plan your project, decide whether to collect the data yourself (from **primary sources**) or use **secondary sources**, such as books or newspapers. Decide on your **sample size**, that is, the number of experiments you will do or the number of people taking part in a survey, and justify your decision.

In the examples below, and in the rest of Unit 13, we will look at how two students (Siobhan and Ron) investigate reaction times for catching a ruler.

Example 1   Siobhan's hypothesis and plan.

Practising catching a ruler several times helps reduce the reaction time when catching a ruler.

Hold a ruler touching a person's open hand and instruct them to catch it as soon as it is released. Release the ruler and record the measurement immediately above the index finger to the nearest mm. Repeat. Ask subjects to practise this 10 times, then repeat the test one more time.

Do this with a sample size of 15 people.

Data collection sheet

Name	Trial 1 (mm)	Trial 2 (mm)	Trial 3 (mm)

Ask a friend to trial the data collection sheet to make sure the instructions are OK.

Siobhan's hypothesis can be tested to see if it is right or wrong.

Siobhan's instructions are clear and she has said what sample size she will use. She can make changes if her trial is not successful.

This is **continuous data** – data found by measuring.

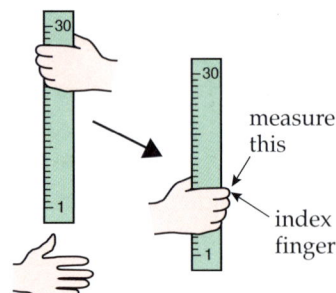

measure this

index finger

Example 2   Ron's hypothesis and plan.

Practising catching a ruler – people will get faster.

My plan:

Get three friends to practise catching a ruler, then see what

distance it measures for each of their tries.

Ron's hypothesis is too vague – he has not said what he is trying to find out.

Ron's instructions are not clear enough, and his sample size is too small.

Exercise 13.1

Choose one of the investigations below. Write a hypothesis and a plan.

1. What is the 'average' size of people's clothes?

2. Investigate the number of times a popular news item is talked about in different newspapers or other media.

3. Investigate how accurate people are at estimating the size of angles or weights.

4. Are more goals scored 'at home' than 'away' in football?

5. Which CDs or magazines should the school library stock?

6. Compare the weather in two different parts of the country.

7. Plan a questionnaire looking at a local or school issue, e.g. vandalism or facilities for young people.

8. In 2004, Cambridge won the annual University Boat Race. Are they the better team? Investigate. (Ask your teacher for the data sheet about the finishing times for the University Boat Race.)

9. Investigate primary and secondary school pupils' journeys to school. (Ask your teacher for the data sheet about travel to school in Scotland.)

Your teacher may allow you to choose your own investigation to explore.

Include in your plan how you will collect the data (is it from a primary or secondary source?), how much data you will collect, where you will collect the data, and anything else you think is important.

Design a data collection sheet for your investigation.

Carry out your investigation.

Processing data 2

⊕ Calculate the summary statistics
⊕ Group data into appropriate classes
⊕ Construct stem-and-leaf diagrams

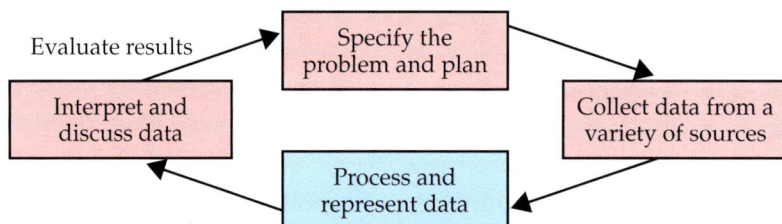

```
            Evaluate results          ┌─────────────────┐
                              ←──────  │  Specify the    │
                                       │ problem and plan│
         ┌─────────────────┐          └─────────────────┘
         │ Interpret and   │                                 ┌──────────────────┐
         │ discuss data    │                                 │ Collect data from a│
         └─────────────────┘          ┌─────────────────┐   │ variety of sources │
                                       │  Process and    │   └──────────────────┘
                              ←──────  │ represent data  │  ──────→
                                       └─────────────────┘
```

When you have collected your data, the next stage of the data handling cycle is processing and representing your data.

This involves putting your data into a useful format and then calculating the ==**summary statistics**== .

Not all investigations require the same statistical calculations. Sometimes it is not necessary to calculate all averages, especially if the data is already grouped.

You will not get a higher mark or grade simply by using a skill that is not needed for your investigation. You must only use skills appropriate to the investigation.

Example   Siobhan has entered her data as a two-way table into a spreadsheet.

	A	B	C	D	E	F	G	H	I	J	K	L	M	N	O	P	Q
1																	
2																	
3	Trial 1	5.8	9	3.2	7.8	9.4	8.7	6.7	9.7	8.3	9.8	7.3	8.2	5.3	7.7	8.3	
4	Trial 2	6.1	9.3	4.9	7.8	9.1	8.8	8.2	8.3	8.5	7.5	9.8	7.5	5.9	7.2	7.6	
5	Trial 3	5.2	6.2	4.7	7.2	8.3	8.1	6.0	6.2	7.3	8.3	6.1	7.1	5.2	6.8	6.9	
6																	
7	Sorted data.							median									mean
8	Trial 1	3.2	5.3	5.8	6.7	7.3	7.7	7.8	8.2	8.3	8.3	8.7	9	9.4	9.7	9.8	7.68
9	Trial 2	4.9	5.9	6.1	7.2	7.5	7.5	7.6	7.8	8.2	8.3	8.5	8.8	9.1	9.3	9.8	7.77
10	Trial 3	4.7	5.2	5.2	6	6.1	6.2	6.2	6.8	6.9	7.1	7.2	7.3	8.1	8.3	8.3	6.64

She also groups her data.

Distance caught in (cm)	3 ⩽ Distance < 5	5 ⩽ Distance < 7	7 ⩽ Distance < 9	9 ⩽ Distance < 11
Trial 1	1	3	7	4
Trial 2	1	2	9	3
Trial 3	1	8	6	0

Siobhan groups her data into a new, two-way table before doing calculations.
Her groups are equal size and do not overlap or have gaps.

Siobhan draws three stem-and-leaf diagrams for her data.

Trial 1		Trial 2		Trial 3	
3	2	3		3	
4		4	9	4	7
5	3 8	5	9	5	2 2
6	7	6	1	6	0 1 2 2 8 9
7	3 7 8	7	2 5 5 6 8	7	1 2 3
8	2 3 3 7	8	2 3 5 8	8	1 3 3
9	0 4 7 8	9	1 3 8		

key: stem = cm   leaf = mm

Siobhan is ordering her data before working out averages.

Exercise 13.2

1   A mean can be calculated using a frequency table. Explain why Siobhan cannot do this for her data.

2   Lata is also carrying out the investigation. She has collected her data to the nearest centimetre.

   a)   Copy and complete the frequency table.

Distance caught (cm)	Number of pupils	Distance caught × number of pupils
7	3	21
8	7	
9	8	
10	6	
11	14	
12	10	
	Total number of pupils =	Total distance =

   b)   Using the table, calculate the mean of the distance caught to one decimal place.

3   Helen has also recorded her data to the nearest centimetre. Copy and complete the table to use an assumed mean of 10 cm to calculate the mean.

Distance caught	7	10	12	9	7	14	11	8	11	8
Distance − 10	⁻3									

   Now calculate the mean from this data.

4   If it is appropriate for your investigation you should now draw stem-and-leaf diagrams, calculate summary statistics (averages and range), group the data if it was collected in ungrouped form.

   Remember, you must only use skills that are suitable for your investigation. If you are unsure, ask your teacher for advice.

Representing data 1

⊕ Illustrate data using appropriate diagrams

Key words
hypothesis
pie chart
bar chart
line graph
frequency diagram
compound bar chart

Evaluate results → Specify the problem and plan

Interpret and discuss data

Collect data from a variety of sources

Process and represent data

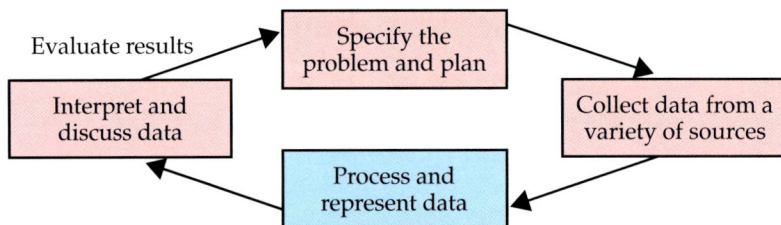

When drawing diagrams, think about the following points:

  i) Will the diagram help to test the **hypothesis**?
  ii) Is there a title and are the axes numbered and labelled?

Which diagram is suitable?

Pie chart: categorical data. It should have at least three sectors, but not too many.

Bar chart/line graph: usually discrete data, which may be grouped.

Frequency diagram: usually grouped, continuous data.

Compound bar chart or frequency diagram: useful for comparing two or more distributions.

If two or more frequency diagrams are to be used to compare data, use the same scales on both axes to help the comparison.

Example   Siobhan draws three different diagrams to show her data.

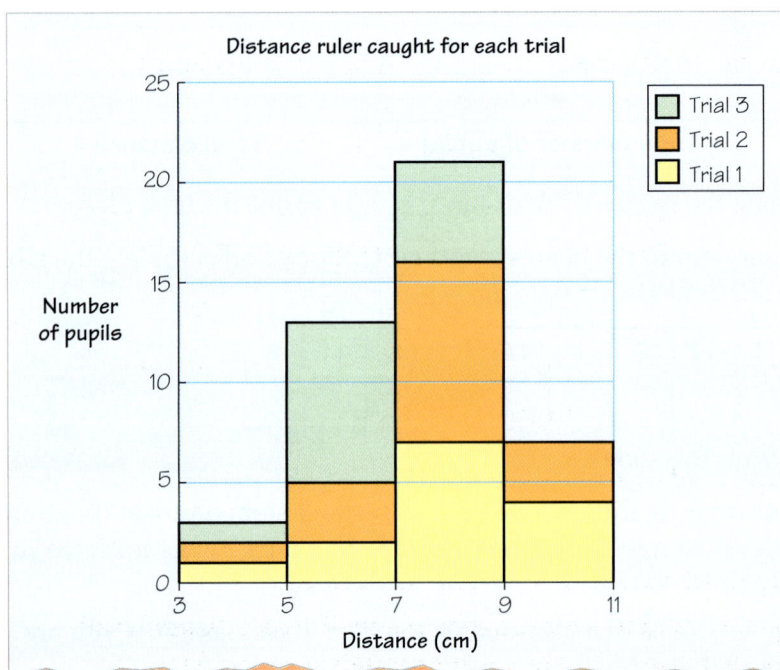

Distance ruler caught for each trial

Siobhan draws a compound bar chart to show the spread of her grouped data.

Siobhan has included a title, a key, and has labelled her axes correctly.

The diagram makes it easy to compare the three trials on the same axis at a glance.

She draws a pie chart.

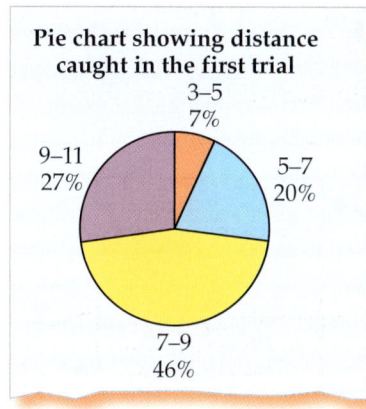

Pie chart showing distance caught in the first trial

3–5
7%

9–11
27%

5–7
20%

7–9
46%

A pie chart is not the most suitable diagram to show this type of data.

She also draws a bar chart.

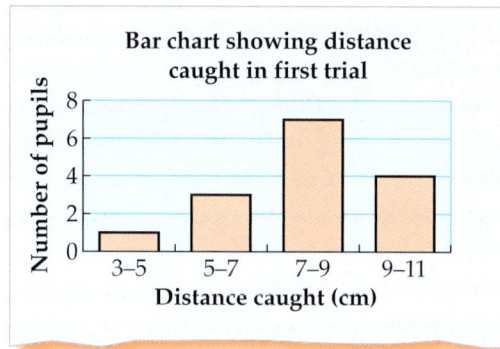

Bar chart showing distance caught in first trial

Number of pupils

Distance caught (cm)

3–5   5–7   7–9   9–11

Bar charts should be used for discrete data, but the distance caught is continuous data.

Exercise 13.3

1 Use the compound frequency diagram in the Example to draw three separate frequency diagrams for Siobhan's data.

2 Another pupil draws two frequency diagrams for the first two trials in the investigation.

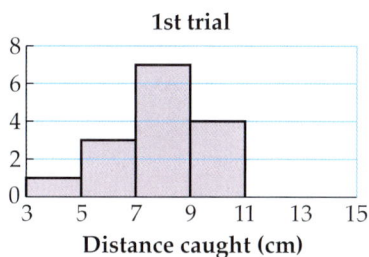

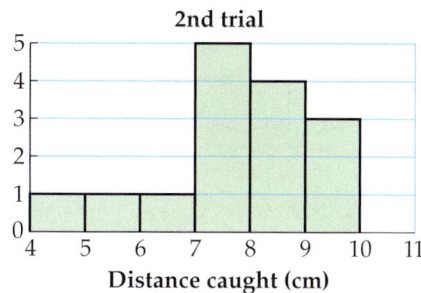

1st trial

Distance caught (cm)

2nd trial

Distance caught (cm)

What mistakes has the pupil made with the diagrams?

3 Draw suitable diagrams to illustrate the data you have collected.

Remember, you will not get extra marks for drawing many different diagrams all showing the same thing or diagrams that are not appropriate for your data.

⊕ Interpret data

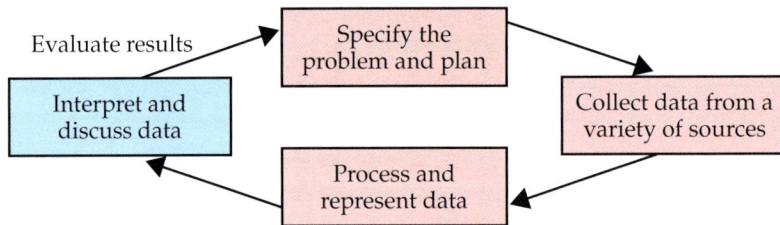

You must include a written explanation or **interpretation** with your diagrams to show what they mean. Always communicate clearly – write your report so that it can be understood by someone who has not been in your class or seen your working.

For example, in an investigation comparing the times that boys and girls take to run 100 metres, writing "The boys' smaller mean and median shows that boys are faster runners than girls" will get higher marks than "The mean and median for the boys are smaller than the girls".

Example   Siobhan's data.

	Mean	Median	Range
Trial 1	7.68	8.2	6.6
Trial 2	7.77	7.8	4.9
Trial 3	6.64	6.8	3.6

Siobhan has put her **summary statistics** (e.g. mode, mean and median) into a table. She uses them to decide if her original hypothesis that 'practising catching a ruler several times will reduce the reaction time' is correct or not.

There is not enough evidence to support the hypothesis that there is an improvement between trials 1 and 2, as the mean for trial 2 increases slightly, showing that people's times were slower. However, the median decreases, showing that people's times were faster. This is not surprising as these were the first two attempts by the people who took part in the experiment.

She discusses her hypothesis, using the evidence she has found.

The averages for trial 3 show that there was an improvement in the ability of people to catch the ruler as both the averages are smaller.

The range for trial 3 is smaller than the ranges for trials 1 and 2, showing that there was greater variation in people's reaction times in the earlier trials.

Distance caught in cm (D)	3 ≤ D < 5	5 ≤ D < 7	7 ≤ D < 9	9 ≤ D < 11
Trial 1	1	3	7	4
Trial 2	1	2	9	3
Trial 3	1	8	6	0

When I group my data, this again supports the hypothesis that people will improve their ability to catch the ruler with practice.

Both trials 1 and 2 have a modal class of 7 ≤ Distance caught < 9, but in trial 3, the modal class has decreased to 5 ≤ Distance caught < 7.

Siobhan explains what her statements mean. She could have added that this difference in modal class implies that the slower people gained most from the practice.

Exercise 13.4

1 Steve has also carried out the investigation.

His hypothesis was that there would be no difference in the ability of boys and girls to catch the ruler.

Here are his statistics.

	Mean	Mode	Median	Range
Boys	9.64	8.2	9.4	8.1
Girls	7.01	No mode	8.35	5.6

Distance caught in cm (D)	4 ≤ D < 6	6 ≤ D < 8	8 ≤ D < 10	10 ≤ D < 12	12+
Boys	0	8	16	10	6
Girls	5	14	21	0	0

a) There is no mode for the girls. Explain why this is possible.

b) Compare the averages for boys and girls. Do they show a difference between them?

c) The boys have a larger range. What does this show?

d) What is the modal class for
  i) boys?   ii) girls?

e) Does the grouped data show that the boys caught the ruler on the whole in a shorter or greater distance than the girls?

f) Is Steve's hypothesis true or false? Explain your answer.

2 Look at the statistics you have calculated and diagrams you have drawn for your own investigation. Explain carefully what each of them means. Remember to link what you are writing back to your original hypothesis or starting point.

Writing your report

⊕ Communicate interpretations and results of a statistical enquiry using selected tables, graphs and diagrams in support, using ICT as appropriate

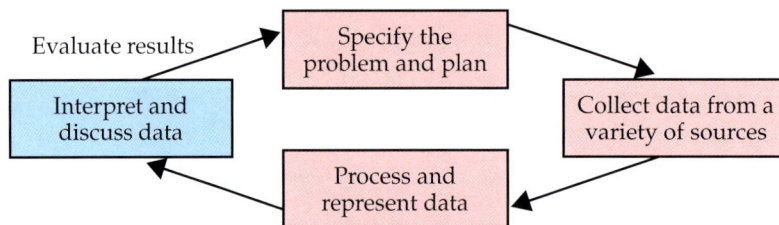

Key words
hypothesis
sample size
analysis
evidence

Evaluate results → Specify the problem and plan → Collect data from a variety of sources → Process and represent data → Interpret and discuss data → (Specify the problem and plan)

When you have finished your investigation, bring together all the information in your report. Your report should enable anyone to understand what you have done and why, without knowing anything about it previously.

Check that you have included the following in your report:

Introduction
Project title
An explanation of the problem
Your **hypothesis**

Planning
What information you needed
The **sample size** (amount of data collected)
Explanation of why you chose to collect this amount of data
What special equipment was needed

Collection of the data
How you collected the data
Where the data was collected
The accuracy of your data (e.g. nearest cm) and an explanation of why you chose this

Processing and representing the data
Any necessary calculations
Relevant diagrams (with an explanation as to why a particular diagram was appropriate)
Tables of results

Interpreting and discussing the data
A link from your **analysis** back to your original hypothesis
Evidence that backs up any statement that you make

Remember:
Make sure your project can be easily understood. Is there enough explanation?

You will not get extra marks or a higher level by including diagrams or statistics that are not relevant to your project.

Example   This is the beginning of Siobhan's report.

Ruler Catching Investigation

A ruler is held at arm's length in front of a person and dropped. The person must catch the ruler as quickly as possible, and the distance the ruler has dropped before being caught is measured.

My hypothesis is that people's reaction time to catch the ruler will improve with practice.

The information I need to collect is about each person (age, boy/girl, class) and the distance they catch the ruler each time. I need to collect information about each person so I can talk to him or her again if I need to, and also I may have time to look for differences between different ages, etc.

I will ask each person to perform the experiment twice without practice, and record the results. They will then be able to practise more times. I will then perform the experiment one more time, again recording the result. I do not expect any improvement between the first and second times that each person catches the ruler.

I will ask 15 people as my sample size, which gives me 45 results in total. I have chosen this as my sample size as I think a smaller number will not give me very reliable results. Choosing a bigger sample size will mean that I have a lot of data and it will take a long time to analyse.

The only equipment I need is a ruler, marked in cm and mm. I will record my measurements to the nearest millimetre. This means that I can round each one to the nearest centimetre later on if I want to.

She explains clearly what her investigation is about.

She explains how she will carry out her investigation.

Exercise 13.5

Write a report explaining your investigation.

Use the checklist opposite to help you include important information.

13.6 Evaluating your investigation

◈ Evaluate an investigation

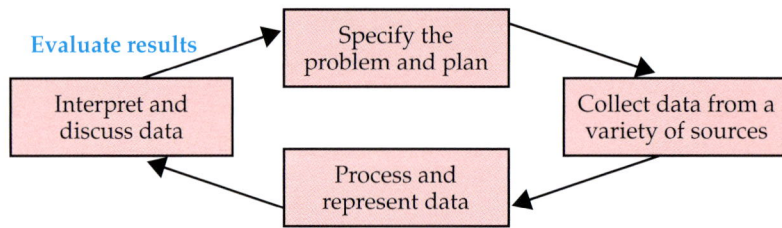

The data handling cycle is continuous. You need to evaluate your investigation and write down how you would improve it, or extend it, if you had more time.

Points to include in your evaluation

Are my results fair?

Is the data representative of all the possible information I could have chosen?

Were there any problems with the data?

How did I solve these problems (e.g. data that did not seem to fit in with the rest)?

How could I continue or extend my investigation?

If I was doing the investigation again, what changes would I make to my original plan?

Example 1   Siobhan's evaluation.

I think that my sample size was too small and so may not be representative of everybody.

If I were to repeat the investigation, I would increase the number of people I asked to 25 or 30.

She says how she could improve her investigation.

To extend the investigation, I would try to find out if other factors were important in people's ability to catch a ruler. For example, are girls better than boys?

She includes a number of ideas about how to extend or continue her investigation.

Looking to see if there is a relationship between people's ability to catch the ruler with their writing hand and their other hand would mean that I could look at a connection between these two results.

One person kept missing the ruler altogether, so I decided not to include her results in my investigation as I would either need a longer ruler or her very big distance would affect my calculations.

Example 2 Ron's evaluation.

> I really enjoyed this investigation. It was very interesting. If I
> were to do it again, I would choose some other people to do
> it, as my friends are really good at catching rulers now, so it
> wouldn't be fair. I would record more of their results, so I
> would have more data to look at.

This is not what *evaluating your investigation* means!

Exercise 13.6

❶ Complete your report with an evaluation of your work.
Use Siobhan's evaluation to help you.

❷ In her evaluation, Siobhan suggested that she could extend her investigation by looking at reaction times of boys and girls. Write down three other ideas for extending her evaluation.

❸ Why do you think Siobhan decided not to use a longer ruler for one of the people in her experiment?

❷ Look back at Steve's results on page 177 – suggest some points he could have included in his evaluation.

Cuboids

⊕ Be able to describe properties of cuboids and shapes made from cuboids
⊕ Be able to use plans and elevations

Key words
face
vertex
edge
plan view
front elevation
side elevation

A cuboid has 6 **faces**, 8 **vertices** and 12 **edges**.

Vertices is used when we talk about more than one **vertex**.

Face   Vertex

Edge

The **plan view** of this cuboid is a rectangle as seen looking down on the shape from above.

Plan view

The **front elevation** is a square as seen from the direction shown here:

Front elevation

The **side elevation** is a rectangle as seen from the direction shown here:

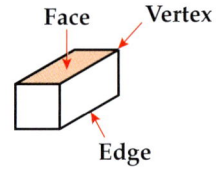

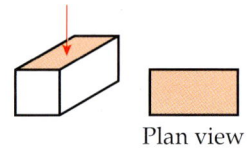

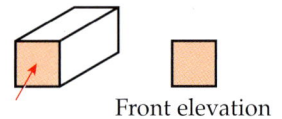

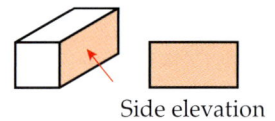

Side elevation

Example   a) How many faces, vertices and edges has the shape in the diagram?

b) Draw the plan view, front elevation and side elevation of the shape.

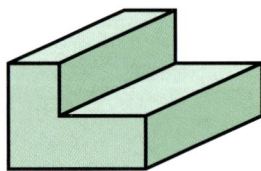

a) 8 faces, 12 vertices and 18 edges.

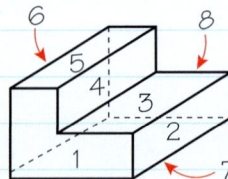

Labelling the faces make them easier to count.

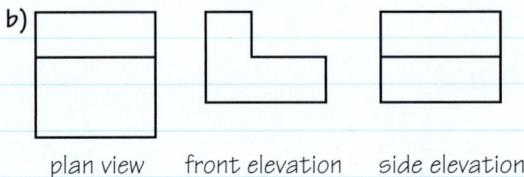

b)

plan view   front elevation   side elevation

Exercise 14.1

1 Make a copy of the diagram.
   a) On your copy colour two edges that are parallel in red.
   b) Colour two edges that are perpendicular in blue.

   > Perpendicular means at right angles.

   c) Colour two edges that are neither parallel nor intersect each other in green.

   > Parallel means lines that go in the same direction and never meet.

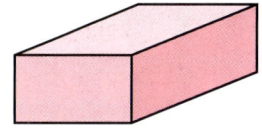

2 Look carefully at this cuboid.
   The faces that are opposite each other are the same colour.
   a) How many edges occur where a red face meets a blue face?
   b) How many edges occur where a red face meets another red face?
   c) How many edges occur where a blue face meets another blue face?

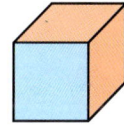

3 The diagram shows a Rubik's Cube with faces coloured red, blue, green (hidden), yellow, orange and white. It is made up with 27 small cubes.
   a) How many small cubes have three faces with different colours?
   b) How many small cubes have two faces with different colours?
   c) How many small cubes have only one face coloured?
   d) How many of the small cubes have no faces coloured?

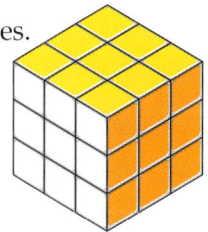

4 Draw the plan view, front elevation and side elevation of this shape.

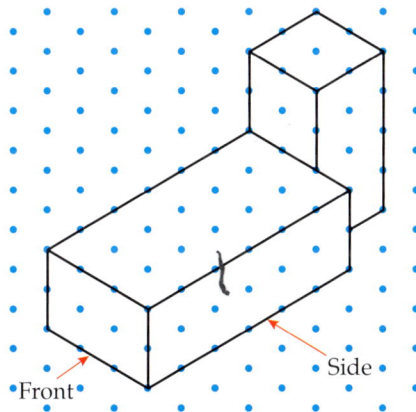

Side

Front

5 Here is the plan view, front elevation and side elevation of a shape. Draw a sketch of the shape.

plan   front   side view

6 Here are three views of the same cube.
   Which colours are opposite each other?

2-D representations of 3-D objects

Key words
cross-section

⊕ Be able to visualise and use 2-D representations of 3-D objects
⊕ Be able to analyse 3-D shapes through 2-D projections

This is a plan view of a solid shape.

The shape could be a cube or a cuboid.

A cube and a cuboid could be placed on an overhead projector to show the plan view is a square.

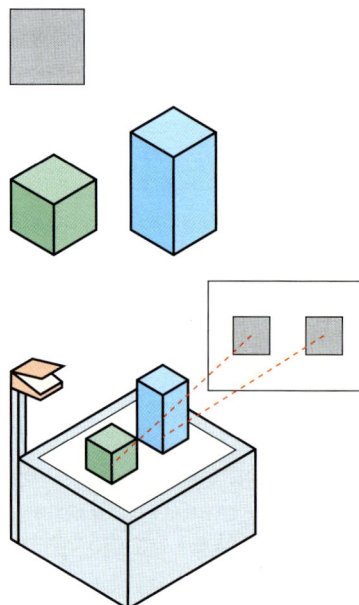

A **cross-section** of both the cube and the cuboid is a square.

The cuboid also has a rectangular cross-section. This rectangular outline is the same shape as the plan view of the shape.

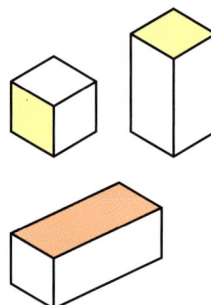

Example 1 The diagram shows two different views of the same shape.

a) Draw a possible shape on isometric paper.
b) Draw another possible shape on isometric paper.

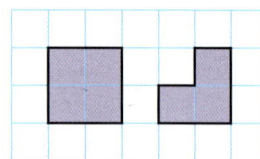

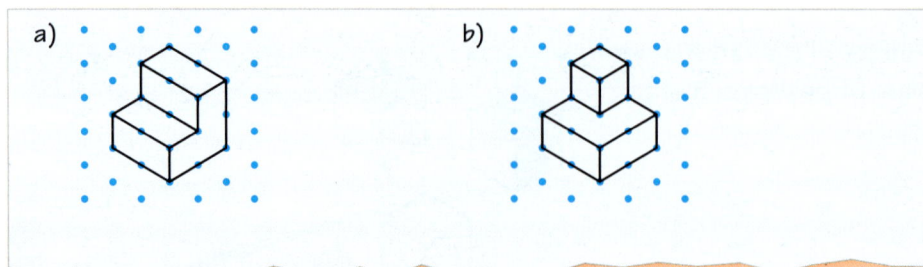

a)

b)

Example 2   The following is the plan view of an object.
Describe the possible objects
(there may be several solutions).

i)   ball (or sphere)

ii)   Ice-cream cone (or cone)

iii)   drinks can (or cylinder)

Exercise 14.2

1 The diagram shows three different views of the
same shape.
Draw a possible shape on isometric paper.
Make your shape with linking cubes to check them.

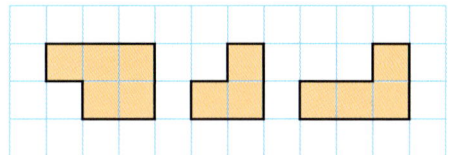

2 The following are views of objects. Describe a possible object for each one (there may be
several solutions).

a)   b)   c)   d)   e)   f)

3 The side view of a roll of sticky tape has the shape of a
rectangle. Draw sketches of five other objects that give a
rectangular side view.

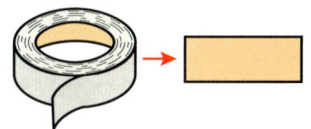

4 A cube casts a shadow. Which of the following are possible shadows of the cube? Which
are impossible?

a)   b)   c)   d)   e)

5 Make a cuboid with two linking cubes as shown in the diagram.
Discover what shapes can be seen from different views of this cuboid.
Draw each view that you find.

3-D reflection symmetry

⊕ Be able to identify reflection symmetry in 3-D shapes

A **plane** is a flat surface.

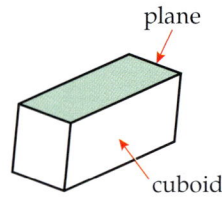

plane

cuboid

A cuboid has 3 planes of reflection symmetry.

Think of the **plane of symmetry** as a mirror. The mirror cuts the 3-D shape into half so that each half of the shape is a reflection of the other.

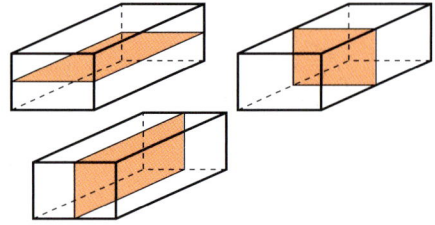

A **cross-section** is the surface made by slicing through a 3-D object.

By slicing a cube in different planes, we can create different shaped cross-sections.

Cross-section

Slicing the corner off this cube gives a triangular cross-section.

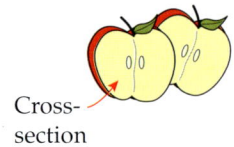

Example   Copy this shape and draw the planes of symmetry.

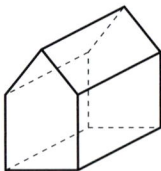

Draw each plane on a separate diagram.

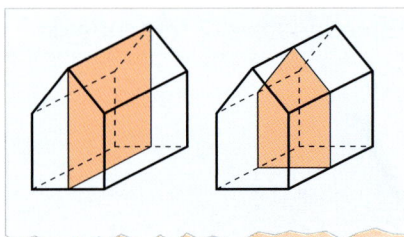

Exercise 14.3

1 The drawings show half a 3-D solid. Copy and complete each solid so that the shaded face forms a plane of symmetry.

a) 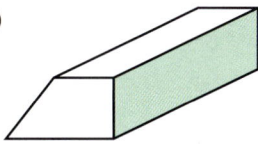 **b)** 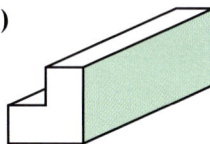 **c)**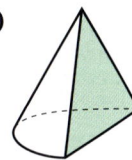

2 Use tracing paper to copy these shapes and draw the planes of symmetry. Draw each plane on a separate diagram.

a) 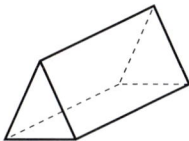 **b)** 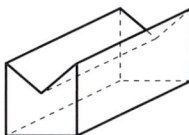 **c)**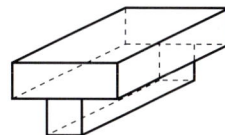

3 Draw some cubes on isometric paper.

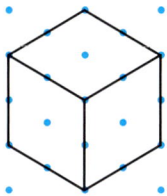

Show how to slice the cube so that the cross-section is:

a) a rectangle

b) an equilateral triangle.

4 Use four cubes to make as many different shapes as possible. Two shapes are shown in the diagram.

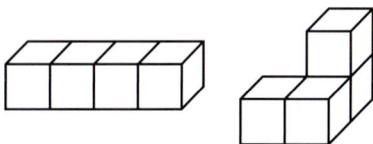

For each shape identify any planes of symmetry.

⊕ Be able to construct and make nets of 3-D shapes

A **net** folds up to make a 3-D shape.

A cuboid has six faces.

This is an example of a net of a cuboid.

The cuboid looks like this:

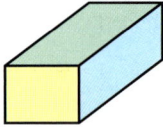

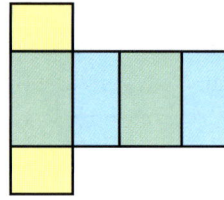

Always draw a sketch before constructing a net.

Example 1 The diagram shows a triangular prism.
Draw the net of the prism.

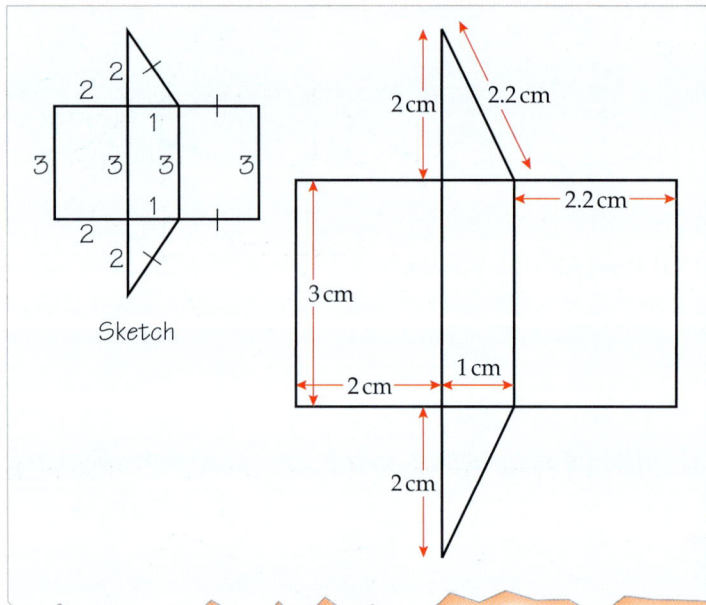

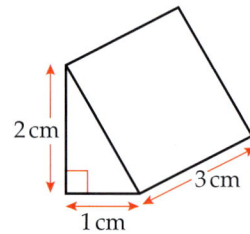

2 cm
3 cm
1 cm

Remember to draw a sketch first.

Sketch

2.2 cm
2 cm
2.2 cm
3 cm
2 cm 1 cm
2 cm

Example 2 The diagram shows a sketch of a net of a square based pyramid.
Draw the pyramid on isometric paper.

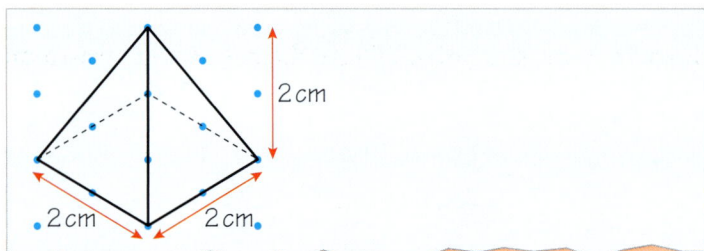

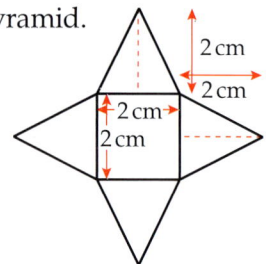

2 cm
2 cm
2 cm

2 cm
2 cm
2 cm

You need 1 cm square paper, plain paper and isometric paper for this exercise. You will also need card, scissors, glue and sticky tape.

1 The diagram shows the sketch of a net of a cuboid. Draw the cuboid on isometric paper and label the width, length and height.

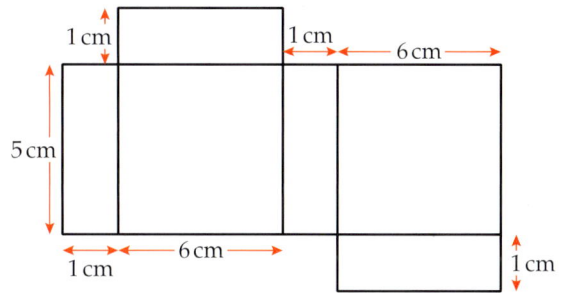

2 On plain paper draw an accurate net of the shape in **Q1**. Stick it to card and cut it out. Fold up the net and use sticky tape to hold it together.

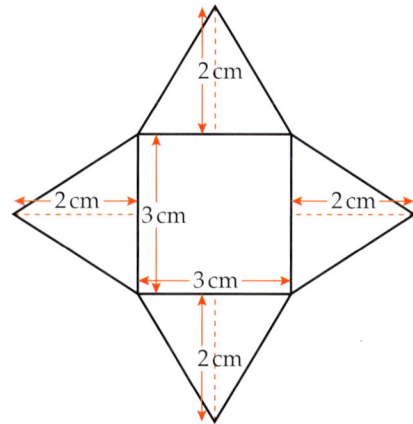

3 Draw an accurate net for this shape on 1 cm square paper. Stick it to card and cut it out. Fold up the net and use sticky tape to hold it together.

4 Choose one of the shapes shown here and draw the net on 1 cm square paper, then make it.

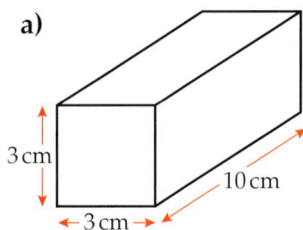

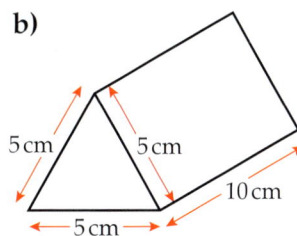

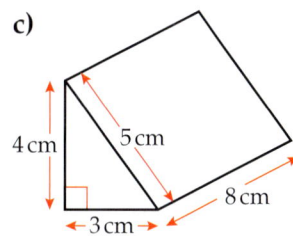

a)

b)

c)

5 Using Clixi and working with a partner, make a prism. Draw the net of your prism on squared paper.

14.5 More nets

◈ Be able to draw a net for a shape made of cubes or cuboids

◈ Be able to draw a sketch of the shape from a net

This is a sketch of a **net** of a cuboid.

The lengths that are needed to make an accurate drawing of the net are marked.

There are six **faces**.

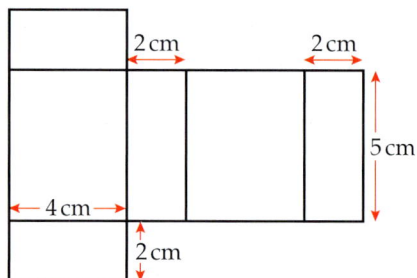

Opposite faces have dimensions:

5 cm by 4 cm

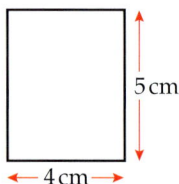

4 cm by 2 cm

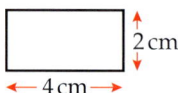

5 cm by 2 cm

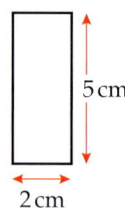

This shows us that the dimensions of the cuboid are 5 cm × 4 cm × 2 cm.

A sketch of the cuboid can now be drawn.

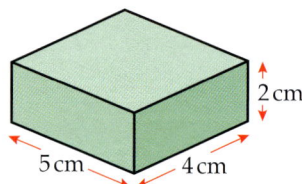

Example   The diagram shows a net of a shape. Draw the shape on isometric paper and label the dimensions.

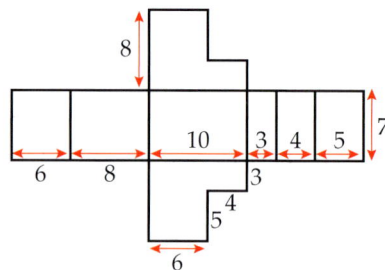

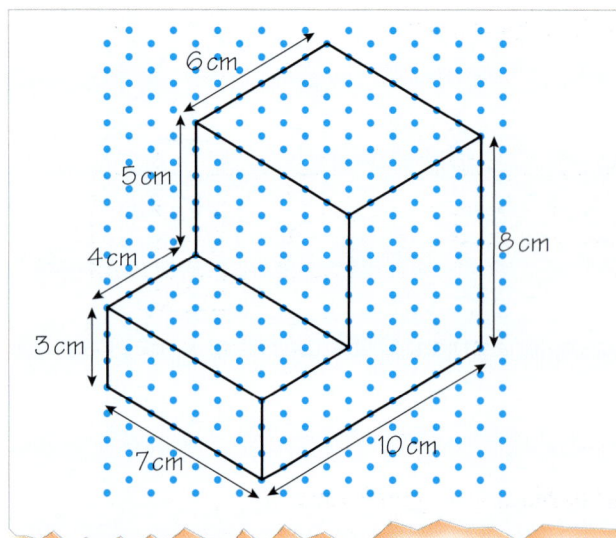

Exercise 14.5

1 Make this shape using Clixi. Open up your shape, keeping each face whole, and draw a sketch of the net for this shape

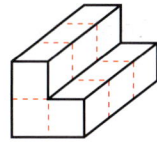

2 Make a shape of your own using Clixi.

    a) Draw a sketch of your shape.

    b) Write down the number of faces, edges and vertices of your shape.

    c) Open up your shape and draw a sketch of the net.

    d) Show by drawing arrows which edges join together.

3 The diagram shows the net of a shape.
Draw the shape on isometric paper and label the dimensions.

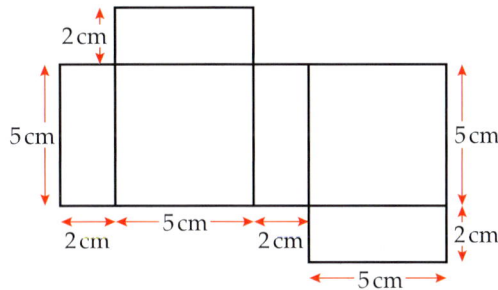

4 The diagram shows a shape and its net.

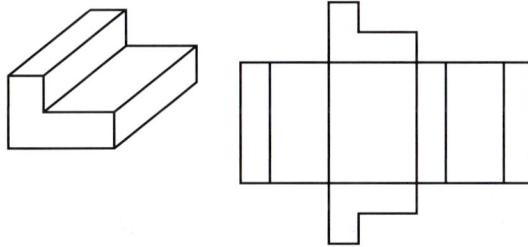

    a) Make a copy of the net. Show, by drawing arrows, which edges join together.

    b) How many faces, edges and vertices has the shape?

5 Peter draws some nets for a cuboid.

    a)   **b)**   **c)**

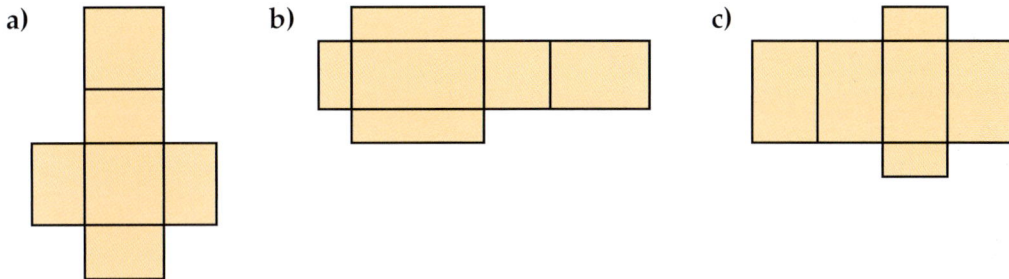

Some will not make a cuboid.
Write which will not make a cuboid and explain how you know.

14.6 Surface area

◈ Be able to calculate the surface area of cuboids and shapes made from cuboids

◈ Be able to solve problems involving volume and surface area

Cubes and cuboids have six faces. The total area of the faces is called the **surface area**.

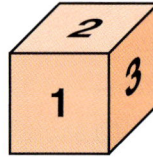

Think of a dice: the faces are numbered from 1 to 6.

Here is a cuboid of width 3 units, length 5 units and height 2 units.

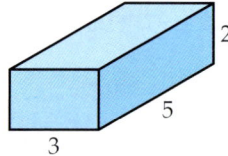

Drawing the **net** of a cuboid shows the area of each face.

The surface area of this cuboid is:

$15 + 10 + 6 + 6 + 15 + 10 = 62$ square units.

Since a cuboid has three pairs of matching faces, you can think of the surface area as:

$2 \times 15 + 2 \times 10 + 2 \times 6$ square units.

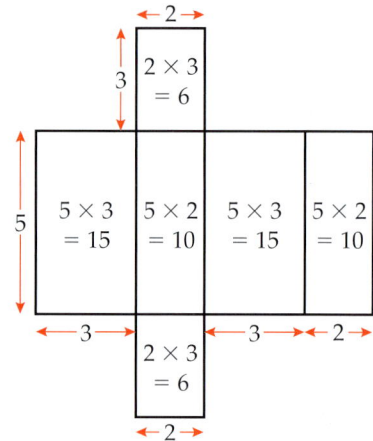

Example   Find the surface area of these shapes:

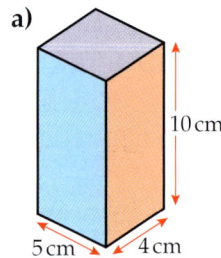

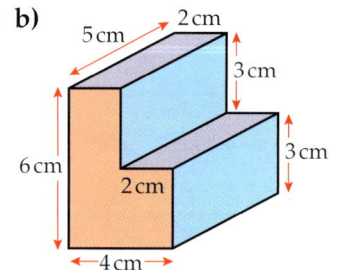

a)

10 cm
5 cm   4 cm

b)

2 cm
5 cm
3 cm
3 cm
6 cm
2 cm
4 cm

a) Area of blue rectangle = $5 \times 10 = 50$ cm²
    Area of red rectangle = $4 \times 10 = 40$ cm²
    Area of purple rectangle = $5 \times 4 = 20$ cm²
    Total surface area = $2 \times 50 + 2 \times 40 + 2 \times 20 = 220$ cm²

b) Area of red face = $6 \times 2 + 3 \times 2 = 18$ cm²
    But there are two of these so the area of 2 red faces = 36 cm²
    Area of 2 blue faces = $5 \times 3 + 5 \times 3 = 30$ cm²
    Area of 2 purple faces = $2 \times 5 + 2 \times 5 = 20$ cm²
    Area of base = $4 \times 5 = 20$ cm²
    Area of back = $6 \times 5 = 30$ cm²
    Total surface area = $36 + 30 + 20 + 20 + 30 = 136$ cm²

You may find it helpful to sketch the different faces of the shape with their dimensions.

Exercise 14.6

1 Calculate the surface area of each of these cuboids.

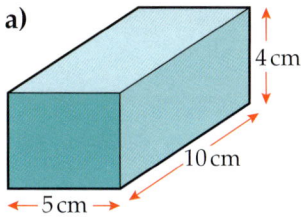

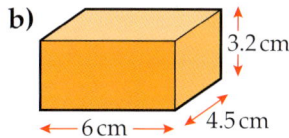

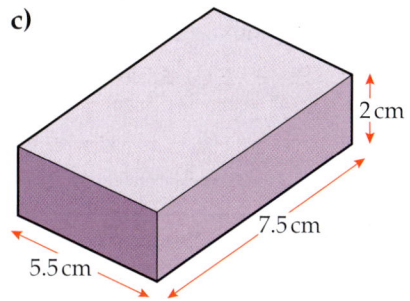

a)

4 cm
10 cm
5 cm

b)

3.2 cm
6 cm
4.5 cm

c)

2 cm
7.5 cm
5.5 cm

2 Calculate the surface area of each of these shapes.

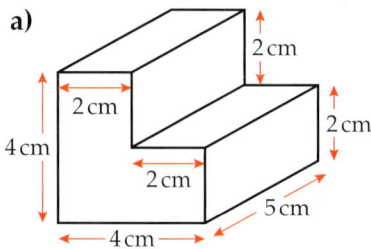

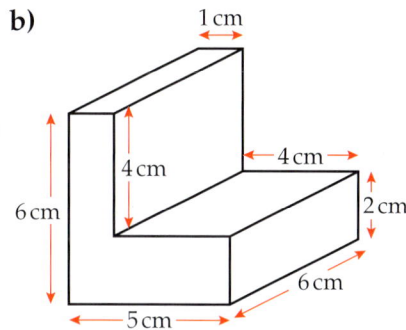

a)

2 cm
2 cm
4 cm
2 cm
2 cm
5 cm
4 cm

b)

1 cm
4 cm
4 cm
6 cm
2 cm
6 cm
5 cm

3 Work out the volume and surface area of this shape.

> Remember the volume of a cuboid is the area of the cross-section multiplied by the length.

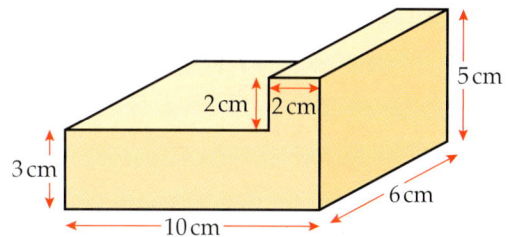

2 cm   2 cm
5 cm
3 cm
6 cm
10 cm

4 A manufacturer wants to design a box with a volume of 24 cm³. Each one of these cuboids has a volume 24 cm³. Which one uses the least amount of card?

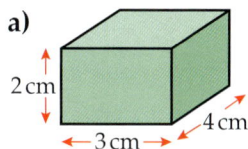

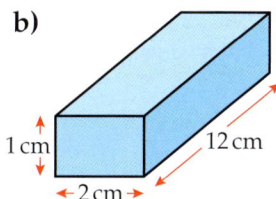

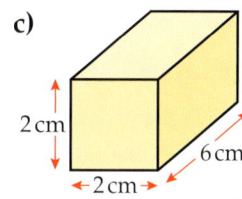

a)

2 cm
3 cm
4 cm

b)

1 cm
2 cm
12 cm

c)

2 cm
2 cm
6 cm

5 There are four different cuboids which can be made with a volume of 30 cm³. One is shown in the diagram. Draw three more on isometric paper. Which one has the smallest surface area?

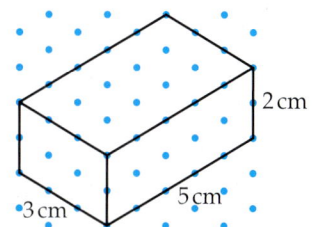

2 cm
3 cm
5 cm

6 On isometric paper draw as many different cuboids as you can that have a volume of 60 cm³. Label all the dimensions clearly.
Which cuboid has the smallest surface area and which has the greatest?

⊕ Design a survey or experiment

⊕ Design, trial and refine data collection sheets

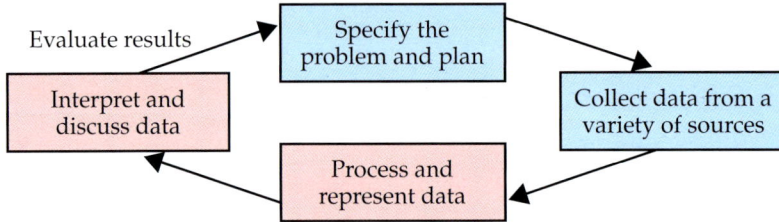

When carrying out a statistical investigation, use the data handling cycle to help guide you.

Start your investigation by specifying the problem and making a plan to show how you will investigate the problem.

Include in your plan:

- a description of the problem
- a suitable hypothesis
- a description of how you will collect the data
- the **sample size** (how much data you will collect)
- a data collection sheet.

The examples below show how two students investigate the number of *heads* and *tails* when tossing three coins.

Example 1   Harriet's plan

Throw 3 coins in 8 groups of 20. This will give me a sample size of 160 trials.

Each time record the number of heads.

Compare theoretical probabilities to the experimental ones.

Use a two-way table for the data collection sheet.

Number of trials \ Number of heads	0	1	2	3
20				
40				
60				
80				
100				
120				
140				
160				

Harriet should also include a hypothesis.

She has stated the sample size.

It is a good idea to try out the data collection sheet, before starting your investigation.

Example 2 Lata's problem

Look at what happens when I throw 3 coins.

> This is not detailed enough. Lata should say what she thinks her experiment will show.

This is Lata's plan:

Throw the coins; counting how many heads I get each time.

Exercise 15.1

Choose one of the investigations below.

For your chosen investigation suggest a hypothesis to test (if appropriate) and write a plan. Include how you will collect the data, the sample size and if you will split this number into groups, where you will collect the data and anything else you think is important.

Design a data collection sheet for your investigation.

Carry out your investigation.

1 Two dice are thrown. Find the probability of the dice showing the same numbers.

2 Design a spinner. Compare the theoretical probabilities to the experimental ones.

3 Investigate this statement:

'The average throw for a dice is 3.5, because $\dfrac{(1 + 2 + 3 + 4 + 5 + 6)}{6} = 3.5$'.

4 Using digit cards, investigate the probability that they will be in numerical order when they are shuffled and dealt out in a row.

5 Four red and one white counter are put into a bag. A counter is chosen at random, its colour noted and then replaced. Explore how the probability of choosing the white counter changes as you increase the number of times you repeat the experiment.

6 Investigate the number of throws it takes to throw a coin until it shows a *tail*.

7 Use random numbers to explore the outcomes when throwing two coins.

Experimental probabilities

- ⊕ Calculate experimental probabilities
- ⊕ Calculate summary statistics

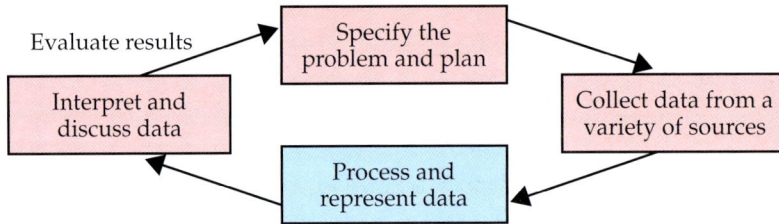

Once you have collected your data, you will need to process the data.

This involves putting your data into a useable format, calculating the **experimental probabilities** and then finding **summary statistics** such as the mean.

$$\text{Experimental probability} = \frac{\text{number of times an outcome happens}}{\text{number of times the experiment was carried out}}$$

You will not need to use the same statistical techniques for all investigations.

You must only use techniques appropriate to the investigation.

Example   Harriet's data

Frequency table after first 20 trials.

Number of heads	Frequency	Number of heads × frequency
0	1	0
1	5	5
2	8	16
3	6	18
	Total = 20	Total number of heads = 39

It is a good idea to show your working.

The mean number of heads after 20 throws =

$$\frac{(0 \times 1 + 1 \times 5 + 2 \times 8 + 3 \times 6)}{20} = \frac{(0 + 5 + 16 + 18)}{20} = \frac{39}{20} = 1.95.$$

Experimental probabilities after first 20 trials.

Number of heads	0	1	2	3
Frequency	1	5	8	6
Experimental probabilities	$\frac{1}{20} = 0.05$	$\frac{5}{20} = 0.25$	$\frac{8}{20} = 0.4$	$\frac{6}{20} = 0.3$

Mean number of heads as the number of trials increases.

Number of trials	20	40	60	80	100	120	140	160
Mean number of heads (2 d.p.)	1.95	1.40	1.53	1.49	1.55	1.57	1.51	1.58

Harriet has repeated the same calculation for each group of throws.

Exercise 15.2

1 Brian is carrying out the same experiment as Harriet and Lata. He draws a frequency table for his experiment looking at the probability of getting 2 *heads* and 2 *tails* when throwing the 4 coins.

	2 *heads*, 2 *tails*	Other
Frequency	28	52
Experimental probability	0.28	0.52

$0.28 + 0.52 \neq 1.0$

Explain what Brian has done wrong.

Calculate the correct experimental probabilities.

2 This is Harriet's frequency table after 160 throws.

Number of *heads*	Frequency	Number of *heads* × frequency
0	17	
1	58	
2	61	
3	24	
	Total frequency =	**Total number of *heads* =**

Calculate the mean, median, mode and range for the number of *heads*.

3 Complete the table to calculate the experimental probabilities for Harriet's investigation after 160 trials.

Number of *heads*	Frequency	Experimental probability (2 d.p.)
0	17	$\frac{17}{160} =$
1	58	
2	61	
3	24	

4 Calculate the experimental probabilities for your investigation.
If you have split your sample size into small groups you can calculate these probabilities as your sample size increases.

5 If it is appropriate for your investigation you should now calculate summary statistics such as the mean, for each group of trials.

Remember, you must only use skills that are suitable for your investigation. If you are unsure, ask your teacher for advice.

15.3 Possible outcomes 2

⊕ Find all possible outcomes of an experiment

⊕ Calculate theoretical probabilities

Once you have calculated the experimental probabilities from the data you have collected, it is important to also calculate the **theoretical probabilities** for comparison. This will often involve finding all the possible outcomes for the experiment.

Remember, the theoretical probability (P) is:

$$P(\text{outcome}) = \frac{\text{number of ways the outcome can happen}}{\text{the total number of outcomes}}$$

You are less likely to make mistakes if you work in a **systematic** (or ordered) way, for example, draw a sample space diagram, table, tree diagram, etc.

Example   Harriet lists all possible outcomes when throwing three coins.

0 heads:	ttt		
1 head:	htt	tht	tth
2 heads:	hht	hth	thh
3 heads:	hhh		

Harriet writes down the outcomes in a systematic way.

Possible outcomes.

Number of heads	Frequency (number of ways this can happen)	Number of heads × frequency
0	1	0
1	3	3
2	3	6
3	1	3
	Total frequency = 8	Total number of heads = 12

She puts this information into a frequency table and calculates the theoretical mean for the number of *heads*.

The mean number of heads $= \frac{12}{8} = 1.5$.

Number of heads	Frequency	Theoretical probability
0	1	$\frac{1}{8} = 0.125$
1	3	$\frac{3}{8} = 0.375$
2	3	$\frac{3}{8} = 0.375$
3	1	$\frac{1}{8} = 0.125$

Exercise 15.3

1 Complete the table to show the theoretical frequencies when two coins are thrown 160 times.

Number of *heads*	Theoretical probability	Theoretical probability × 160
0	$\frac{1}{8} = 0.125$	$0.125 \times 160 =$
1	$\frac{3}{8} = 0.375$	
2	$\frac{3}{8} = 0.375$	
3	$\frac{1}{8} = 0.125$	

2 **a)** Find all of the possible outcomes when two coins are thrown and the number of *heads* recorded.

> Use a systematic method to find these outcomes: 0 *heads*, 1 *head*, 2 *heads*.

b) Use your results to complete the table.

Number of *heads*	Frequency (number of outcomes)	Number of *heads* × frequency
0		
1		
2		
	Total frequency =	Total number of *heads* =

c) Use the table to calculate the mean number of *heads* when two coins are thrown.

3 **a)** Complete the sample space diagram to show the possible outcomes when four coins are thrown.

> The outcomes from 2 coins being thrown have been used as headings for the table.

	hh	ht	th	tt
hh	hhhh			
ht				
th				
tt			thtt	

b) Copy and complete the table to show the frequency of each outcome.

Number of *heads*	Frequency (number of outcomes)	Number of *heads* × frequency
0		
1		
2		
3		
4		
	Total frequency =	Total number of *heads* =

c) Use the table to calculate the mean number of heads when four coins are thrown.

4 Find all of the possible outcomes for your experiment and use them to find the theoretical probabilities so you can compare them later on to the experimental ones.

Representing data 2

◈ Illustrate data using appropriate diagrams

Key words
pie chart
bar chart
line graph
frequency diagram
compound or comparative bar chart

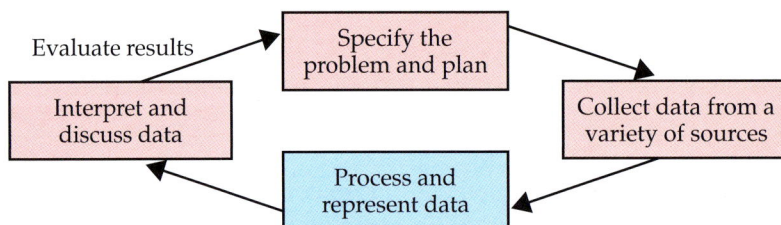

When drawing diagrams, ask yourself the following:

- Is the diagram suitable for the data?
- Is there a title?
- Are the axes numbered and labelled?

Which of the following diagrams is most suitable?

Pie chart: categorical data, in more than two groups

Bar chart/line graph: discrete data, which may be grouped

Frequency diagram: usually grouped, continuous data

Compound or comparative bar chart: useful for comparing two or more distributions.

If two or more frequency diagrams are to be used to compare data, use the same scales on both axes to help the comparison.

Example

Harriet draws different diagrams for her results.

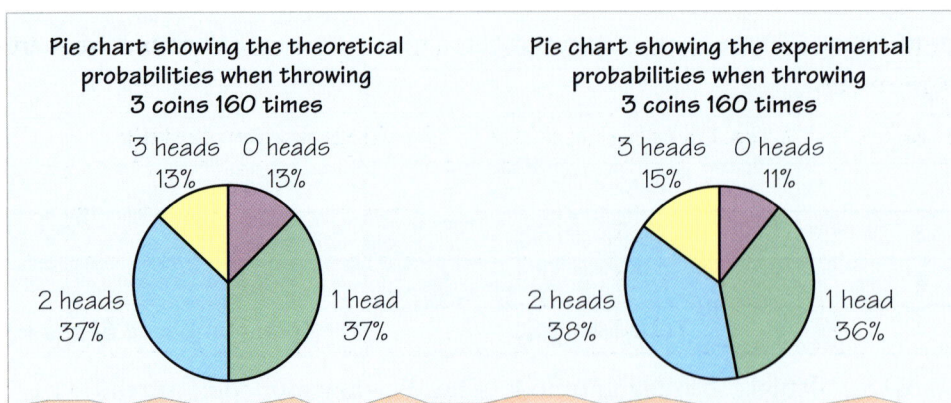

Pie chart showing the theoretical probabilities when throwing 3 coins 160 times

3 heads 13%   0 heads 13%   2 heads 37%   1 head 37%

Pie chart showing the experimental probabilities when throwing 3 coins 160 times

3 heads 15%   0 heads 11%   2 heads 38%   1 head 36%

It is difficult to compare probabilities using these two pie charts.

Comparative bar chart showing the number of heads when 3 coins are thrown for 160 throws

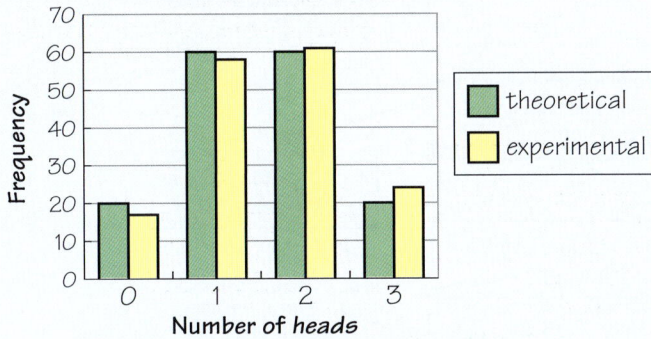

This diagram shows the probabilities more clearly.

Bar-line graph showing the mean number of heads as I increase the number of throws

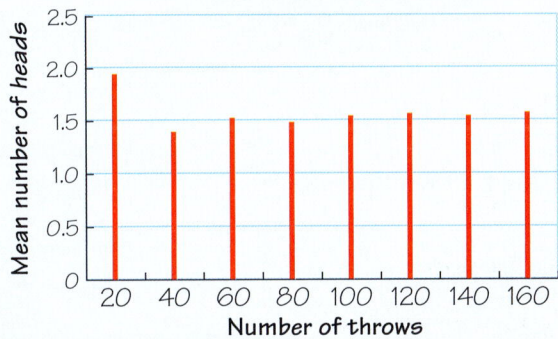

The bar-line graph shows that the mean gets closer to the value of 1.5 as the number of throws increases.

Exercise 15.4

1 Discuss the usefulness of each of Harriet's diagrams, for showing her data.

See Lesson 13.3 for help.

2 Redraw the comparative bar chart as two separate bar charts.

Use the same scale on both sets of axes.

3 Draw a suitable diagram to compare the theoretical and experimental probabilities from Harriet's experiment.

Number of *heads*	Experimental probability	Theoretical probability
0	0.11	0.125
1	0.36	0.375
2	0.38	0.375
3	0.15	0.125

4 Draw suitable diagrams to illustrate the data you have collected.

Remember, you will not get extra marks for drawing many different diagrams all showing the same thing or diagrams that are not appropriate for your data.

Interpreting data 2

⊕ Interpret diagrams

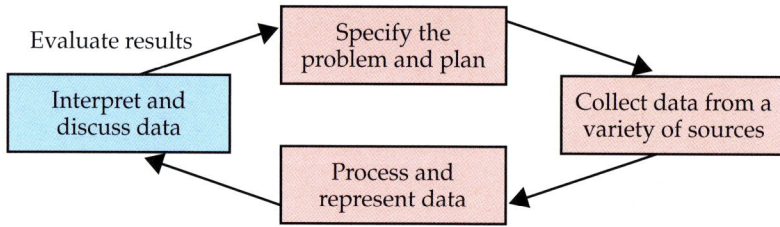

Evaluate results → Specify the problem and plan → Collect data from a variety of sources → Process and represent data → Interpret and discuss data → Evaluate results

A diagram or table is meaningless without written explanation or **interpretation**.
Try to explain what your results show rather than just repeating your table of results.
Remember to link your interpretation to your original **hypothesis**.

Example   This is part of Harriet's interpretation of results.

Table comparing frequencies.

Number of heads	0	1	2	3
Theoretical frequency	20	60	60	20
Experimental frequency	17	58	61	24

This shows the frequency we expect.

This shows the data from the experiment.

This shows that the frequencies for my experiment and what we would expect to happen in theory, if the experiment was carried out 160 times, were quite close.

Harriet has linked her results to her hypothesis.

Table comparing probabilities.

Number of heads	0	1	2	3
Theoretical probability	0.125	0.375	0.375	0.125
Experimental probability	0.106	0.363	0.381	0.150

She has found the probabilities by dividing frequency by 160, the number of trials.

The table comparing the probabilities of the theoretical and experimental probabilities after 160 trails shows more clearly how close the two types of probability were.

I would not expect them to be the same. If I carried out the experiment more times, my results might be more accurate.

Bar-line graph showing the mean number of heads as I increase the number of throws

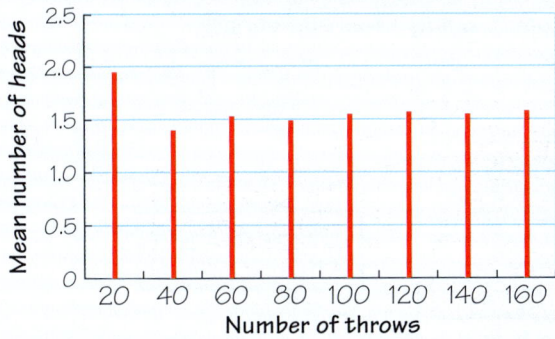

The bar-line graph of the mean number of *heads* against number of throws shows that this value is starting to settle around the value of 1.5, which is the theoretical number of heads in this experiment.

Exercise 15.5

1 Brian was investigating the frequencies of two coins showing either both *heads* or both *tails*.

His hypothesis was that he thought the probability of two coins showing the same would be $\frac{1}{2}$.

Here are some of his results.

Outcome	Coins showing 2 *heads* or 2 *tails*	Coins not showing 2 *heads* or 2 *tails*
Frequency	52	48
Experimental probability	0.52	0.48

Bar-line graph showing the probability of two coins showing 2 *heads* or 2 *tails* as the number of trials increases

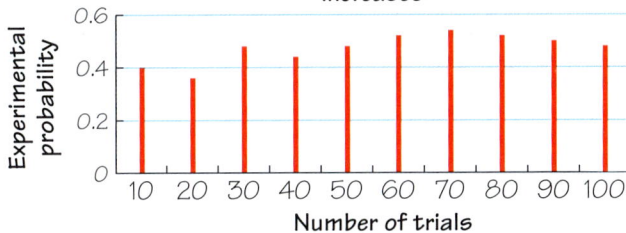

Was Brian's hypothesis correct? Use information from the table and graph to explain your answer.

2 Look at the statistics you have calculated and diagrams you have drawn for your own investigation. Explain carefully what each of them means. Remember to link what you are writing to your original hypothesis or starting point.

◈ Communicate interpretations and results of a statistical enquiry using selected tables, graphs and diagrams in support, using ICT as appropriate

◈ Evaluate an investigation

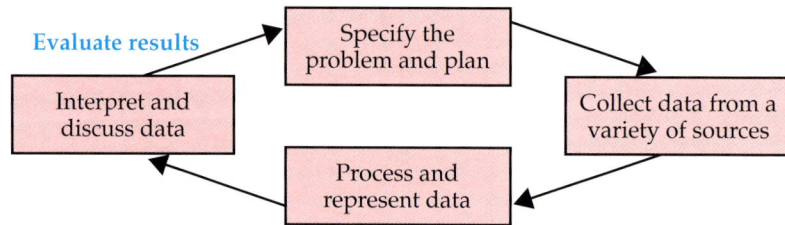

When you have analysed your results, gather all the information together as a report. Your report should enable anyone to understand what you have done and why, even if they do not already know anything about your investigation.

The data handling cycle is continuous and does not stop once you have written your report. **Evaluate** your investigation by writing down how you could improve or extend your work. Say how **representative** you think your results are. For instance, if your hypothesis is about students aged 11–18 and you have only included members of your year group in your investigation, you need to discuss this.

Example 1   These are some of the comments from Harriet's report.

An investigation looking at the number of heads when 3 coins are thrown

Three coins are thrown and the number of heads counted each time.

I will be looking at the mean number of heads and also comparing the experimental results with the theoretical ones, looking for similarities.

I will throw the coins 160 times, in groups of 20. This will enable me to analyse how the distribution of the number of heads changes as the sample size gets larger.

160 times is not too small so my results should be reliable, but also not too big so I will not take too long analysing my results.

I only need 3 coins for my experiment.

Evaluation

I think my results were quite fair and typical for this experiment.

I would have liked to increase my sample size so the accuracy of my experimental results may have been improved.

To extend the investigation, I would look at different numbers of coins, not just 3.

She explains what this investigation is about.

She includes a detailed plan, and explains her sample size.

She suggests improvements and ideas for further work.

Example 2   Lata writes:

> This was a good investigation that was easy to carry out. I did get a bit bored
> sometimes with all that throwing.
>
> If I were to do it again, I would do it less times so I could get it finished sooner.

None of this belongs in a report.

Check that you have included the following in your report:

Introduction
Project title
An explanation of the problem
Your **hypothesis**

Planning
What information you needed
The **sample size** (amount of data collected)
Explanation of why you choose to collect this amount of data
What special equipment is needed

Collection of the data
How you collected the data
Where the data was collected
The accuracy of your data (e.g. nearest cm) and an explanation of why you chose this

Processing and representing the data
Any necessary calculations
Relevant diagrams (with an explanation as to why a particular diagram was appropriate)
Tables of results

Interpreting and discussing the data
A link back to the original hypothesis
Evidence to back up any statements that you make

Evaluation
This should include a discussion of the following:
- Are my results fair?
- Is the data representative of all the possible information I could have chosen?
- Was my sample size big enough? Mention any problems you had with the data.
- Say how you solved these problems (e.g. data that did not seem to fit in with the rest).
- Say how you could continue or extend your investigation.
- Changes that you would make to your original plan.

You will not get extra marks or a higher level by including diagrams or statistics that are not relevant to your project.

Exercise 15.6

Write a report explaining your investigation. Include an evaluation.
Use the checklist above to help you include important information.

This is a set of revision questions covering Units 11–15. If you have a problem with a question, look back at the lesson shown in the box to refresh your memory.

Questions 1–15 are non-calculator questions.

1 Expand the brackets in each of these expressions.

Lesson 11.1

   a) $4(t + 3)$ **b)** $r(r - 2)$ **c)** $3(x + 2) + 2x - 4$

2 Length AB is equal to length AC

Lesson 12.2

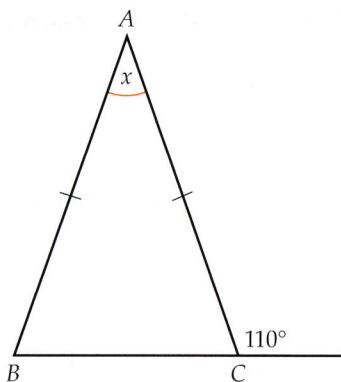

Find the size of angle x.
Write down any angles you find and the angle facts you used.

3 Plan an investigation into how accurate people are at estimating the size of angles. Make sure your plan includes:

Lesson 13.1

- A hypothesis you can test to see if it is right or wrong
- What information you will collect (is it primary or secondary data?)
- How you will collect it and what data collection sheet you will use.
- Who you will collect it from and how many people you will ask.

4 **a)** How many faces, vertices and edges does this shape have?

Lesson 14.1

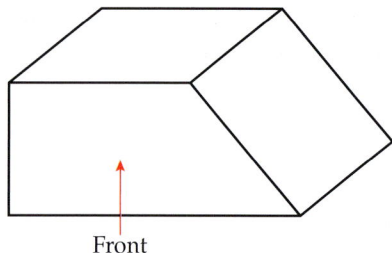

Front

   b) Draw a plan view, front elevation and side elevation.

5 Simplify the following:

Lesson 11.2

   a) $y^3 + y^3$ **b)** $a^2 + a^3 + a^2$

   c) $6m^4 - 4m^4$ **d)** $6f^2 + 7f^3 - 3f^3$

6 Two coins are tossed 40 times and the number of *tails* recorded.
The results are:

Lesson 15.2
Lesson 15.3

Number of *tails*	Frequency
0	12
1	16
2	12

   a) Find the mean number of *tails* per throw.

   b) Find the experimental probability for each result as a fraction.

   c) List all the possible outcomes from tossing 2 coins.

   d) What is the theoretical probability of getting exactly 1 *tail*?

7 Zoë goes for a cycle ride. She leaves home and cycles 5 miles in $\frac{3}{4}$ hour.
She then gets a puncture and stops to try and repair it.
After $\frac{1}{2}$ hour she gives up and walks her bicycle home.
She walks at a speed of 5 miles per hour.

Lesson 11.5

   a) Draw a distance–time graph to illustrate her journey.
Use 2 cm to represent $\frac{1}{2}$ hour along the *x*-axis and 1 cm to represent 1 mile on the *y*-axis.

   b) How long was Zoë out of the house?

   c) How far did she go in total?

8

Lesson 12.3

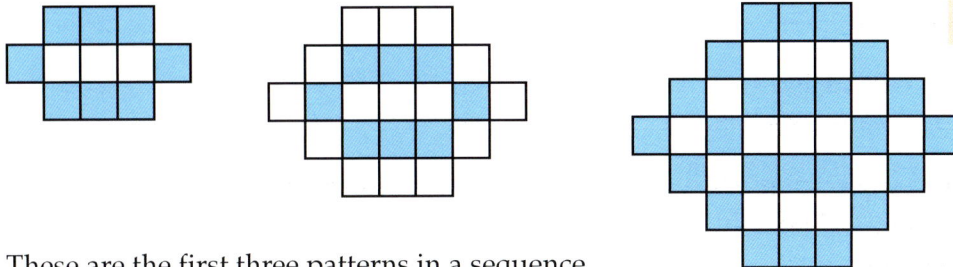

These are the first three patterns in a sequence.
Each pattern is created by adding an increasing number of squares.

   a) How many extra squares are added each time?

> Make a number sequence.

   b) How many blue squares will be needed for the 7th pattern?

   c) How many squares in total will be in the 4th pattern?

9 Boys and girls competed in throwing a small ball into a target hole.
Each person had 5 throws and the frequency of hitting the target
was recorded. The summary statistics of the results were:

Lesson 13.4

	Mean	Mode	Median	Range
Boys	2.2	2	2	2
Girls	2.5	1	2	5

   a) Compare the ranges. What does this tell you?

   b) Compare the modes. What does this tell you?

   c) Compare the means. What does this tell you?

   d) Are boys or girls better at hitting the target? Give reasons for your answer.

⑩ The diagrams show three different views of the same shape.
Draw a possible shape on isometric paper.

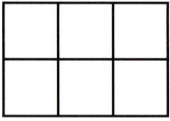

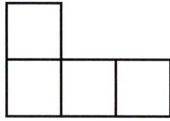

Lesson 14.2

⑪ This graph shows Ali's walk to school one Monday morning.

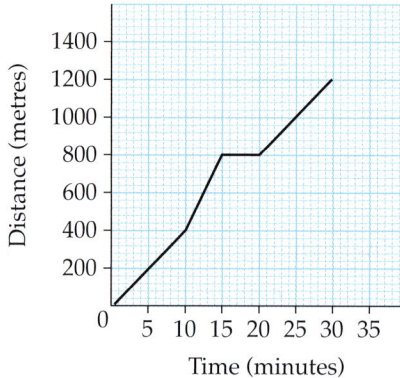

Lesson 11.6

a) How far does Ali walk to school each day?

b) How long did it take him to get to school this Monday?

c) Ali stopped at a friend's house to wait for him to get ready. How far away from Ali's house does his friend live?

d) How long did Ali wait for his friend?

e) Between which times did Ali walk the fastest? How do you know?

⑫ Everyone in a class makes a 5-sided spinner. John says his is a fair spinner but Ben's is not. Plan an investigation to test John's hypothesis. Include in your plan a data collection sheet and explain in detail how you will undertake the investigation.

Lesson 15.1

⑬ a) Copy this cuboid and show all planes of symmetry. Draw each plane on a separate diagram.

Lesson 14.3

b) Show how to slice the cuboid so that the cross-section is a triangle.

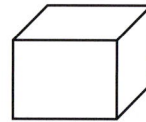

⑭ Which of the following should NOT be included in an evaluation.

Lesson 13.5

a) I would increase the sample size next time as mine was too small and did not represent my data.

b) I really enjoyed doing this investigation with my friends.

c) To extend my investigation I would compare the results of males and females.

⑮ Two 3-sided spinners numbered 1 to 3 are spun and the results added together. After 90 trials the results were:

Lesson 15.4

Total	Experimental frequency	Theoretical frequency
2	7	10
3	22	20
4	28	30
5	24	20
6	9	10

Draw a suitable diagram to compare these results.

16

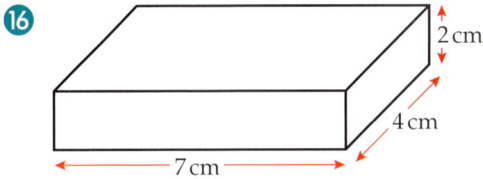

a) Draw an accurate net of this cuboid.

b) Find its surface area.

Lesson 14.4
Lessson 14.6

17 Look back at **Q6** part **b)**. Change your fractions into decimals and use your answers to complete this table.

Lesson 15.5

No. of *tails*	Theoretical probability	Experimental probability
0	0.25	
1	0.5	
2	0.25	

Do you think that the coins were biased? Use the information in your table to explain your answer.

18 Using the formula $t = s^2 - 4r$, find the value of t when:

Lesson 11.3

a) $s = 5$ and $r = 3$ b) $s = 4$ and $r = 4$ c) $s = 3$ and $r = 2$

19 a) These are the heights of Adam's tulips, measured to the nearest centimetre.

Lesson 13.2

31 34 25 27 31 18 28 32 30 19
37 29 27 31 34 31 29 40 26 41

i) Draw a stem-and-leaf diagram for this data.

ii) Find the median.

John also has tulips which he measures, and puts the results into a table:

Height (cm)	Frequency	Frequency × height
27	2	
28	3	
29	5	
30	6	
31	3	
32	1	
	Total =	Total =

b) Find the mean height of John's tulips.

20 This is the net of a 3-D shape. Make a sketch of the shape showing the measurements.

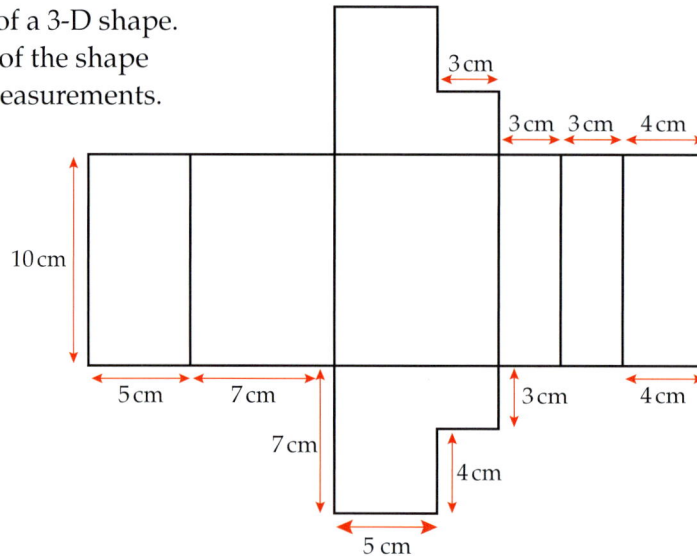

Lesson 14.5

3 cm

3 cm 3 cm 4 cm

10 cm

5 cm 7 cm

3 cm 4 cm

7 cm

4 cm

5 cm

21 A survey asked 200 people about their favourite flavour of ice-cream. These are the results.

Lesson 13.3

Flavour	Vanilla	Strawberry	Chocolate	Other
Frequency	80	46	50	24

Draw a pie chart to represent this data.

22 A record shop is closing down and everything has 20% off the original price. The sale price of a DVD is £12.
What was its original price?   What percentage is equal to £12?

Lesson 12.1

23 a) Using Adam's data from **Q19**, group the heights into equal sized groups using $15 \leqslant$ height < 20 for the first group.

b) Draw a frequency diagram to represent your grouped data.

Lesson 13.2

24 The cost of hiring a car is £40 plus £25 per day.

a) What would be the cost to hire a car for 6 days?

b) Construct a formula to hire a car. Let C stand for the cost in pounds and d stand for the number of days.

c) If I spent £140 on hiring a car, how many days had I hired it for?

Lesson 11.4

25 Class 3G are making toys for their charity stall at the fair.
A bear costs 70p to make and sells for £2.
A dog costs 50p to make and sells for £1.50.
They spend exactly £5 on materials and make 8 toys in total.

a) How many of each toy did they make?

b) How much profit did they make for charity?

Start with number combinations that make 8.

Lesson 12.4

Index

addition
    decimals 96–9
    fractions 16–19
adjacent angle 162
algebraic expressions
    collecting like terms 146–51
    equation forming 34–5
    expanding brackets 146–9
    simplifying 146–51
    substituting values 40–1,
        114–15
    terms involving powers
        of x 150–1
alternate angle 44–5, 50–1, 162
angles
    adjacent 162
    alternate 44–5, 50–1, 162
    bisector 52–3, 60–1
    corresponding 44–5, 50–1, 162
    exterior 46–7
    interior 46–7
    obtuse 53
    problem solving 50–1
    sum of, at a point 162
    sum of, in a quadrilateral 46–7
    sum of, in a triangle 46–7, 162
    vertically opposite 44–5, 50–1,
        162
arc 52
area
    circle 153
    compound shapes 82–5
    parallelogram 84–5
    rectangle 82–3, 153
    trapezium 84–5
    triangle 82–3
arithmagon 34
arrowhead 46–9, 135
axes for graphs 116–17, 120–1

bar chart 70–1, 174–5, 200–1
bar-line graph 70–1, 174–5, 200–1
billion 106–9
bisector of angle between two
        lines 60–1

centre of enlargement 136–9
circle, area 153
class interval 66–7
collecting like terms 146–51

common denominator 16–17,
    16–19
comparative bar chart 200–1
compound bar chart 174–5, 200–1
cone 185
congruent shapes 136–7
conjecture 168
construction
    bisector of angle 52–3
    formulae 154–5
    perpendicular bisector of
        line 52–3
    perpendicular from a point on a
        line 54–5
    perpendicular from a point to a
        line 54–5
    quadrilateral 56–9
    triangle 56–7, 56–9
continuous data 66–7, 170–1
corresponding angle 44–5, 50–1,
    162
cross-section
    cube 184
    cuboid 86–7, 184
    different shapes 186
cube root 106–7
cube [numbers] 106–7
cube [shape]
    cross-section 184
    volume 86–7
cuboid
    cross-section 86–7, 184
    front elevation 182
    net 186–93
    overview 182–3
    plan view 182
    shapes 182–3
    side elevation 182
    surface area 192–3
    volume 86–7, 192–3
    volume of shapes 86–9
cylinder 185

data
    bar chart 70–1, 174–5, 200–1
    bar-line graph 70–1, 174–5,
        200–1
    class interval 66–7
    collection sheet 129
    collection, trial 62–3

comparative bar chart 200–1
compound bar chart 174–5,
    200–1
continuous 66–7, 170–1
diagrams 70–1
discrete 66–7
frequency diagram 70–1, 174–5,
    200–1
handling, investigation 62–3
hypothesis 72–3
interpretation 202–3
interpreting information 72–3
mean 64–5
median 64–5
modal class 66–7
modal group 66–7
mode 64–5
pie chart 66–9, 70–1, 174–5
primary source 62–3, 170–1
processing 64–5
range 64–5
sample size 62–3, 170–1
secondary source 62–3,
    170–1
statistics 64–5, 172–3
stem-and-leaf diagram 64–5,
    173
summary statistics 64–5, 172–3,
    176
data representation 174–5,
    200–1
decimals
    addition 96–9
    division 102–3
    fractions 16–17, 26–9
    multiplication 100–1
    number line 22–3
    ordering 22–3
    percentages 26–9
    rounding 96–7
    subtraction 96–9
delta 46–9, 135
denominator 16–17
direct proportion
    graphs 42–3
    ratio 26–7
discrete data 66–7
distance–time graphs
    basics 156–7
    interpreting 156–9

division
by 0.1 and 0.01 94–5
decimals 102–3
fractions 20–1
integers 14–15
negative numbers 14–15
numbers less than 1 94–5

enlargement 136–41
equation forming
algebraic expressions 34–5
real-life situations 34–5, 36–9
using algebra 36–9
equation solving
by balancing the equation 32–5
by inverse operation 32–3
collecting together unknown
values 36–7
unknown on both sides 36–7
unknown on one side only
32–3
equilateral triangle, symmetry
135
equivalent fractions 16–19
equivalent point 132–3
equivalent ratio 24–5
evaluating investigation 180–1
event 124–5
expanding brackets 146–9
experimental probability 126–31,
196–7
exterior angle 46–7

factor pair 110–11
factorisation 104–5, 110–11
formula
construction 154–5
definition 152, 154
substitution into 152–3
fractions
addition 16–19
cancelling 20
common denominator 16–17,
16–19
decimals 16–17, 26–9
denominator 16–17
division 20–1
equivalent 16–17, 16–19
improper 18
multiplication 20–1
numerator 16–17
ordering 16–17
percentages 26–9
subtraction 16–19
frequency diagram 70–1, 174–5,
200–1
front elevation 182

function
graphical representation 12–13
input 10–11
inverse 13
linear 12–13
machine 10–11
output 10–11
relationship between two sets
of values 6–9

geometry, problem solving
162–3
gradient 116–19
graphs
axes 116–17, 120–1
curved 120–3
direct proportion 42–3
distance–time 156–9
gradient 116–19
interpreting 122–3
linear functions 12–13
plotting 120–1
quadrants 116–17
relationship between variables
122–3
scales 120–1
straight-line 116–19
y-intercept 116–19

hundredths and percentages 26–9
hypotenuse 56–9
hypothesis 72–3, 170–1, 202–3

imperial and metric measure
equivalents 80–1
improper fractions 18
index [of number] 106–7
index [of number] notation
110–13
integers
division 14–15
multiplication 14–15
interior angle 46–7
interpreting graphs 122–3
inverse function 13
investigation
data representation 174–5
data type and grouping 66–7
diagrams 70–1
evaluating 180–1
hypothesis 72–3, 170–1
interpreting information 72–3,
176–7
pie chart 66–9
planning outline 62–3, 170–1
processing data 64–5, 170–1
report writing 176–9

investigation, probability
data representation 200–1
experimental probabilities
196–7
hypothesis 202–3
interpreting data 202–3
planning 194–5
report writing 204–5
sample size 194–5
summary statistics 196–7
theoretical probabilities 196–9
isosceles trapezium 46–9, 79, 135
isosceles triangle 51, 134–5

kite 46–9, 134–5

line
mid-point of segment 76–9
perpendicular bisector 52–3
perpendicular from a point on
the line 54–5
perpendicular from a point to
the line 54–5
line of symmetry 134–5
locus 60–1
lowest common multiple (LCM)
18

magic squares 41
mapping diagram 6–9
mean 64–5
median 64–5
mental arithmetic
doubling 90–1
estimating by rounding
96–9
halving 90–1
multiplication 90–3
near tens 92–3
partitioning 92–3
metric and imperial measure
equivalents 80–1
mid-point of segment 76–9
million 106–9
modal class 66–7
modal group 66–7
mode 64–5
multiplication
by 0.1 and 0.01 94–5
decimals 100–1
estimating by rounding 100–1
fractions 20–1
integers 14–15
mental arithmetic 90–3
negative numbers 14–15
numbers less than 1 94–5
standard method 100–1

negative numbers
    division 14–15
    multiplication 14–15
nets
    cuboid 186–93
    square-based pyramid 188
    3-D shapes 186–91
    triangular prism 188
notation
    approximately equal to ^{a} 80
    index/power 110–13
    sequences general term $T(n)$ 4
    symbols $<, >, \leqslant, \geqslant$ 22–3
numerator 16–17

obtuse angle 53
order of operations 40–1, 114–15
order of rotation symmetry 134–5
ordering
    decimals 22–3
    fractions 16–17
outcome 124–7

parallel lines 44–5, 162
parallelogram
    angles 163
    area 84–5
    properties 46–9
    symmetry 134–5
partitioning 92–3
path traced out by moving point
    60–1
pentagon 51, 163
percentages
    decimals 26–9
    decrease 30–1
    fractions 26–9
    hundredths 26–9
    increase 30–1
    problem solving 160–1
    unitary method 26–9, 30–1
perpendicular
    bisector of line joining two
        points 60–1
    bisector of line segment 52–53
    from a point on a line 54–5
    from a point to a line 54–5

pie chart 66–9, 70–1, 174–5
place value 106–9
plan view 182
plane 186
plane of symmetry 186–7
polygons, regular 51
possible outcome 124–7
power 106–7
power notation 110–13

powers of 10 106–9
primary source 62–3, 170–1
prime factors 110–11
prime number 110–11
prism, triangular 188
probability
    comparison 130–1
    estimating 126–9
    event 124–5
    experimental 126–9, 130–1,
        196–7
    outcome 124–7
    possible outcome 124–7
    random event 130–1
    systematic approach 126–7
    theoretical 124–5, 126–31, 196–9
probability investigation
    data representation 200–1
    experimental probabilities
        196–7
    hypothesis 202–3
    interpreting data 202–3
    planning 194–5
    report writing 204–5
    sample size 194–5
    summary statistics 196–7
    theoretical probabilities 196–9
proportion
    problem solving 160–1
    ratio 24–7
pyramid, square-based 188

quadrants 116–17
quadrilaterals
    construction 56–9
    sum of angles 46–7
    types 46–9

random event 130–1
range 64–5
ratio
    cancelling 24–5
    direct proportion 26–7
    enlargement 140–1
    equivalent 24–5
    problem solving 160–1
    proportion 24–7
    scale drawings 142–3
    transformations 140–1
    unitary method 26–7
rectangle
    area 82–3, 153
    properties 46–9
    symmetry 134–5, 186
reflection 132–3
reflection symmetry 134–5, 186
report writing 176–9, 204–5

revision exercises
    units 1–5: 74–7
    units 6–10: 144–7
    units 11–15: 206–9
rhombus 46–9, 134–5
right-angled triangle construction
    56–7
rotation 132–3
rotation symmetry 134–5
rounding
    to decimal places 96–7, 102–3
    to nearest whole number 96–7
    to power of 10 96–7
    use for estimates 96–9, 100–3

sample size
    background 62–3
    deciding 170–1
    probability investigation
        194–5
sample space diagram 131
scale drawings 142–3
scale factor 136–41
secondary source 62–3, 170–1
sector 66–9
sequences
    consecutive terms 6–7
    general term, finding 6–7
    general term, using 4–5
    generating 4–5
    term-to-term rule 2–3
side elevation 182
sphere 185
square root 104–7
square [number] 104–7
square [shape]
    cross-section of cube or cuboid
        184
    properties 46–9
    symmetry 134–5
square-based pyramid 188
stem-and-leaf diagram 64–5,
    173
straight-line graphs 116–19
strategies
    extended problems 166–9
    geometrical problems 162–3
    harder and mixed problems
        164–5
    multistep problems 166–7
    problem solving 160–1
    surface area problems 192–3
    systematic approach 166–8
    volume problems 192–3
substitution into expressions 40–1,
    114–15
substitution into formulae 152–3

subtraction
    decimals 96–9
    fractions 16–19
summary statistics
    data 172–3, 176
    measures 64–5
    probability investigation 196–7
surface area of cuboid 192–3
symmetry
    arrowhead 135
    delta 135
    equilateral triangle 135
    isosceles trapezium 135
    isosceles triangle 134–5
    kite 134–5
    line of 134–5
    order of rotation 134–5
    parallelogram 134–5
    plane of 186–7
    rectangle 134–5, 186
    reflection 134–5, 186
    rhombus 134–5
    rotation 134–5
    shapes 134–5
    square [shape] 134–5

trapezium 135
triangle, equilateral 135
triangle, isosceles 134–5

term-to-term rule 2–3
tessellation 135
theoretical probability 124–5,
    126–31, 196–9
3-D objects represented in 2-D
    184–5
3-D reflection symmetry 186–7
3-D shapes, nets 186–91
transformations
    centre of enlargement 136–9
    enlargement 136–41
    equivalent point 132–3
    image 132–3
    object 132–3
    ratio 140–1
    reflection 132–3
    rotation 132–3
    scale factor 136–41
    translation 132–3
    types 132–3
translation 132–3

trapezium
    area 84–5
    isosceles 46–9, 79
    symmetry 135
triangle
    area 82–3
    construction 56–9
    equilateral, symmetry 135
    isosceles, properties 51
    isosceles, symmetry 134–5
    sum of angles 46–7
triangular prism 188
2-D representations of 3-D objects
    184–5

unitary method
    percentages 26–9, 30–1
    ratio problems 26–7

vertically opposite angle 44–5,
    50–1, 162
volume
    cube 86–7
    cuboid 86–7, 192–3
    cuboid shapes 86–9

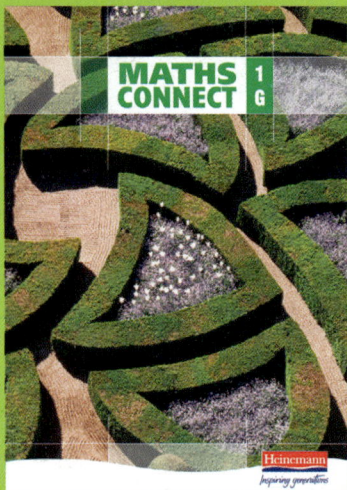

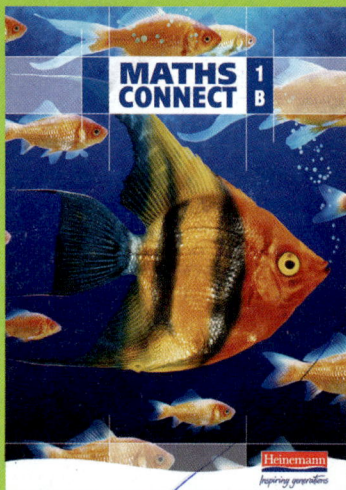

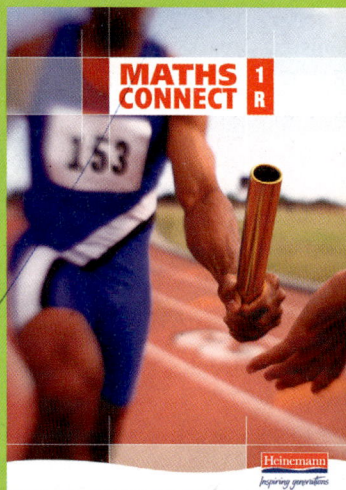

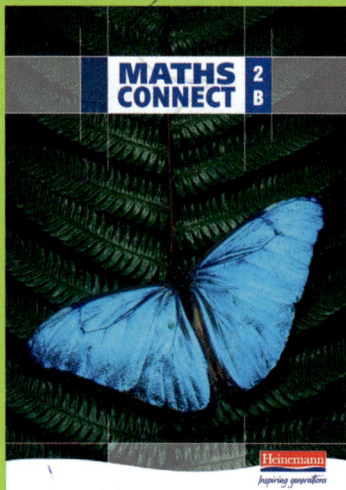

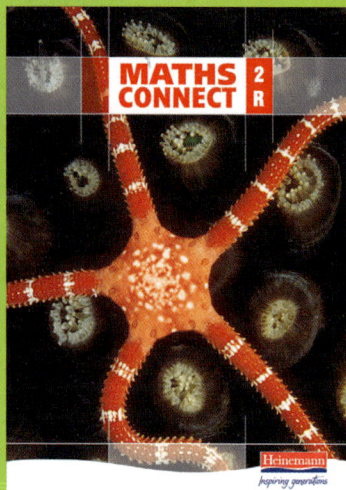

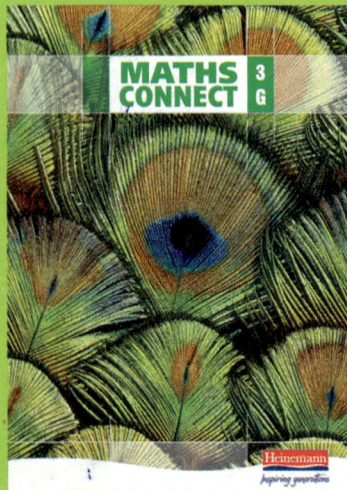

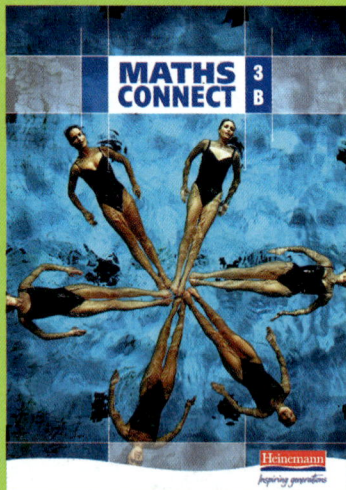

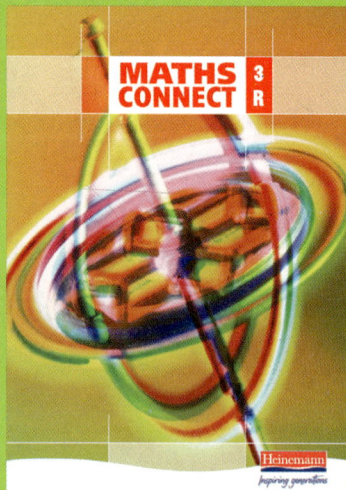